POWER, TEACHING, AND
TEACHER EDUCATION

Higher Ed

Questions about the Purpose(s) of Colleges & Universities

Norm Denzin and Shirley R. Steinberg
General Editors

Vol. 22

The Higher Ed series is part of the Peter Lang Education list.
Every volume is peer reviewed and meets
the highest quality standards for content and production.

PETER LANG
New York • Washington, D.C./Baltimore • Bern
Frankfurt • Berlin • Brussels • Vienna • Oxford

CHRISTINE E. SLEETER

POWER, TEACHING, AND TEACHER EDUCATION

Confronting Injustice with Critical Research and Action

PETER LANG
New York • Washington, D.C./Baltimore • Bern
Frankfurt • Berlin • Brussels • Vienna • Oxford

Library of Congress Cataloging-in-Publication Data

Sleeter, Christine E. [Essays. Selections.]
Power, teaching, and teacher education: confronting injustice with
critical research and action / Christine E. Sleeter.
p. cm. — (Higher ed: questions about the purpose(s) of colleges and universities; vol. 22)
Includes bibliographical references and index.
1. Critical pedagogy—United States. 2. Multicultural education—United States.
3. Education—Standards—United States. I. Title.
LC196.5.U6S58   370.11'5—dc23   2012042563
ISBN 978-1-4331-2144-9 (hardcover)
ISBN 978-1-4331-2143-2 (paperback)
ISBN 978-1-4539-1040-5 (e-book)
ISSN 1523-9551

Bibliographic information published by **Die Deutsche Nationalbibliothek**.
Die Deutsche Nationalbibliothek lists this publication in the "Deutsche
Nationalbibliografie"; detailed bibliographic data is available
on the Internet at http://dnb.d-nb.de/.

The paper in this book meets the guidelines for permanence and durability
of the Committee on Production Guidelines for Book Longevity
of the Council of Library Resources.

© 2013 Peter Lang Publishing, Inc., New York
29 Broadway, 18th floor, New York, NY 10006
www.peterlang.com

Printed in the United States of America

Contents

Foreword

Arnetha Ball & Cynthia Tyson

Issues of injustice and inequality in teaching and teacher education present one of the central challenges facing 21st-century education. It is impossible to change the balance of power unless we confront existing injustice and inequalities and explore ways that teachers and teacher educators can better comprehend their critical role in maintaining or breaking through the barriers and removing the structures of institutional inequalities. As an increasingly diverse student population is becoming more and more the norm in culturally and linguistically complex classrooms while, at the same time, a predominantly white, middle-class, monolingual, female teaching force *remains* the norm, critical research and action are one viable approach to confronting the injustices that persist in our educational system. It is also critically important to understand the historical forces that have brought us to where we are today.

Currently, we are immersed in a global information society in which technology has increased the amount and transmission speed of information beyond all expectations. Yet, it is difficult to perceive the paradigm shifts while those shifts are actually occurring. In today's society everyone is expected to be able to move easily through the information and develop the cognitive and critical thinking skills to distinguish between "useful" and "useless" information. However, such skills are seldom explicitly taught in our schools. Nonetheless, in our global 21st-century society, a critical factor in confronting injustice will be the ability to harness the knowledge needed to improve education for all students and to serve the public good in socially just ways. At one point in our educational history we were able to use the information available to challenge the system to be responsive to the multicultural and multiethnic needs of students. However, our challenges and responses have now been effectively stalled and replaced by a narrative of neoliberalism. Understanding this realignment is *the* key factor that will allow us to focus on socially-just teaching and teacher education that places generativity, innovation, and knowledge creation at the core of an emerging educational future for all. Teachers and teacher education programs unaware of the implications of the current shift in the national narrative for our K–12 educational systems will find it difficult to understand, positively impact, and advocate for those students whose experiences do not resemble their own.

We need new knowledge, new alliances, new competencies, and critical innovations in teaching and teacher education in order to address the current neoliberal assault. Christine Sleeter's powerful collection brings research insights and historical contextualization to the battle that lies ahead. The chapters challenge the reader to look critically at current reform movements and to question simplistic conceptions of culturally responsive pedagogy so as to understand its true relevance to student achievement.

In her previously published articles and book chapters herein, Christine Sleeter frames all of these issues for teachers and teacher educators in multicultural education, social justice education, and urban education. The book presents considerable research evidence that well-designed and well-taught ethnic studies can produce positive academic and social outcomes for both students of color and White students. Based upon this research, Sleeter questions the current move away from ethnic studies and toward a test-driven, accountability-focused education, particularly in certain school settings.

Through case studies, essays, and research reports, Sleeter challenges teachers who advocate teaching for and about democracy and explores the extent to which teachers are actually (dis)empowered to enact democratic practices in their classrooms in the current accountability context. The book documents neoliberalism's assaults on social justice teaching and examines how curriculum is classified and framed to reconfigure power relations among racial, ethnic, language, and social classes.

Christine Sleeter challenges the reader to think about who has a right to define what schools are for, whose knowledge has most legitimacy, and how the next generation should think about the social order and their place within it. She calls particular attention to the ways in which culturally responsive, multicultural approaches to teaching have been supplanted by standardized curricula and pedagogy derived from neoliberal business models.

These essays illustrate how culturally and linguistically diverse students, many of whom have been underprepared for rigorous academic work, can still attain high levels of academic excellence in a challenging and supportive context using critical pedagogy, critical race theory, antiracist education, and multicultural education. The book closes with a discussion of how we can equip the next generation of multicultural, social justice teachers.

Just as Sleeter herself was once not consciously aware of the national paradigm shift taking place, most teachers and teacher educators are as yet unaware of these shifts. She asks, *"How did a reform movement that reduced broad equity issues to test score gaps and that redefined equality to mean teaching everyone the same thing in the same way at the same time manage to drown out multicultural and social justice paradigms?"* and then provides powerful insights into this dilemma.

Power, Teaching, and Teacher Education sounds an alarm and reminds us of the history and magnitude of the forces we face as well as the strategies we will require if we are to have any traction in the struggle. The book also reframes current dialogue by providing examples of what is possible in elementary and secondary classrooms and in teacher education programs and links these examples to research and theory. The author further argues for an expanded dialogue across critical traditions to strengthen their power and guide practice, examines the barriers Whites encounter when confronting racism, and shares approaches to challenge institutionalized classism, racism, and oppression.

The power of this book lies in the way it effectively strips away the haze that obscures our vision as the author forcefully and unapologetically documents how the No Child Left Behind Act of 2001 and the broader accountability movement are products of neoliberalism even though often camouflaged by the language of democracy, civil rights, standards, accountability, and market competition among schools. In these pages, the unobscured reality emerges, and we can discern that the national school reform agenda is currently embodied in the movement towards privatization and marketization, particularly in those failing schools that have been converted into charter schools, many run by private management companies. Such schools are located disproportionately in impoverished communities, and many of them are now run by private management companies. As we saw most dramatically in New Orleans after Katrina, education has, indeed, become an arena for profit-making, with the expansion of these management companies and testing becoming a multi-billion dollar industry that consumes sizable chunks of school budgets every year.

All of these issues become clear in this ground-breaking collection. *Power, Teaching, and Teacher Education* will have a far-reaching impact. It contains a critically important revelation, a much-needed historical backdrop and contextualiza-tion, a succinct appeal, and a call to action that demands our response. As Christine Sleeter notes, it is not too late: Reform movements have risen in the past, and despite organized efforts to blunt them, are being created today. We certainly hope so. Because our response—or the lack of response—has the potential to change teaching and teacher education as we currently know it.

—November 26, 2012

Acknowledgments

The following chapters have been reprinted with permission of the original publishers.

Ch. 2: "Teaching for democracy in an age of corporatocracy." Reprinted from *Teachers College Record*, 2008, *110* (1): 139–159.

Ch. 3: "Standardizing knowledge in a multicultural society" (with J. Stillman). Reprinted from *Curriculum Inquiry,* March 2005, *35* (1): 27–46.

Ch. 4: "Confronting the marginalization of culturally responsive pedagogy." Reprinted from *Urban Education,* May 2012, *47* (3): 562–584.

Ch. 5: "Transgressing boundaries for socially just teaching." Reprinted from M. C. Fehr & D. E. Fehr, eds., 2009, *Teach Boldly! Letters to Teachers about Contemporary Issues in Education,* pp. 1–12. New York: Peter Lang.

Ch. 6: "The academic and social value of ethnic studies: A research review." Reprinted monograph of the National Education Association, 2011. Washington, DC: The National Education Association.

Ch. 7:   "Working an academically rigorous, multicultural program" (with B. Hughes, E. Meador, P. Whang, L. Rogers, K. Blackwell, P. Laughlin, & C. Peralta-Nash). Reprinted from *Equity & Excellence in Education*, 2005, *38* (4): 290–299.

Ch. 8:   "Critical pedagogy, critical race theory, and antiracist education: Implications for multicultural education" (with D. Delgado Bernal). Reprinted from J. A. Banks & C. A. M. Banks, eds., 2003, *Handbook of Research on Multicultural Education*, 2nd ed., pp. 240–260. San Francisco: Jossey-Bass (now owned by J. Wiley & Sons). Reprinted with permission of J. Wiley & Sons.

Ch. 9:   "Teacher education, neoliberalism, and social justice." Reprinted from W. C. Ayers, T. Quinn, and D. Stovall, eds., *The Handbook of Social Justice in Education*, 2008. New York: Routledge.

Ch. 10:   "Teaching Whites about racism." Reprinted from R. J. Martin, ed., *Practicing What We Teach: Confronting Diversity in Teacher Education*, pp. 117–130. Albany, NY: SUNY.

Ch. 11:   "Researching successful efforts in teacher education to diversify teachers" (with H.R. Milner). Reprinted from A. F. Ball & C. A. Tyson, eds., 2011, *Studying Diversity in Teacher Education*, pp. 81–104). Lanham, MD: Rowman & Littlefield.

Ch. 12:   "Developing teacher epistemological sophistication about multicultural curriculum: A case study." Reprinted from *Action in Teacher Education*, 2009, *31* (1): 3–13. Reprinted by permission of Taylor & Francis Ltd, http://www.tandf.co.uk/journals).

Ch. 13:   "Te Kotahitanga: A case study of a repositioning approach to teacher professional development for culturally responsive pedagogies" (with A. Hynds, R. Hindle, C. Savage, W. Penetito, and L.H. Meyer). Reprinted from *Asia-Pacific Journal of Teacher Education*, 2011, *39* (4): 339–351.

1

Introduction

In 1995, I came to California as a founding faculty member of California State University Monterey Bay (CSUMB). I was strongly drawn by its vision of educating students from racially and ethnically diverse working class families through paradigms that value multiculturalism, ethnic studies, gender studies, and postcolonial studies. Like the other faculty members who came because of this vision, I was eager to work with a diverse group of colleagues to bring to life the contours of education I had been writing about and experimenting with for years in Wisconsin. While we were able to enact (unevenly) much of this vision in the university, P-12 education was heading in quite a different direction. My experience of the jarring clash between corporate-driven reforms shaping education and the multicultural, democratic vision faculty members brought to CSUMB gave rise to the essays in this book.

I began my teaching career in 1972 in Seattle, about when Seattle public schools were developing early curriculum and pedagogy for teaching diverse students and sending teachers (including me) to workshops and institutes on multicultural teaching. Although terms like *culturally responsive pedagogy* and *teaching for social justice* had not yet been invented, ethnic studies and women's studies programs were growing, the concept of cultural deficiency was openly challenged, and approaches to schooling that responded constructively and proactively to culturally and linguistically diverse students were visibly in development (Gay, 1983). My sensibilities about race and anti-racism, equity and justice, multicultural education, critical pedagogy, bilingual education (bodies of thought and action that although related, too often compete with each other) were formed initially in this context of optimistic democratic struggle. Like many other teachers and teacher educators, I became especially immersed in classroom and school practice, exploring possibilities for engaging students in intellectual inquiry projects, multiple cultural perspectives, and democratic processes. I was also interested in how such practices interact with the research and theory that was deepening my own understanding of culture, difference, and power.

Because the core concepts we were working with at CSUMB seemed so very well suited to the vibrantly diverse students in California and increasingly the U.S. in general, and the tremendous social justice issues facing this nation, initially I did not recognize the seismic shift taking place in education policy on the national stage. It was a conversation with a bilingual Chicana teacher in about 1999, in my graduate-level Multicultural Curriculum Design course, that brought home to me the reality of this national paradigm shift. She was expressing frustration that our class was talking about civil rights movements, particularly the Chicano movements of the 1960s and 1970s, when there seemed to be so little progress in improving the quality of education and life in general for the Latino students she was teaching in middle school. I asked her what lessons or insights from these movements were included in her school's curriculum. Surprised by my question, she pointed out that schools were focusing on aligning the curriculum to the state standards and tests. When I asked if there was any attention in her school, in which over 90% of the students were Latino, most of whom were underachieving, to building on the cultural backgrounds of students, or to whose knowledge is in textbooks, she replied that these kinds of things no longer received attention. The entire focus of professional development now was on alignment, which she had decided would be the topic for her master's thesis.

Although I was familiar with California's new state curriculum standards and the general thrust of standards-based reform nationally, I had anticipated finding in California more widespread pushback against reforms that silence attention to multicultural social justice issues. This conversation jarred me because this teacher, had there been pushback from teachers locally, would likely have been part of such an effort. Instead, she seemed to accept the idea that attention to such issues in schools had not led anywhere. At the time, I asked myself: What have "we" (those of us working in critical multicultural and bilingual education) not been doing well? How did a reform movement that reduces broad equity issues to test score gaps, and that redefines equality to mean teaching everyone the same thing in the same way at the same time, manage to drown out multicultural and social justice paradigms? Addressing these questions requires a historical context.

Neoliberalism and the Restoration of Power

A graph in *A Brief History of Neoliberalism* (Harvey, 2005) displays shifts in the share of national income of the top 0.1% of the populations of the U.S., France, and the U.K., in five-year increments, between 1913 and 1998 (p. 17). The display, appropriately titled "The restoration of power," directs us toward the roots of the seismic shift I found myself bumping up against.

By the conclusion of World War I, according to Harvey (2005), the wealthiest 0.1% of the U.S. population had almost 10% of the national income (according to Saez [2010] the figure was closer to 5%, although the trends he describes are the same). After a postwar drop in income that briefly rebounded right before the Great Depression, that wealthiest group's share of the national income declined sharply until the early 1940s, after which it plateaued at about 2% for the next forty years.

What happened during the 1930s and 1940s that resulted in some income redistribution? The primary engines at work were President Roosevelt's New Deal policies and the subsequent labor union growth that the New Deal supported. Concerned about the need to pull the nation out of the Great Depression, provide relief to unemployed people, and reform the financial system, Roosevelt led the adoption of several related measures, including emergency job relief, public works programs such as the Tennessee Valley Authority, public safeguards such as social security, progressive taxation and the inheritance tax to help pay for public services, regulations on corporations, and the National Labor Relations Act. The National Labor Relations Act guaranteed workers the right to organize and established a framework for organized labor to negotiate wage agreements and other conditions of employment. While White Americans disproportionately benefited—Jim Crow was still alive and well—these developments narrowed the chasm separating the wealthy from the poor and facilitated the right of working people to organize.

Neoliberalism was born in the context of reduced and stagnating fortunes of the super-rich. Neoliberal philosophy was initially articulated in 1947 during a meeting led by Austrian political philosopher Friedrich von Hayak (see Harvey, 2005). The group's core principles, derived from classical liberal philosophy, were individual liberty, private property, and market competition. The group believed that a society built on these principles flourishes but worried that they were being undermined by state intervention policies. Neoliberal economic theory gradually gained strength as it was embraced by wealthy corporate leaders and individuals who strongly opposed state interventions, viewing these as thwarting prosperity. By the 1970s, neoliberalism had become influential in some universities, particularly at the University of Chicago, and both Hayek and Milton Friedman were awarded the Nobel prize in economics.

While neoliberalism was incubating, the U.S. Civil Rights movement had gone into full swing. Prompted by events that included desegregation of the military during World War II, the U.S. Supreme Court decision *Brown v. Board of Education* in 1954, and Rosa Parks refusing to give up her seat on a bus in 1955, African Americans (with some White allies) organized massively to challenge racism. The Black Civil Rights movement prompted movements by other historically marginalized groups, including Mexican Americans, American Indians, women, and people with disabilities. It was not always clear that progress toward equity for diverse groups was being made—the work was difficult and at times life-threatening, and victories were always followed by more challenges. Yet, the victories that were won by organized movements, in the context of growing racial and ethnic diversity, felt threatening to many Whites.

So, during the late 1980s and early 1990s, a barrage of public critiques of multiculturalism, many funded by conservative think tanks, began to appear (for a review, see Sleeter, 1995a), at about the same time states were being urged to establish curriculum content standards. These critiques charged multiculturalism with damaging education and social cohesion by appealing to the divisiveness of ethnic cheerleading, weakening the school curriculum, and addressing minority student achievement by appealing mainly to self-esteem rather than hard work and academic challenge.

The 1980s can be regarded as a watershed during which gains of the labor movement, followed by the Civil Rights movements, were challenged and began to be reversed, although I did not realize this at the time. Hacker and Pierson (2010) pinpoint 1978 as the beginning of that watershed. That year, despite Democratic control of Congress and the presidency, Congress passed deep capital gains tax cuts and raised the payroll tax rate, thus retreating from the use of taxes to temper economic inequalities. (That same year, California voters passed Proposition 13, limiting property taxes that helped to fund schools.) How did such tax cuts happen when Democrats controlled Washington? Hacker and Pierson explain that wealthy businesspeople had organized almost a decade earlier, establishing lobbies to oppose government regulations of business, PACs to make large campaign donations, and think tanks such as the Heritage Foundation to shape public opinion.

Globally, neoliberalism was presented as the solution to "stagflation," or lack of economic growth. Neoliberal economic theory had been implemented on a national scale during the 1970s in Chile under Pinochet, as spearheaded by economists from the University of Chicago; it was a disaster for the poor but a boon for the middle and upper classes (Harvey, 2005; Klein, 2008). Mechanisms for pressuring economies around the world into neoliberalism were established in the form of structural adjustments required for International Monetary Fund loans: deregulation, privatization of publicly owned companies, conversion to export economies, export of natural resources, social spending cuts, weakening of organized labor, and removal of restrictions on foreign investment. These pressures paved the way for large corporations to expand globally—a system that Perkins (2004) aptly terms "corporatocracy."

For those at the top of the economic pyramid, these activities, both internationally and domestically, began to pay off during the 1980s. Reagan was elected president in 1981. He immediately slashed capital gains taxes and led the rewriting of tax codes to benefit corporations on the theory that benefits would trickle down (Hacker & Pierson, 2010). By 1988, the share of national income of the wealthiest 0.1% had jumped from around 2% to about 5% (Harvey, 2005).

Neoliberalism Goes to School

In 1983, the National Commission on Excellence in Education published *A Nation at Risk*, which was followed by highly visible national discussions and reports that depicted schools, and U.S. society generally, as being in a state of crisis. These reports and discussions framed the main purpose of schools as regaining the U.S.'s international economic competitive advantage. The main argument was that technological advances and global restructuring were transforming the nature of production and work, requiring the U.S. to prepare many more workers for the demands of this new economy.

The business community, which had alerted us to the crisis, offered its solutions: standards, assessment, and accountability emerged as the three components most central to its school reform plan (Business Roundtable, 1999, p. 1). In response to the Business Roundtable's systematic pressure, the states began to construct disciplinary content standards and testing programs. For a time there were attempts to do so at a national level: the state governors' National Education Goals Panel, *Goals 2000: The Educate America Act,* and the *Improve America's Schools Act* called for national curriculum standards in math, science, history, and English and other disciplines. (Today's Common Core Standards are a continuation of this earlier work.) To varying degrees, states used drafts of national standards documents to inform the writing of their own state content standards.

The *No Child Left Behind Act* of 2001, and the broader accountability movement, is a product of neoliberalism, although this is obscured somewhat through use of language of democracy and the Civil Rights movement (Emery & Ohanian, 2004). In addition to standards, tests, accountability, and market competition among schools, by 2000 the dominant national school reform agenda had embodied privatization and marketization in additional ways. Concluding that private schools in Third World nations "are of higher quality than the public alternative, achieving higher standards at a fraction of the cost of public education" (Tooley & Dixon, 2006, p. 27), the Heritage Foundation recommended expansion of private schooling as a tool for addressing poverty. Pushed by wealthy venture capitalists, partially privatized charter schools and vouchers for private schools emerged in the United States as favored strategies for school improvement (see, for example, Dakari, 2009). Failing schools, located disproportionately in impoverished communities, began to be converted into charter schools, many run by private management companies (Berliner, 2005; Saltman, 2007). This shift toward privatization played out most dramatically in New Orleans after Katrina (see Buras, 2010).

Education itself had become an arena for profit-making, as is the case with expansion of private management companies. Testing, now a multi-billion dollar per year industry, also takes sizable chunks of school budgets. According to the Government Accounting Office, the main beneficiaries of testing requirements are the largest textbook publishing corporations: CTB-McGraw-Hill, Harcourt, Pearson, and Houghton Mifflin (Bracey, 2005). In 2010, Pearson alone, the largest company involved in testing, reported revenues of $9 billion from sale of tests (Singer, 2012).

But at the same time, as teachers are well aware, public education has been subject to severe funding cuts. By 2012, per-pupil funding for schools had fallen to below 2008 levels in 35 states—in many cases, far below (Oliff, Mai & Leachman, 2012). While the recession is the most immediate cause, a general decline in public willingness to fund public services through taxes—pushed by anti-tax groups—is also a cause. For example, with reference to higher education, Lyall and Sell (2006) found that, between 1980 and 2000, the percent of states' budgets spent on higher education shrank from almost 10% to about 7%. They emphasized that, "through a series of incremental, unplanned, and largely undebated decisions, we are privatizing American higher education" (p. 78).

Restoration of Power?

The Occupy Movement has it right: wealth has been moving upward in the economic hierarchy rather than trickling downward. By 2009, the share of national income of the wealthiest 0.1% of the U.S. population had risen to 7.8% (Logan, 2011), while the middle class had shrunk. Between 1971 and 2011, the proportion of adults in the middle class dropped from 61% to 51%; the proportion at both the upper- and lower-income ranges grew (Pew Research Center, 2012). The Pew Research Center reports that during the recession, incomes at the bottom fell four times faster than incomes at the top, bringing income inequality in the U.S. to levels comparable to that of Ivory Coast and Pakistan. Actually, for the bottom 80% of the population, real incomes had barely nudged upward and would have fallen if the average American worker were not working more hours (Hacker & Pierson, 2010). The assault on unions, which had begun in earnest under Reagan, was taken up actively with Tea Party support, most visibly in Wisconsin (ironically, Wisconsin was the birthplace of much of the earlier labor movement).

Whether or not these patterns represent a permanent restoration of the power of the wealthiest remains to be seen. The wealthiest had organized, using various means such as lobbying, establishment of PACs and the American Legislative Exchange Council (ALEC) to influence legislation, and development of various media outlets (including Fox News) to shape public opinion accordingly. The question is when and how people will organize powerfully enough to push back as they have done in the past.

The U.S. is arguably the most diverse nation on the planet. Its diversity may be its greatest strength in struggles for social justice despite its legacy of racism and patriarchy and efforts of conservative coalitions to use divisions to leverage power. The success of the Occupy Movement has been its articulation of a clear reading of the world, as Freire would have put it, which connects with the everyday experiences of millions of people. A weakness has been its taken-for-granted Whiteness (Sen, 2011). Not only have many of its White spokespeople assumed the right to speak, but the movement has been uneven in forming alliances with already-existing movements of people of color. Much work is yet to be done building coalitions across lines of race, gender, religion, and sexual orientation in a context in which conservative media attempt to exploit divisions. But movements have been built in the past and, despite organized efforts to blunt them, are being built now.

Overview of This Book

Like Dewey, I view schools as essential to building a just, multicultural, democratic society. Despite efforts to privatize, regulate, and de-unionize schooling, I believe that education is one of the essential ingredients both to struggles for social justice and to our personal and community well-being. Hence, the chapters in this book, which consist of lightly edited previously published articles, situate the work of teachers within the larger context I have sketched out. Writing from the vantage point of a teacher educator, I focus particularly on the work of teachers in their classrooms as well as research that supports that work.

Part I, Neoliberalism's Assaults on Social Justice Teaching, examines how neoliberal school reforms attempt to "rein in" pedagogy and curriculum that support students from diverse backgrounds, particularly students of color and immigrant students. Through case studies of two teachers in California (an elementary school teacher and a middle school teacher), Chapter Two explores the tensions between attempts to enact democratic practice in the classroom, and limits the accountability context places on them. Chapter Three (with Jamy Stillman) reports a critical analysis of the reading/language arts and history-social science standards documents in California to explore how the neoliberal standards movement has reconfigured curriculum codes and in whose interests. We argue that the standards movement is not simply trying to improve student learning but also reasserts the right of the wealthiest to define what schools are for, whose knowledge has most legitimacy, and how the next generation should think about the social order and their place within it. Chapter Four examines why attention to culturally responsive, multicultural approaches to teaching has largely been supplanted by curricula and pedagogy that derive from neoliberalism. I discuss three factors that contribute to its marginalization: (1) a persistence of faulty and simplistic conceptions of what culturally responsive pedagogy is, (2) too little research connecting its use with student achievement, and (3) elite and White fear of losing national and global hegemony.

Part II, Teaching Back to Power, shifts from situating the work of teachers within a larger context of power relations, to possibilities of practice that challenge those relations. Chapter Five illustrates student-centered, culturally and politically relevant teaching in three different contexts: a first-grade bilingual classroom, a high school English classroom, and a school district ethnic studies program. Chapter Six supports such teaching through a review of the research on the impact of ethnic studies. This review, commissioned by the National Education Association, analyzes published studies that systematically document the impact of ethnic studies on students, Pre-K through higher education, concluding that well-designed and well-taught ethnic studies has positive academic and social outcomes for students. Chapter Seven (with Bob Hughes, Elizabeth Meador, Patricia Whang, Linda Rogers, Ka-ni Blackwell, Peggy Laughlin, & Claudia Peralta-Nash) shows the design and inner workings of a graduate program that offered an academically challenging curriculum, grounding teacher-leaders in multicultural social justice education. The program successfully graduated a student population as racially and ethnically diverse as that of California itself. As eight faculty members who designed and worked this program, we show how culturally and linguistically diverse students, many of whom have been underprepared for rigorous academic work, can attain high levels of academic excellence in a challenging, empowering, and supportive context. Chapter Eight (with Dolores Delgado Bernal) explores implications of three critical traditions for multicultural education: critical pedagogy, critical race theory, and anti-racist education. We argue the need to expand dialogue across critical traditions for the purpose of strengthening their power to guide practice.

Part III, Equipping the Next Generation of Multicultural, Social Justice Teachers, explores teacher education in a neoliberal context. Chapter Nine develops three goals of social justice for teacher education: (1) supporting access for all students to high-quality, intellectually rich teaching that builds on students' cultural and linguistic backgrounds; (2) preparing teachers to foster democratic engagement among young people; and (3) preparing teachers to advocate for children and youth by situating inequities within a systemic sociopolitical analysis. These goals have implications not only for the design and substance of teacher education programs but also for who is recruited into teacher education. Chapter Ten drills down into a process for teaching White preservice teachers about racism so that they might become allies for social justice teaching. After briefly examining barriers White people encounter when learning about racism, I share an approach that I have used many times that interweaves various pedagogical strategies designed to help White people recognize ways in which racism and other forms of oppression are institutionalized, how they play out locally in everyday life, and how they can be challenged. Chapter Eleven (with H. Richard Milner) takes up diversifying who goes into teaching. The chapter reviews programs to recruit and prepare teachers of color, critically examines the nature of research on such programs, and sketches what a research agenda might look like.

The last two chapters directly link teacher professional development for multicultural social justice with its impact on the work of classroom teachers. Chapter Twelve explores the impact of a teacher professional development course on a novice teacher's understanding of multicultural curriculum and her enactment of pedagogy in the classroom. Chapter Thirteen (with Anne Hynds, Rawiri Hindle, Catherine Savage, Wally Penetito, and Luanna Meyer) reports a case study of a professional development program in New Zealand. I became intrigued with work in New Zealand partly because, although the students there are diverse, schools are not as controlled by neoliberal reforms as they are in the U.S., making culturally based reform efforts more possible. In this study, we found a professional development program that begins with teachers learning to form relationships with their indigenous Maori students, relationships that are associated with positive shifts in teachers' understandings of their positioning within classrooms and their expectations for their Maori students.

Ultimately, the work of pushing back against neoliberalism, especially as it is connected with racism, patriarchy, and radical religious fundamentalism, is a political project. Research, however, helps to support work that pushes back. This book, then, represents an attempt to reframe dialog by showing examples of what is possible in elementary and secondary classrooms and in teacher education programs and linking those examples to research and theory.

PART I

Neoliberalism's Assaults on Social Justice Teaching

2

Teaching for Democracy in an Age of Corporatocracy

A sixth-grade teacher of English language learners, teaching standards-based content in social studies, was covering the five forms of government included in her text: oligarchy, direct democracy, monarchy, tyranny, and representative democracy. What unfolded over the next 45 minutes illustrates a clash between conflicting paradigms and their implications for teaching.

I had known the teacher, Nancy, since she had enrolled as a graduate student in two of my courses four years earlier. I was visiting her classroom in the context of a study of teachers working with multicultural curriculum in standards-based environments (Sleeter, 2005). Nancy is a White woman with over twenty years of teaching experience. The middle school in which she taught, located in a predominantly White middle- to upper-class neighborhood, had diversified its population by bussing almost half of its students from low-income, very diverse neighborhoods. This year, English-language learners brought 13 languages to Nancy's morning two-hour language arts and social studies block.

As shown later in this chapter, Nancy is philosophically strongly committed to cultivating democratic citizenship, and had built a classroom environment in which students were invited regularly to consider controversial issues and participate in decision-making. She is passionate about helping students learn to name and address problems they face collectively in their own lives and had learned to embed standards-based skills in reading and writing within significant, real-world problem-based learning.

I had not been in her classroom for several weeks. On the morning in which the incident I will describe occurred, she informed me that her new principal had directed her to adhere strictly to the state's content standards and state-adopted text for both language arts and social studies. This morning, she would be starting a unit on ancient Greece by covering the five forms of government presented in her text.

Using an overhead projector, Nancy reviewed definitions of oligarchy, direct democracy, monarchy, tyranny, and representative democracy. She divided students into five groups, assigned one form of government to each group, and directed the groups to read textbook passages about the form of government they were assigned, and then construct a description of it in their own words. After a few minutes, she asked a volunteer from each group to stand and present the group's work. Initially, she had to ask questions to draw out students' descriptions. As they talked, she wrote their main ideas on the overhead to assist the class in taking notes, and those who were new to English in following the lesson.

When elaborating on monarchy, Nancy used the term *royal blood*, a new term to some students. One asked, "How do you get royal blood? I've never heard of royal blood, I have type B blood." She explained that royal blood means you come from a family in charge. A few minutes later, in the context of discussing what representative democracy is, another student observed that President Bush's father had also been president, so was that royal blood? A moment later, in the context of discussing tyranny, a student wondered whether Arnold Schwarzenegger's election as governor of California exemplified democracy or tyranny, since he epitomized use of force, and another underscored this point by observing, "He touched the ladies." Nancy commented that the students' observations were interesting, but that people had voted for Bush and for Schwarzenegger. She tried to get students to question why people vote as they do and to see voting as something we have control over.

Later Nancy told me that these questions would have been worth opening up for consideration: "Just a little comment like Arnold Schwarzenegger, and you just realize, wow, there's a whole lesson there about political process and democracy, and you know, citizenship, and how we choose our leaders and why, and it's wonderful that that happens, and that they're thinking about it and talking about it" (personal communication, January 30, 2004). But doing so would not be viewed positively by members of the school administration, were one of them to drop into her class, so she did not pursue students' thoughts. In a high-stakes testing context, test-score production took precedence over issue exploration.

There is a profound irony in what happened during those 45 minutes. The text-book and content standards Nancy was to follow teaches that the U.S. is based on democracy, and that U.S.-style democracy is the world's best form of government. But despite that message as well as Nancy's commitment to participatory democracy, she was told to follow directions from others over what to teach, transmitting content to students they would be able to reproduce on tests. In other words, the context of teaching had become distinctly undemocratic, an irony that was not lost on her. Further, neither the standards nor the textbook offered extensive analytical tools for examining power and decision-making as they actually function, particularly connections between political processes and the economic structure (Sleeter, 2002).

Teachers who are committed to democratic teaching are faced with two tasks: negotiating increasingly undemocratic systems in order to find space for democratic teaching, and critically examining what democracy is, including gaps between its ideals and actual practice. After distinguishing between democracy and its antithesis "corporatocracy," I will examine the classroom practice of two teachers to illustrate potentials and limits of democratic teaching in accountability contexts where teachers are under pressure to raise test scores.

Education for Democracy or Corporatocracy?

Because the U.S. is actively exporting its conception of democracy to the world, one might imagine that its citizens would have a robust conception of what democracy is. But that is not the case. In his book *First Democracy*, Paul Woodruff (2005) observed,

> Even educated Americans seem to be confused about democracy, seduced by its doubles, and complacent in their ignorance. When I ask my learned colleagues about democracy, they often say it is 'majority rule,' or they speak vaguely of putting matters to a vote, as if this made a decision democratic. Sometimes they simply point to the Constitution of the United States, forgetting that this was written by men who feared government by the people and were trying to keep it at bay. (p. 4)

Woodruff examined seven features that are central to democracy, based on an analysis of ancient Athens. They include the following: 1) freedom from tyranny; 2) the rule of law, applied equally to all citizens; 3) harmony (agreement to adhere collectively to the rule of law while simultaneously accepting differences among people); 4) equality among people for purposes of governance; 5) citizen wisdom that is built on human capacity to "perceive, reason, and judge" (p. 154); 6) active debate for reasoning through uncertainties; and 7) general education designed to equip citizens for such participation.

At an abstract level, across the political spectrum one finds broad agreement about these features. From the left, for instance, Beane and Apple (1999) enumerated similar features that enable a democratic way of life, including 1) "open flow of ideas" that enable people to be broadly informed, 2) faith in the "individual and collective capacity of people" to resolve problems, 3) evaluation of ideas and policies through critical reflection, 4) "concern for the welfare of others and the 'common good,'" 5) "concern for the dignity and rights" of everyone, 6) understanding of democracy as an ongoing process, and 7) organization of social institutions in a way that supports democratic processes and values (p. 7). From the right, Ravitch (2002) proclaimed the value of equality and human rights, protection of the right to disagree and debate, the right to vote and to be represented in government, and citizens taking responsibility for sharing burdens and acting for the common good.

Yet, these values and features are given form and substance through very different political paradigms, making it reasonable to query the extent to which political decision-making in the U.S. actually uses democratic processes and institutional structures. Woodruff (2005) argued that U.S. citizens often confuse democracy with three deceptive doubles: voting, majority rule, and elected representation. Voting can be so rigged that it does little more than justify the wishes of tyrants; majority rule negates the rights and interests of minorities; and electing representatives leads to bloc competition for power. Democracy is thwarted when domination takes forms such as above-the-law privilege, coercive power, or "self- and familial-indulgence at the expense of the common good" (Parker, 2003 p. 33). Where one stands on the extent to which the U.S. embodies democracy depends on how one interprets the relationship between democracy, capitalism, and power.

Advocates of capitalism link the ideal of free enterprise with democratic freedoms, extolling the primacy of individualism, property rights, and personal responsibility. As Tom Feeney (2004) noted, the Republican Study Committee of the U.S. Congress adopted six principles for governance, four of which are individual freedom, personal responsibility, less government, and lower taxes. Feeney explained that these principles enable individuals to make creative choices that build prosperity and quality of life. Similarly, writing an annual publication of the Heritage Foundation, Miles (2006) explained: "In an economically free country, individuals can pretty much determine their natural abilities, figure out how best to use them, and go about their business" (p. 23). The publication itself goes on to support the idea that the more freedom individuals have to use resources as they wish, the more creatively they will be able to generate wealth; further, privatized institutions out-perform public institutions by placing few restrictions on the entrepreneurial talents individuals can bring to bear on problems (Tooley & Dixon, 2006). From this perspective, democracy and prosperity thrive when individuals have maximum liberty to make their own decisions about how to deploy their property and talents.

Critics of capitalism view concentrated wealth as leading to minority control of power, which undermines governance by the people; critics argue that a limited conception of democracy leads people to equate it with the right to vote for representatives, which tacitly has become capitulation to rule by an elite (Apple, 2001; Parker, 2003; Woodruff, 2005). As Boyte (2003) pointed out, "Traditional citizenship education has been dominated by 'liberal' theory" that forefronts the role of the state in balancing rights of individuals against fair distribution of goods and resources, under the rule of law (p. 88). Liberalism, as embodied in the U.S. Constitution, limits the ability of ordinary people to self-govern, centralizing power in the hands of those who presumably "know" what is best for the whole. Critics argue that increasingly the U.S. is governed not through democracy, but rather through a particular form of oligarchy.

While working as an "economic hit man" promoting U.S. foreign policy and corporate interests, John Perkins (2004) coined the term "corporatocracy" to describe the form oligarchy now takes. According to Perkins, corporatocracy involves linking three powerful institutions that are run by a small elite whose members move "easily and often" across institutions: major corporations, government, and major banks (p. 26). Linking these institutions concentrates power, enabling an increasingly powerful elite to build a global empire to which most people in the world are subservient. Reflecting on his role as an economic hit man for the power elite, Perkins explained that, "We were driven by greed rather than by any desire to make life better for the vast majority" of the people in the countries to which he was sent (p. 26). Rooted in the primacy of property rights over human rights, corporatocracy protects the rights of corporations as well as wealthy individuals to determine how resources will be used, by whom, and to what ends.

Corporatocracy thrives under neo-liberalism, as discussed in the Introduction to this book. Neo-liberalism holds that human well-being can best flourish within a framework of individualism, free markets, free trade, and competition, under which the role of government shifts from regulating markets to enabling them, and privatizing public services (see Harvey, 2005). Ordinary people generally accept these assumptions, since market freedom is touted as the result of "thousands of years of human social evolution" (Perkins, 2004, p. 216), enabling a better life for the majority of people in the world. As Perkins explained, an unquestioned corollary is "that people who excel at stoking the fires of economic growth should be exalted and rewarded, while those born at the fringes are available for exploitation" (p. 216). Perkins argued that most people do not question these assumptions because most have learned to view a wealthy lifestyle as a highly desirable goal and increasingly are employed by the corporatocracy. Further, until recently, U.S. citizens have been relatively protected from the impact of corporatocracy's global empire, as much of the rest of the world has been experiencing it (see Klein, 2008). Trained to see corporatocracy as progress, we shape our conceptions of justice, freedom, liberty, and democracy to fit within the contours of corporatocracy.

Democracy and corporatocracy both value student learning, but define what is to be learned, how, and for what purpose quite differently. The differences rest largely on the extent to which education is seen as serving a public or a private purpose. Let us contrast education for democracy with education for corporatocracy in relationship to four central, persisting questions about schooling (Kliebard, 1982).

1. What purposes should education serve?
2. What is the nature and source of most significant knowledge, and who decides?
3. What is the nature of students and learning, and what teaching processes best promote learning?
4. How should the success of education be judged?

Democratic educators view education as a resource for the public good (Dewey, 1938). A task of education is to help young people learn to connect their own self interest and future with that of a broad, diverse public, and learn to engage productively with this public to address social concerns, including how society's resources might be distributed most fairly and in accordance with human rights (Deakin, Coates, Taylor, & Ritchie, 2004; Parker, 2003). Democratic educators strive to build "a sense of shared purpose" that is not simply license to pursue one's "own goals at the expense of others," on the one hand, nor erasure of community, cultural, and linguistic differences (Beane & Apple, 1999, p. 12), but rather ongoing negotiation of differences.

Under corporatocracy, education is a resource for national global competition and for private gain. According to Lezlee Westine, president and CEO of TechNet, "We cannot take for granted America's continued technological and economic preeminence....If we are to maintain our nation's global leadership in this new era, we must redouble our commitment to innovation" (Business Roundtable, 2005). Education affords credentials (valued differently based on where they were obtained) that can be used to purchase entry into the economic sphere. In that sense, education is a profit-generating commodity for which individual students and families compete (Hess, 2001). Education also prepares workers and socializes them to connect their own self-interest and future with those of employers. Education itself can be privatized to support individual and corporate accumulation of profit and power.

Democratic educators believe that there is no single body of knowledge everyone must learn. Rather, multiple ideas, perspectives, and funds of knowledge that originate in diverse communities have value; diverse perspectives and viewpoints should be opened to debate and dialog (Freire, 1973). Diverse funds of knowledge are seen as a social resource to be drawn on, cultivated, and learned from; perspectives from diverse social locations are valued as lenses for examining issues for ethics and justice (Banks, 2004a). As Beane and Apple (1999) put it, "Since democracy involves the informed consent of people, a democratic curriculum emphasizes access to a wide range of information and the right of those of varied opinion to have their viewpoints heard," including non-mainstream points of view that are often silenced (p. 14–15).

Corporatocratic educators value teaching content and skills that are needed by the nation-state and the economy, assuming sufficient consensus within each discipline that experts can codify it. Ravitch (2001), for example, frequently argued that "the public schools should teach a common culture," based on the presumption that there is consensus about what that common culture is. Teaching everyone the same skills, facts, and discipline-based concepts is intended not only to upgrade the rigor of the curriculum to improve U.S. international standing and prepare young people for the work force (Business Roundtable, 1997), but also to promote patriotism, and cultural and linguistic assimilation (Ravitch, 2001).

For democratic educators, teaching/learning processes that develop critical thinking precede and trump mastery of particular content. Democratic educators value mastery of academic skills and concepts, but believe these must be embedded in thinking; thinking is not something to do later on (Kohn, 1999). Since learning to live and participate in democratic life is inherently social, the teaching/learning process should engage young people with others who are both similar to and different from themselves (Dewey, 1938). In addition, it should engage everyone in learning to produce as well as consume knowledge.

For corporatocracy, teaching/learning processes that emphasize mastery of particular content precede or trump thinking; teaching processes that emphasize problem-solving and solution-generation are characterized as "fuzzy" if they leave students without a sense of correct, factual knowledge.[1] Corporatocratic reform proposals conceptualize young people as empty vessels to fill with knowledge, partly because their authors tend to conceptualize schools as businesses, and young people as products. Implicitly, young people are taught to look to "experts" as the primary source of knowledge, and to consume expert knowledge rather than to produce it. Those who master state-approved disciplinary knowledge can become the knowledge creators.

Democratic educators evaluate education based on how well it serves a diverse public, diverse communities, and the public interest. This cannot be directly measured, although it can be judged using multiple indices of community and societal well being, such as the thoughtfulness of its citizens (Meier, 2004). Democratic educators also advocate multiple measures of student learning, valuing diversity among students. Corporatocracy evaluates according to "performance or market share," seeing "career advancement and financial rewards" as incentives for employees to work toward cost-effective means of reaching measured goals (Hess, 2001). Using standards-based curriculum and tests, the success of education is judged based on how well scores go up, similar to judging the success of business based on increased profit margin.

Drawing from this discussion, several key characteristics of teaching for democracy would include: 1) students considering social issues in relationship to the public good, 2) students using democratic decision-making processes in the classroom, 3) teachers embedding content in critical thinking about real issues, 4) teachers engaging students in multiple perspectives and multiple funds of knowledge, 5) schools affording all students access to high-quality education, and 6) students' cultural and linguistic identities being supported and viewed as legitimate aspects of citizenship.

No Child Left Behind

No Child Left Behind and the broader accountability movement reflect structures and processes of corporatocracy and neoliberalism, although with some cooptation of the language of democracy and the Civil Rights movement. The slogan "Leave no child behind" was first used by Marian Wright Edelman (1996) of the Children's Defense Fund when, speaking of society's eroding financial support for children as money shifted increasingly away from social programs and into the military and tax cuts, she implored: "Can America come home before it's too late to its founding creed of God-given human equality and act to leave no child behind?" The "achievement gap" had long been framed in terms of glaring inequitable opportunities to learn (e.g., Yeakey & Bennett, 1990), including chronic under-funding of schools attended by students of color and from low-income backgrounds, with school funding tied to local tax revenues despite continued neighborhood segregation on the basis of race and class (Berliner, 2005). Other inequities include access to teaching excellence, instructional time, challenging curriculum, up-to-date materials and resources, and resources in students' primary language (Oakes, Blasi & Rogers, 2004), and high expectations (Hauser-Cram, Sirin & Stipek, 2003; Pang & Sablan, 1998). The language and requirements of *No Child Left Behind*, however, rather than addressing this broad range of access issues, have narrowed the focus to school-level gaps in measured outcomes only, implicitly supporting resurgence of the "culture of poverty" for interpreting race and class achievement gaps (Noguera & Akom, 2000).

Created in an ascendancy of neoliberalism, *No Child Left Behind* makes use of many of its tools and assumptions. Following models of business management, states have been directed to set clear, high standards districts are to align curriculum to them and teachers are to teach to them and test student mastery of them. Test results are then to bring consequences, such as whether a student receives a diploma or whether a school receives good or bad publicity. Schools with scores that do not go up, like businesses whose profits do not expand, are subject to closure. *No Child Left Behind* facilitated privatization of schooling, which, as discussed in the introductory chapter of this book, is part of a larger neoliberal project of privatizing public services (Valenzuela, 2005). While some schools and school leaders have used data on the achievement gap as a tool to improve teaching (e.g., Fuller & Johnson, 2001; Haycock, 2001; Roderick, Jacob & Bryk, 2002; Skrla, Scheurich, Johnson, & Koschoreck, 2001), many others have narrowed curriculum so that teaching to the test substitutes for deeper intellectual inquiry, and concepts that are not tested are simply dropped (Hillocks, 2002; Jones, Jones & Hargrove, 2003; Lipman, 2004; McNeil & Valenzuela, 2001; Valli et al., 2008). *Race to the Top*, which presses states to include student test data in teacher evaluation, continues this emphasis of reform by market competition and testing.

There is need to invigorate a discussion of what schools are for in a society that purports to value democracy. And clearly, there is need to engage in democratic processes to reverse the erosion of democracy and conditions that support engaged learning. As Wood (2004) argued, "Educators, parents, and students need to come together to challenge what is happening to the daily quality of school life for our children as a result of the pressure on testing" (p. 48). Democratically minded teachers have the immediate dilemma of what to do, especially if they work with low-income children.

Teaching for Democracy in Standards-based Classrooms

How can democratically minded teachers navigate an accountability context that is rooted more in corporatocracy than democracy? The remainder of this chapter examines the practice of two teachers, drawn from a larger set of a case studies study of eight excellent teachers in California, who had a strong interest in democratic and multicultural teaching (Sleeter, 2005). All of them had been my graduate students.

Rita and Nancy (pseudonyms) both taught English-language learners from low-income backgrounds in schools that did not meet Adequate Yearly Progress (AYP) targets for 2003–2004 set by *No Child Left Behind*. Rita taught second grade, and Nancy taught sixth grade. I wanted to find out what they were able to do to enact a vision of engaged, democratic teaching. During 2003–2004, I spent six hours observing and taking notes in each of their classrooms. I also tape-recorded an hour-long interview with each teacher, and analyzed papers they had completed in my courses as well as their master's theses. Both teachers reviewed an earlier draft of this chapter for accuracy of facts and validity of interpretation. The portraits that follow show how each of them navigated a clash between their own vision of education and demands placed on them.

Using Standards Strategically

Rita, a fifth-year second-grade bilingual teacher, exemplified using standards strategically to try to build student achievement and teach for democracy simultaneously. All of her students were of Mexican descent; their families elected to place them in a bilingual classroom. The students' parents were mostly low-skill laborers, working in agricultural fields or packing plants.

Strategic use of standards meant studying and prioritizing the standards to decide which to emphasize and which to deemphasize or even skip. Rita explained that she used this strategy to find space to go beyond the standards. She used the grade-level standards as a guide, but expected and taught more than they require: in both math and language arts, she moved students into parts of the third-grade curriculum, for example, by teaching them to write multiple-paragraph rather than one-paragraph essays, and in math to divide with remainders. In order to do this, she carefully studied the standards and adopted texts, prioritizing them to figure out what is key and what she could skip, using experience and staff development as a guide. She commented,

> Now, there are some things in the standards that I don't cover by the end of the year. Some of them I don't get to cover, there's just a ton of stuff, if you were to cover every standard, you would be 70 years old by the time I finished with all of them! (interview, February 10, 2004)

Rita viewed teaching as a mission to empower her students. By "empowerment," she meant both preparing them for college, and also preparing them to speak their minds. She explained:

We're expecting students to get power in college. College doesn't—college gives you power, but you must bring it with you, from when you're little. That's when I realized, wait a minute!…I need to teach my students to be creative people, responsible citizens, independent thinkers, people who speak their minds, all of those things. I need to teach my little ones all of that and more (interview, February 10, 2004).

To empower her students as best she could, she organized her classroom to teach her students to be knowledge producers, independent collaborators, and cross-cultural navigators.

Rita started teaching students to produce books when she realized that too much of the standard instructional program was boring. As a university student, she had come to see herself as an author in courses in which books were created with student writings. Through learning to use computers, produce knowledge, and write for an audience, she had become both engaged and empowered. As a teacher, she realized that she could, in turn, empower her working-class students. As she explained, "I need my kids to know they can be writers" (interview, February 10, 2004).

By her fourth year of teaching, Rita had figured out how to teach them to write and research using the computer; her class was producing five books per year. She taught students to use Microsoft Word and do Internet research. For example, for a biography project, each child chose a person to research, wrote a page about the person's life, and inserted a downloaded photo of the person. Most chose pop stars, but some chose people such as presidents, sport stars, and inventors. Rita connected book production with units in her reading/language arts text, so that she could teach standards and knowledge production simultaneously.

Rita organized her classroom into stations (including a computer station), and taught her students to work both independently and collaboratively. Although initially she developed this organizational structure to enable integration of computers into language arts, she then used it as a way of teaching students to help each other and to problem-solve independently. She explained that it required experimentation and persistence to figure out how to make this classroom organization work, since students were not used to working in small groups. She also occasionally invited students to challenge and question authority. As the teacher, she embodied authority in the classroom and periodically she invited students to critique her and offer input into the operation of the classroom.

Rita viewed it as important that her students embrace their own culture and language and not succumb to pressures to assimilate. She stressed respect for one's own family, and taught family and community respect through activities such as interviewing grandparents and learning Aztec dance. She also regarded it as critical that students learn to engage with people who differ from themselves. She was convinced that racial and ethnic minority groups need to learn to collaborate in order to address common concerns together: "If they don't know about other cultures, if they're arguing with the Chinese, how are they going to fight about any issue?" (interview, February 10, 2004). As an immigrant from Mexico, it had taken her several years to realize that communities of color face similar issues and can advocate more strongly together than separately. She was struggling with how to teach this broad idea, however, since her school was ethnically fairly homogeneous, and her access to substantive multicultural curriculum materials was limited. She also admitted that, "Most teachers get caught in this chaos of *No Child Left Behind*, accountability and you name it, we forget" (interview, February 10, 2004).

Rita was determined, however, to ensure that her students have access to the highest quality of education possible, since she viewed low-income communities' democratic participation as thwarted by an inferior education. For that reason, she spent extra time working with parents, locating computers to construct a computer center, and pushing her second-graders into the third-grade curriculum.

Although Rita was critical of many manifestations of the standards movement—scripted curricula, excessive testing, lack of attention to multicultural education, devaluing of bilingualism, and pressure on teachers, the standards movement supported her conviction that children from low-income homes are capable of full participation in society and need to be prepared accordingly. Further, by resisting prescriptions that she felt worked against engaged teaching (such as following a script), she was able to enact, to some extent, her vision of what it means to teach for democracy. As a result, her students' test scores were considerably higher than scores of other second-grade teachers teaching similar students, which supported the latitude her principal gave her for working with standards strategically.

Teaching for Democracy Collides with Demands of Corporatocracy

Discerning readers will note limits in the extent to which Rita enacted democratic teaching. By working strategically with standards, Rita was able to teach critical thinking and knowledge creation, offer low-income students a college-preparatory curriculum, affirm students' cultural and linguistic identities, and, to a much lesser extent, involve students in collaborative decision-making. The fact that most of her curriculum was determined through top-down decision-making, however, and that her students would need to demonstrate mastery of that curriculum on tests limited the extent to which she was able to engage students in classroom-based decision-making processes.

In her many years of teaching, Nancy developed considerable skill in teaching for democracy prior to the standards movement. She described her teaching goals as both developing academic learning and preparation for democracy. She strongly believed that schools should cultivate citizen participation and had worked to build a classroom in which students speak up, debate, listen, and think. She had also learned to open up controversial issues, encouraging debate without preaching her own point of view. She was passionate about helping students learn to name and address problems they face collectively in their own lives.

For example, in 2001–2002, she had designed and taught a unit related to ancient Egypt that examined hierarchical versus egalitarian social structures in history and the present, including the student social structure in her school. The unit was connected to the district's curriculum goals, and it used the adopted social studies and literature texts. But it highlighted analysis of social organization in various contexts and the role citizens can play to access political participation where they live; it used additional readings in literature and social studies and various activities to engage students in these issues. For her master's thesis, Nancy worked with students in one of her classes to investigate a school problem regarding how students treat each other, and to generate solutions. The students helped to formulate the research question, design interview and survey questions, gather data, and analyze it; students then proposed solutions. Nancy explained that she involved students in asking questions about equity "because I wanted to bring the issues of democracy and discrimination to the surface in my school environment. I involved my students because I believe, as Freire did, that, 'as they look at their environment, they will find the autonomy to become the problem solvers of institutional inequality'" (Freire, 1998, p. 128, cited by Pipes, 2002, p. 15).

Right after September 11, 2001, Nancy described the personal and political power of students not only in discussing issues, but also in getting to know each other as people in the process:

> I was having a debate with my students about whether we should bomb Afghanistan. The majority of my students said, No, we shouldn't, because we would be bombing innocent civilians, we would be doing what was done to us, it wouldn't solve anything, et cetera. But I had two boys who said, Yeah, we just need to bomb them, look what they did to us, we just need to bomb them. And I let the kids dialog and talk, and all the different people tried to convince these boys that they didn't feel that this was right. Every day I try to create an atmosphere in the classroom where we can have this kind of discussion, where students feel free to disagree respectfully with one another as they explore their ideas. I'm not going to tell the students my own personal opinions…I want them to think for themselves. Finally one of the girls said, Well, what about Ahmed? (Ahmed was a Pakistani student who disappeared two days after September 11. I think he went back to Pakistan.) And so the students asked,

What about Ahmed? He's over there. What will happen to him? And those same two boys changed their minds and said, Then we've got to come home…We shouldn't bomb them. No great arguments, no amount of rationale would change their minds, only the human connection they had with their friend Ahmed. (interview, October 19, 2001)

This story supported Nancy's conviction that democracy requires people who can debate, speak their minds and listen, that young people can learn to build empathy and listen with their hearts as well as their minds, and that knowledge should be selected in a way that helps students learn to hear and understand multiple perspectives: "That's what I'm doing here, is helping to create, helping to motivate people to be responsible citizens" (interview, January 30, 2004).

In Nancy's view, teaching for democracy includes offering all students an academically rich curriculum, taught in a way that builds access to college. "My job is to educate. They need to be able to read, they need to be able to write, they need to be able to analyze in order to become effective in society" (interview, January 30, 2004). She also believed that knowledge should come, in part, from the students themselves, as they ask questions and pursue interests that relate to broad curriculum goals. "It's a two-way street, we all learn from each other," she explained (interview, January 30, 2004). Prior to passage of *No Child Left Behind*, Nancy had been used to working with textbooks and broad curriculum goals, along with additional resources, to build interdisciplinary thematic curriculum units that connect contemporary issues and students' questions with history and literature. Her two-hour language arts and social studies bloc lent itself well to this.

Nancy's previous principal had supported her in what she was doing. However, conditions pushed her toward the more constrained and conventional approach to teaching that was evident the day I watched the incident that opens this article. Those conditions included escalating performance targets that direct administrators to concentrate on test scores (sometimes to the exclusion of other considerations), and the school having a new principal. Nancy had also been challenged for taking some of her students to a school board meeting so they could speak to a controversial local issue the board was considering. For these reasons, Nancy had been directed to stick to the standards and the textbook and to omit other material.

Claiming Space for Democracy in Student Academic Engagement

Teaching for democracy converges with teaching for corporatocracy in one important area: both aim to develop student learning. The assumptions differ about why this is important, what should be learned, and how students learn. But their emphasis on student learning provides limited space in which democratically minded teachers can work by using standards strategically.

Students achieve in schools and classrooms that engage them in well planned, interesting, and complex projects that embed basic skills and content in higher-order thinking (Berger, 2003; McCombs, 2003; Taylor, Pearson, Peterson, & Rodriguez, 2003). When the pressure toward teaching to standards and tests results in rote teaching to low levels of thinking, however, students become disengaged. For example, based on a study of over one thousand elementary teachers of students classified as gifted in various parts of the country, Moon, Brighton and Callahan (2003) found that accountability pressures discourage effective classroom practices. They noted that, "A prevalent pattern across classrooms and teachers is the belief that the standards, as operationalized by the state assessment, are the gospel, and most teachers feel unable to deviate from them. In many cases, this belief is validated by school and/or district policies, strictly monitored pacing guides, and/or administrative mandates." Pressured to teach to tests, teachers substantially reduced their use of projects and other creative teaching strategies, aiming their instruction mainly at their lowest achievers, and leaving much of the rest of the class "bored and disengaged from learning."

Pedagogical approaches that support student achievement also support teaching for democracy. Teaching for democracy is more, however, than good teaching. Multicultural and democratic educators have long envisaged schools as servants of democratic life helping young people cultivate knowledge, intellectual tools, and experience working across diverse viewpoints and identities to address shared social concerns. As Banks (2004a) emphasized, "Students must attain democratic values in school if we ever hope to change the political, social, and economic structures of stratified societies and nation-states because they are the future citizens and leaders" (p. 10). Now, perhaps more than ever before, it is vital to retain and act on this vision.

Currently the economy, particularly at the upper levels, does not have room for everyone, and there is no evidence that closing achievement gaps will close opportunity gaps that have widened for reasons unrelated to student achievement. For example, in 2009, the wealthiest 1% of the population took home 21% of the nation's income and held 43% of the nation's financial assets, while the bottom 90% of the population took home only a little more than half (53%) of the nation's income and held only 17% of the nation's financial assets (Allegretto, 2011). Tax codes, reduction of organized labor, and policies that favor wealth acquisition over public wellbeing support widening gaps. Testing and standardizing knowledge do not close such gaps. What is needed is consciousness-raising on the part of citizens—

like the Occupy movement has done—leading to public mobilization that questions and resists a growing lopsidedness in wealth distribution.

The accountability movement frames education largely as a commodity for individual consumption rather than as a resource for public good. It is ironic that school knowledge has become exceedingly prescribed and determined at a time when the U.S. is aggressively exporting its version of democracy and personal liberties. While politicians extol U.S. freedoms, teachers like Nancy and Rita—particularly those working with low-income students, students of color, and English language learners—are being told what to teach, sometimes complete with a script to follow. Rita and Nancy illustrate how democratically minded teachers attempt to navigate such pressures. And yet, "individual rights and freedoms come from the very communities that sustain such liberties," rather than those that suppress them (SooHoo, 2004, p. 207).

Parker (2003) pointed out that, "History gives democracy no advantages" (p. 52). Active democracies (at least those of European origin) have been short-lived. If we were serious about sustaining and developing democracy and justice, we would need to "educate for principled activism" (Parker, p. 52), which places responsibilities on schools. These include the responsibility to expect the best from all students and teach to demanding expectations, but also to engage students in curriculum that respects who they are, what they know, and what they bring. It also includes continuing to deepen teachers' pedagogical skill working with diverse populations, which goes beyond identifying "best practices" that can then be scaled up (Lee & Luykx, 2005).

Standards, texts, and tests will not raise political consciousness—indeed, they are designed not to. As the example of Nancy's classroom shows, the standards and texts make available only a limited range of ideas. Directing teachers to follow them blunts critique and questions. Teachers need support in finding spaces to teach for democracy. More importantly, we need to keep alive a vision of participatory democracy for a diverse public, sharpening our own political analysis of the U.S., its institutions, and its place in the world.

Note

1. For example, in 1985, California adopted math framework that "in many ways was the antecedent of the 1989 NCTM [National Council for the Teaching of Mathematics] Standards" (Schoenfeld, 2004, p. 269) in its emphasis on thinking and problem solving. But it was loudly condemned by conservative groups objecting to constructivist pedagogical processes that may allow students to come to incorrect answers through computation errors. Constructivism was caricatured in media as "fuzzy math."

3

Standardizing Knowledge in a Multicultural Society

With Jamy Stillman[1]

> Curriculum in any time and place becomes the site of a battleground where the fight is over whose values and beliefs will achieve the legitimation and the respect that acceptance into the national discourse provides. (Kliebard, 1995, p. 250–251)

Across the U.S., in an attempt to raise standards for student learning, states developed curriculum standards that specify what students are to learn; raising standards has become synonymous with standardizing curriculum. In California, very detailed curriculum standards were developed during the 1990s in History-Social Science, Reading/Language Arts, Mathematics, Natural Science, and Visual and Performing Arts. In 2001, state legislation created a seamless web specifying not only subject matter content in every discipline for K-12, but also university coursework in disciplines that prepare teachers. Standards for teacher credentialing were also aligned to K-12 content standards, making the main role of teacher education preparation to teach state-adopted curriculum. The purpose of this chapter is to examine standards in two disciplines—History-Social Science, and Reading/Language Arts—in order to explore their connection with broader power relationships.

Theoretical Framework

For over a century, curriculum in the U.S. has periodically acted as a lightening rod for debate about what schools should do, and more broadly, about basic values and beliefs about how young people should view society, and what adults expect of them as they enter the adult world. Like Kliebard (1995), Bernstein and Solomon (1999) argued that in any society, groups struggle for the means to control consciousness of people, and that education develops the consciousness of children and youth: "The pedagogic device, the condition for the materializing of symbolic control, is the object of a struggle for domination, for the group who appropriates the device has access to a ruler and distributor of consciousness, identity, and desire" (p. 268).

To examine the legitimation of power and control in two disciplines in California, we used Bernstein's (1975) theory of codes of power in curriculum. Bernstein suggested that codes of power can be uncovered by examining how curriculum is classified and framed. *Classification* refers to the degree to which curriculum contents are separated and bounded, for example, the strength of boundaries among disciplines, or between school knowledge and everyday knowledge. "Where classification is strong, contents are well insulated from each other by strong boundaries" (p. 88). Bernstein distinguished between two basic types of curriculum in relationship to classification: a collection code curriculum, and an integrated code curriculum. A *collection code* reflects strong classification; the stronger the classification, the more hierarchical the structure of knowledge, the more status academic knowledge has over everyday knowledge, and the greater degree to which teaching moves sequentially from basic facts, toward the deep structure of a given discipline. An *integrated code* curriculum is weakly classified, boundaries are blurred, and knowledge is viewed much less hierarchically. Curriculum tends to be organized around themes and emphasizes the knowledge construction process, rather than accumulation of disciplinary facts and concepts. Bernstein suggested that movements away from collection to integrated code curricula may reflect broader social movements that attempt to "alter power structures and principles of control" (p. 111). Conversely, movements that attempt to reestablish collection code curricula may reflect broader movements to reestablish traditional power hierarchies.

Frame refers to "the degree of control teacher and pupil possess over the selection, organization, pacing and timing of the knowledge transmitted and received in the pedagogical relationship" (Bernstein, 1975, p. 89). Under strong framing, teachers and students learn to work within a set of received knowledge; under weak framing, they are encouraged to use their own sense-making process. Curriculum that has strong framing offers little decision-making power to teachers or students; curriculum that has weak framing encourages classroom decision-making. "Framing regulates the form of socialization into the category system, that is, into the positional structure, and into the form of the power relationships which constitute, maintain and reproduce the structure" (p. 179). In other words, teachers and students learn their place in hierarchical power relationships through the degree of power they have over selecting, organizing, and teaching or learning curriculum.

These codes are constructed and play out within structural relationships, which include relationships among teachers (grade level, subject area), between teachers and administrators, and among students (particularly how students are grouped in school). Ultimately, Bernstein was interested in how young people are inducted into a stratified and segmented society. Since he viewed education as a primary regulator of society, he saw classification and framing as tools for examining how regulation is imposed and, at times, disrupted.

The standards movement in the U.S. follows a period in which power relations in the broader society had been disrupted. The Civil Rights movement had spawned various movements to redistribute power, which in education took forms such as school desegregation, multicultural education, and bilingual education. To what extent can the standards movement be understood as an attempt to restore earlier power relations? Bernstein's framework enables us to examine this question as it is reflected in curriculum documents. Below, we situate the standards movement in a historic context, then report our analysis of a set of content standards documents.

From Civil Rights to Standardization

Beginning with the Civil Rights movement in the 1960s, the ethnic studies movement, the women's movement, and other democratically based equity movements challenged collection code curricula that had defined academic knowledge of Europeans and Euro-Americans as superior to other knowledge systems. When schools were initially desegregated, parents and community leaders of color began to demand that the curriculum reflect their communities, and that teachers expect the same level of academic learning of their children as they did of White children (Gay, 1995; Weinberg, 1977). Historically disenfranchised communities argued that textbooks and other sources of curriculum were too often culturally irrelevant to students of color and inaccessible to students of non-English-language backgrounds. Particularly on college campuses, youth demanded ethnic studies courses that related to their own experiences. As discussed in more detail in Chapter Six of this volume, ethnic studies and women's studies scholarship burgeoned; faculty hired to teach such courses found themselves needing to unearth subjugated knowledge to construct new curricula (Gay, 1995a).

By the 1980s, models and approaches to multicultural and bilingual curriculum had been created; they tended to follow integrated curriculum codes and weakened framing in that many of the models emphasized teachers' and students' power over the knowledge construction process. For example, Watkins' (1993) six Black curriculum frameworks and Tetreault's (1989) phases of the integration of women into curriculum dislodged classifications within traditional academic knowledge. Ladson-Billings' (1994) and Gay's (1995a) research on culturally relevant pedagogy, along with bilingual education research, demonstrated how essential it is for all students, and especially second-language learners, to build their academic skills on everyday life experiences and family-based knowledge (e.g., Cummins, 1996; Gutiérrez, et al., 2002; Ruíz, 1995; Tharpe et al., 2000). Bilingual education research demonstrated that primary language literacy among English Learners (ELs) supports second-language acquisition, and that fluency in multiple languages is superior to fluency in only one (e.g., Cummins, 1996; Dicker, 1996; Hakuta, 1986; Thomas & Collier, 1999).

General conceptions of language learning and language arts instruction also shifted. In particular, more holistic and integrated approaches to reading and writing instruction emerged and began to challenge traditional pedagogical models of language arts instruction (Emig, 1971; 1982; Goodman & Goodman, 1979; Graves, 1982; Gutiérrez, 2001). Scholarship that argued for a more social and cultural notion of language learning followed (e.g., Heath, 1983) and influenced the development of, and research about, language arts instructional models that showed effectiveness for culturally and linguistically diverse children. In particular, researchers came to considerable consensus about the most helpful instructional principles and processes, emphasizing the importance of contextualized rather than skill-driven instruction, and the connections between language, thinking, values, culture and identity (Center for Research on Education, Diversity and Excellence, 2002; Gibbons, 2002; Wink & Putney, 2002).

Social science was also a subject of debates. The view that the main purpose of social studies is to prepare citizens conflicted with the more traditional view of social science as discipline based, with curriculum drawing from discipline-specific content. Yet a third view defined social science as a process of reflective inquiry (Brophy & VanSledright, 1997); for example, Wineberg (2001) suggested teaching students to think historically and to analyze historical texts as artifacts of human production in specific contexts, rather than delivering interpretations of the past that historians have constructed.

As noted in the Introduction to this book, the mid-1980s ushered in the standards movement, which viewed the main purpose of schooling as bolstering the U.S. economy and its national sovereignty and security. Its genesis is often traced to the publication of *A Nation at Risk* in 1983 (National Commission on Excellence in Education, 1983). Subsequent reform reports expressed concerns of the business community: that technological advances and global restructuring were transforming the nature of production and work, and that the U.S. would need to develop many, many more workers for demands of this new economy. These new workers would need to master "technological visualization; abstract reasoning, mathematical, scientific, and computer expertise; knowledge of specific technologies and production techniques; individual initiative; and so forth" (Berliner & Biddle, 1995, p. 141). On the heels of these reform reports came a barrage of highly visible conservative critiques of multiculturalism and bilingual education (e.g., Bloom, 1989; Ravitch, 1990; Schlesinger, 1992), which targeted curricular changes and policies that had been instituted in schools and universities (see Sleeter, 1995a).

The reform reports as well as the conservative critiques of multiculturalism depicted schools, and U.S. society generally, as being in a state of crisis. In response, beginning in the 1980s, states began to construct disciplinary content standards. By the mid-1990s, most states had content standards in place, and were designing or beginning to implement statewide systems of testing based on them. Beginning in 2001, *No Child Left Behind* mandated that states receiving federal funding implement accountability systems, with annual testing in reading and math.

The specificity, user-friendliness, and prescriptiveness of content standards vary from state to state. In some states, they are highly detailed and specific, leaving fairly little room for local decision-making, while in others they are very broad and general. For example, in their analysis of fourteen states' language arts standards documents, Wixson and Dutro (1999) compared the structure of standards in Texas and California, both of which serve diverse students. While California's language arts standards comprised three volumes, only one of which explicitly addressed how to teach English Language Learners (ELLs), Texas included both standards and instructional guidelines in one accessible and user-friendly document, which integrated strategies throughout for tailoring instruction to English Language Learners.

Within the standards movement, the general paradigm shifted from integrated code curricula to collection code curricula, and weak framing to strong framing. Science was used to justify certain pedagogies. State and federal governments define science to mean studies that claim to be value neutral and rely heavily on quantitative methods. Reading and language arts, particularly, were affected by the seminal "scientific" study supporting phonics instruction, commonly called *The Foorman Study* (Foorman, et al., 1998) and sponsored by the National Institute of Child Health and Human Development (NICHD).[2] Across the country, "alignment" became a watchword, as schools and school districts worked to align their curriculum with state standards and state testing.

Standardizing Curriculum in California

California has a highly diverse student population. In academic year 2002–2003, students in California public schools were: 51% Hispanic, 27% non-Hispanic White, 7% Black, 9% Asian, 3% Filipino, 1% American Indian/Alaskan Native, and 1% Pacific Islander. One out of every four students was an English Learner, coming to school speaking a first language that is other than English (California Department of Education, 2012).

California is often cited having led the nation's standards movement by drafting curriculum frameworks in the early 1980s, which became the cornerstone of its standards-based reform program. For all content areas, the State Board of Education, appointed by the governor, makes curriculum decisions. Subject-matter decisions are made by committees that report to the Curriculum Commission. Members of the Curriculum Commission are appointed by the State Board of Education, the governor, and the Speaker of the House of the Assembly. Commission recommendations go to the State Board of Education, which then flow down to the colleges and the counties, then to districts, then to schools. In other words, the decision-making structure is decidedly top-down.

Content standards guide adoption of textbooks for grades 1–8 by the State Board of Education and construction of state achievement tests. The Public School Accountability Act of 1999 established a system of achievement testing based on curriculum standards and on rewarding high-performing schools and sanctioning low-performing schools. The 2002 Master Plan for Education, which outlines recommendations for education from preschool through university, makes frequent reference throughout to aligning curriculum and teacher preparation to the state's content frameworks and standards.

Our main question, then, was this: Given the historic context of struggles over curriculum, how has the standards movement re-configured codes of power as manifest in curriculum, and in whose interests?

The standards documents

We conducted a content analysis of the following California frameworks and standards:[3]

- *History-Social Science Framework and Standards for California Public Schools* (California Department of Education, 2001)
- *English-Language Arts Content Standards for California Public Schools* (California Department of Education, 1997)
- *Reading/Language Arts Framework for California Public Schools* (California Department of Education, 1999b)
- *English Language Development Standards* (California Department of Education, 1999a)

Content standards in both disciplines were adopted initially in 1987. The *History Social Science Framework and Standards* document, which has been re-adopted periodically with only minor updates, describes what should be taught in the social studies curriculum in considerable detail for every grade except ninth. (For ninth grade, there are suggested units but local decision-making over curriculum is allowed.) Its initial adoption was highly controversial, contested vigorously by numerous educators, community groups and scholars, particularly African American scholars. The main objection was that it had been written primarily by Euro-American scholars working within a Euro-American perspective that conceptualizes everyone within an immigrant paradigm. In so doing, it ignores perspectives that arise from non-immigrant historical experiences, such as those of Native Americans and African Americans (see Cornbleth & Waugh, 1995; King, 1992), concerns that were never addressed. Ultimately, several school districts (notably San Francisco, Oakland, and Hayward) rejected the adopted texts, or recommended that they be used only with substantial alternatives.

In 1997, California adopted a new set of reading/language arts standards and frameworks to replace those adopted in 1987. These new documents embodied a distinctly different theoretical orientation than those issued previously by shifting away from a constructivist, literature-based approach to reading instruction to a direct instruction approach. This shift is evident throughout all three of the reading/language arts documents we analyzed, mainly in the authors' tendencies to make theoretical claims reminiscent of the previous framework, and then to offer content standards and practical guidelines from the direct instruction approach.

Introductions to the documents in both disciplines address California's diverse students, especially the increasing number of students who are not proficient in

English, where writers made clear their dedication to the academic success of such students, and their perception that the content frameworks and standards are based upon consensus about what California's students need to know. What does an analysis of how they classify and frame curriculum reveal?

Methodology

We used two main processes to analyze these documents. First, we read them for themes, keeping systematic notes on each theme. For the reading/language arts documents, we read for themes reflecting a socio-cultural perspective (operationalized through terms such as *contextualization, scaffolding, primary language instruction, bilingual,* and *bicultural*) and a skill-based perspective (operationalized through terms such as decode, phonics, phonemic awareness, and phoneme). For the history-social science document, we read for themes reflecting multicultural content (such as depiction of African American history, depiction of women, depiction of European immigration), and pedagogical approaches (such as interdisciplinarity, use of student-generated historical analysis, use of expert-generated historical analysis).

Second, we counted words and items in each document that reflected patterns related to our thematic analysis. We counted the demographic characteristics of people named for study in the history-social science document, but not the reading/language arts documents, which did not name people for study. There, we counted terms representing pedagogical approaches and references to English language learners.

Results of Analysis

Below, we describe how these documents classify and frame curriculum according to Bernstein's analytical framework.

Classification

Our analysis of classification addresses how knowledge boundaries and hierarchies are established. The boundaries we identified include those between disciplines and languages. We also noted distinct patterns in sequencing and structuring knowledge in each discipline.

The standards solidify disciplinary boundaries. Separate disciplinary committees prepared the standards, and even though the covers of the documents are similar, their overall internal structure is not. The English Language Arts standards for every grade level are organized into four areas: Reading, Writing, Written and Oral English Language Conventions, and Listening and Speaking. Standards and sub-standards are then organized into each of these four areas. In History-Social Science, the standards and sub-standards are organized mainly according to theme, time period, and/or geographic location, which differ from one grade level to the next. For example, second grade is organized around the theme of "People who make a difference"; it includes five standards that have up to four sub-standards. Eighth grade is organized chronologically around U.S. history; twelve standards each have between three and nine sub-standards. That each discipline's standards are organized according to a different internal logic would tend to discourage constructing interdisciplinary curriculum.

The *English-Language Arts Content Standards (ELA)* mandate what all students must learn. The *Reading/Language Arts Framework* details how and in what order teachers must introduce language arts material. These two documents separate what students must learn from pedagogy and instructional decision-making.

The three reading/language arts documents solidify language boundaries and the primacy of English. The *English Language Development Standards (ELD)* are mapped against the *English-Language Arts Content Standards* to help California's English Learners to "'catch up' to the state's monolingual English speakers" (p. 1). The English Language Arts (ELA) standards are named 130 times as *the* instructional objectives of the ELD standards. Learning in English is given clear primacy over learning reading, writing, and other language arts skills in any other language. The documents ignore language arts proficiencies that students might have in a language other than English. For example, while the Introduction to the ELD standards document acknowledges research supporting the value of primary language literacy, the standards themselves encourage teachers to tap students' primary language knowledge only with reference to students' familiarity with English phonemes.

The standards set up a complex structure of knowledge for each discipline. In both, knowledge derived from students' experience is subordinated to school knowledge. For example, the English-Language Arts standards refer to students' familiar experiences and interests primarily with reference to their selection of topics in which to practice oral presentation. Otherwise, there is little reference to students' interests and experiences. The History-Social Science Standards refer to students' community and local area in the primary grades, but from fourth grade onward, detail content to learn without reference to students' lived experiences. In the remainder of this section, we examine how disciplinary knowledge is constructed within each of the two disciplines.

Language arts is hierarchically structured into a learning sequence, leading toward classification of students based on mastery of that sequence. Students are to learn skills first and build meaning on skills. This emphasis on sequence is premised on the assumption that, "A comprehensive program ensures that students master foundational skills as a gateway to using all forms of language as tools for thinking, learning and communicating" (California Department of Education, 1999b, p. 4). The authors emphasize their commitment to a *balanced* literacy program, but also state that, "balanced does not mean that all skills and standards receive equal emphasis at a given point in time. Rather, it implies that the overall emphasis accorded to a skill or standard is determined by its priority or importance relative to students' language and literacy levels and needs" (p. 4). Further, the standards embrace balance mainly when addressing the learning needs of native English speakers. They relegate students who are still learning English to a "back-to-basics" program until they master foundational skills.

This is not to preclude a well-trained teacher from delivering high-quality reading/language arts instruction to English Learners. Nonetheless, following the standards' sequencing with fidelity may lead teachers who have received little or no training in this area to a very *imbalanced* program, particularly for English Learners. The *Reading/Language Arts Framework* contends that "Simplified texts should be used only with students with weak proficiency in English" and that "students who use the simplified text need intensive English language instruction to enable them to catch up with their peers" (California Department of Education, 1999b, p. 76). In other words, California's reading/language arts standards enable balanced instruction more for students who read English at or above grade level than for others.

All three reading/language arts documents are heavily weighted towards phonics instruction, and construct literacy largely as word analysis, particularly in the early grades. The words "phonemes," "phonics" and "phonemic awareness" are mentioned 200 times in these documents collectively. They are mentioned only 22 times in the 84-page ELA document (14 of which are in the glossary), but 66 times in the 93-page ELD document (only two of which are in the glossary). Further, the ELD standards emphasize it from kindergarten through the 12th grade, while in the ELA standards most references to phonics-driven instruction appropriately diminish after the fourth grade. Thus, The ELD standards treat phonics-mastery as a gatekeeper for English learners through the twelfth grade.

As a result, language minority students may be precluded from engaging in literary analysis and other intellectual activities that would prepare them for admission to higher education institutions. And although the standards at times suggest to teachers that optimal student learning happens when skill instruction is embedded in authentic texts, discrete skill instruction is consistently separated from comprehension or literary analysis by requiring that activities such as literature-based instruction be introduced only *after* students demonstrate their discrete skill mastery.

Literature is further separated from skills instruction by being developed in yet a fourth document. Each time the authors of the reading/language arts documents suggest using literature, they advise teachers to refer to the state-sponsored list, *Recommended Literature: Kindergarten Through Grade Twelve* (California Department of Education, 1996). None of the titles are integrated into the standards documents.

The *History-Social Science Framework and Standards* gives clear primacy to history, it as "a story well told" (California Department of Education, 2001, p. 4). The story around which the standards are structured develops over about 10 grade levels. Its central idea is that, as an immigrant society, the U.S. has always been multicultural; students need to "understand the special role of the United States in world history as a nation of immigrants" (p. 21). At the same time, "its institutions were founded on the Judeo-Christian heritage, the ideals of the Enlightenment, and English traditions of self-government" (p. 64). Its unfinished story tells "the historic struggle to extend to all Americans the constitutional guarantees of equality and freedom" (p. 21). Much of its content revolves around the political system of the U.S., as outlined in the Constitution, and is developed primarily through the conceptual tools of chronology and geography, as its introduction states.

The dominant story line revolves around European and European Americans, particularly men. For example, we counted representation of people. Of the 96 Americans who were named for study, 82% were male and 18% were female. They were 77% White, 18% African American, 4% Native American, 1% Latino, and 0% Asian American. Authors of the *History-Social Science* framework recommend integrating children's literature with history (a break in the otherwise strong classification system), and gave specific suggestions. We tallied the racial and gender composition of the 88 authors of recommended children's literature. Fifty-seven percent were male, and 35% were female; we were unable to identify the sex of 8%. Sixty-two percent were European or Euro-American; 19% were African or African American; 1% (one author) was Native American; 7% were Asian or Asian American; none were Latino or South American; and we were unable to identify the background of 10%. We saw a noticeable effort to include stories about diverse European ethnic groups, including Swedish, Irish, and Russian immigrants.

Since history-social science was constructed mainly as a story of immigration, stories of conquest were filtered through that paradigm, using the tools of timelines and maps. Students first study European colonialism briefly in fourth grade in the context of California history. In fifth grade, they meet European explorers largely through map study, then they study English settlements in North America. In seventh grade they examine different world regions, concluding with a unit on "The

Age of Exploration to the Enlightenment." European exploration and conquest are mentioned, but political ideals of the Enlightenment receive at least as much attention. This is important, because it casts colonialism not as the taking of land, life and sovereignty, but rather as the spread of reason, ideas, and liberty. In eighth grade, students encounter "the extension of the United States beyond its borders" (California Department of Education, 2001, p. 106), but relationships between the U.S. and Puerto Rico, the Philippines, or islands in the Pacific and Caribbean are not mentioned. In tenth grade, there is some review of "the worldwide expansion that was fueled by the industrial nations' demand for natural resources and markets and by their nationalist aspirations," presented as map study in which students survey colonial possessions of several European nation and the U.S. (p. 126). Thus, it is possible to graduate from high school with only a fuzzy idea of European and U.S. histories of conquest and exploitation.

The conquests of northern Mexico and indigenous peoples are marginalized and sanitized. In third grade, students briefly study indigenous people of the past, then move on. In fourth grade, when studying the history of California, they briefly study American Indian nations in California's past. In fifth grade, students begin to study U.S. history, starting with a unit devoted to pre-Columbian indigenous people. After that unit, indigenous people appear only sporadically, and in relationship to the story of the Westward movement of Euro-Americans. Students study the conquest of Mexico in fourth, fifth, and eighth grades, but do so mainly as map study and timelines. Given that California used to be part of Mexico and became a part of the U.S. through conquest, this casting of history negates family knowledge of many students of Mexican and indigenous descent.

To summarize, the documents set up strong classification, solidifying a collection code. With the exception of the history-social science framework's recommendation to connect history with children's literature, the disciplines are treated as distinctly separate, each having its own internal and hierarchical structure of knowledge. Reading/language arts is conceptualized as an accretion of skills acquired sequentially and in English. As a result, English Learners may well get less access to higher-order thinking than native English speakers, since thinking and literary analysis in students' first language does not count. History-social science is constructed as a detailed story, sequenced over several grade levels, and organized around historically dominant groups' perspectives, experienced, and ways of seeing the world. The high degree of detail in both disciplines, and the differing organizational systems that structure them, would discourage interdisciplinary teaching or development of other integrated code curricula. Further, the privileging of English and use of English proficiency as a gatekeeper, and the privileging of a

European American immigration story as the backbone for academic content in the social sciences, establishes knowledge of White English speakers as dominant.

Framing

Framing refers to the degree to which teachers and students have authority to bring their own questions, points of view, organization, and pacing to the curriculum. We found reading/language arts to be more strongly framed than history-social science.

Compliance with the standards is enforced mainly through testing. This alignment is more direct in reading/language arts than in history-social science. Each year, all second through eleventh grade public school students are required by state law to take standardized tests, which focus heavily on reading. For grades K-3, schools can choose between only two reading series, both of which are heavily skills-based and scripted. Teachers at higher grade levels have a little more choice; for example, at the time of this analysis fourth-grade teachers could select from six reading texts, and eighth-grade teachers could select from among eight texts.

Although some of California's few remaining bilingual education programs are permitted to administer standardized tests in a language(s) other than English, these tests merely supplement English standardized tests and are not used, as the English tests are, to determine class placement, grade promotion, or a school's ranking on the scale used to determine a school's funding and state intervention efforts. Because California's Public School Accountability Act uses English tests as the *only* outcome measures in its school ranking system, it is increasingly difficult for teachers to stray away from the reading/language arts standards, even if their own professional experience leads them to believe doing so would benefit their students.

Compliance with the history-social science content standards is enforced at the elementary level mainly through the state's textbook adoption process. Elementary students are not tested on mastery of this content. However, at grades 8, 10, and 11, social studies is part of the state's standardized testing program; the eighth-grade test is designed to cover the curriculum for grades 6–8. Secondary teachers have more latitude than elementary teachers to choose texts, but are held accountable through student testing.

Both disciplines are strongly framed through the degree to which content and skills are minutely specified, and through use of disciplinary expertise and science to support the standards. The reading/language arts documents mask ideological debates about literacy by using rhetoric of science. For example, the Introduction to the *Reading/Language Arts Framework* states, "Reading/language arts and related disciplines are the beneficiaries of an abundance of converging research that produces a professional knowledge base related to fostering and sustaining competence in the language arts, particularly beginning reading" (California Department of Education, 1996b, p. 3). The authors name a study sponsored by the National Research Council (1998) as "most important" because of its claim that "there is [now] a convergence of evidence to guide instruction in the language arts" (p. 3). All three documents rely heavily on this research to substantiate their emphasis on phonics instruction and phonemic awareness. But, there is a notable absence of references to studies that support alternative approaches to reading instruction, particularly socio-cultural approaches that may be more effective than phonics-driven methods, especially for diverse students.

We examined the documents for the extent to which they frame how teaching is to occur, particularly given the diverse students in California classrooms. Content in reading/language arts is highly prescribed. At several points in the ELD and ELA documents, the authors mention the "special needs" of English Learners and suggest that teachers modify their instruction to better meet them. Paradoxically, neither document suggests how to do this. In fact, neither document mentions the terms "scaffold," "specially designed academic instruction in English (SDAIE)," or "contextualize," all of which are commonly used in literature that details effective ways of teaching second-language acquisition.

The *Reading/Language Arts Framework*, on the other hand mentions the word "scaffold" many times in the section entitled "Universal Access." This section, featured throughout the document, is broken down into three sub-sections in an effort to address the needs of 1) students with reading difficulties or disabilities, 2) English learners and 3) advanced learners. A universal access section is offered at each of the early grade levels, while it is included less frequently at the higher grades. At each grade level, only a few standards are mentioned and discussed in detail; teachers are then given suggestions for adapting the standards to meet their students' needs. For example, project extension guidelines are offered for "advanced learners," and scaffolding interventions are offered for English learners. To the extent that the Universal Access section suggests that teachers tailor their instruction to their students, inviting teacher judgment could be seen as weakening the framing of curriculum. At the same time, we found the 300-plus-page *Reading/Language Arts Framework* so unwieldy, it was difficult to imagine a teacher finding the time or wherewithal to study these suggestions. Overall, the three documents taken together specify so many skills to teach and the order in which they are to be introduced, that one could see drill on the standards as the best way to get through everything.

In addition, the universal access section of the *Reading/Language Arts Framework* emphasizes using students' scores ("standard deviations") on the language arts portion of the state's standardized test to "diagnose" students' gaps in learning.

Accordingly, teachers are then urged to integrate test preparation into their intervention efforts (California Department of Education, 1996b, p. 226–229). Closely tying the standards documents to standardized tests raises questions about the degree to which teachers have the latitude to implement the standards as they deem most effective, particularly for "special needs" students such as English learners and learning disabled students.

The language arts' emphasis on sequencing similarly strengthens the framing of the language arts curriculum, particularly for English learners and their teachers. For example, the *Reading/Language Arts Framework* suggests that when students demonstrate persistent difficulty in mastering the language arts standards for their grade level, teachers ought to be "differentiating curriculum and instruction, using grouping strategies effectively, and implementing other strategies," in order to meet the needs of these students (California Department of Education, 1996b, p. 226). In principle, this would allow for a weaker framing of the curriculum by affording teachers the chance to exercise their own professional judgment about instructional delivery. Yet, the *Reading/Language Arts Framework* also encourages teachers to deliver instruction for special needs students that is even *more* sequential than for other students (p. 229). This sequential format, which reads like a list of skills and instructional activities, would most easily be aligned with a scripted skill-driven program, leaving little room for modification.

The *History-Social Science Framework and Standards* encourage higher-order thinking and active teaching processes throughout the grade levels. The document acknowledges that historians construct history and that students should become aware of debates among them. For instance, a standard for eleventh grade requires that students "evaluate major debates among historians concerning alternative interpretations of the past" (California Department of Education, 2001, p. 142). And, occasionally the *History-Social Science Framework and Standards* mentions how historians work and that they often disagree with each other. But the main learning process it authorizes is consumption of an interpretation of the past prepared by someone else, rather than learning to construct an interpretation using the tools of historical thinking. The standards are largely content driven, spelling out conclusions students should reach. For example, the term "analyze" is used repeatedly to describe what students should do: "At the same time students should analyze periodic waves of hostility toward newcomers and recognize that the nation has in different eras restricted immigration on the basis of racial, ethnic, or cultural grounds" (California Department of Education, 2001, p. 10). But, the authors have already constructed a general analysis for students; their task is to comprehend that analysis rather than learning to construct an original analysis based on historic data. The authors recommend using a variety of teaching strategies such as debates, simulations, role-play, narratives, and video so that students will become engaged in learning the material. It is possible for teachers to alter how they construct their history or social studies curriculum, but since the curriculum as a whole is packed, it is simply easier for teachers to follow what they are given.

California's teacher credential standards, revised to support the state content standards, also strengthen the framing of the curriculum. As discussed elsewhere (Sleeter, 2003), the teacher credential standards explicitly define teacher education as preparation to deliver the state's academic content standards. The phrase "state-adopted academic content standards" appears 34 times in California's Professional Teacher Preparation document, and 26 times in its Professional Teacher Induction Program document. By contrast, the phrases "culturally relevant," "multicultural," or "justice" appear in neither one. Disciplinary content preparation for teachers is also tied to the content standards; the university's disciplinary programs must be approved by the state as being aligned to the content standards for certification programs to be authorized. In this way, what teachers learn in the university should match with what is in the standards, lessening the possibility that teachers will bring to the classroom ideas that conflict.

To summarize, the state standards strongly frame curriculum in both reading/language arts and history-social science. In the reading/language arts documents, the emphasis on sequence, their prescriptive nature, and the strict compliance enforced by high-stakes standardized testing ensure that a back-to basics reading/language arts curriculum will be implemented across the state, and will be the most strictly enforced with "special needs" children. In addition, the dearth of instructional strategies for teachers of English learners and the inaccessibility of guidelines that are included discourage straying from or expanding upon the curriculum, even in the interest of meeting the needs of individual students. Further, because of the theoretical contradictions present throughout all three reading/language arts documents, a teacher may be given the impression that s/he can implement a literature-based and linguistically responsive reading/language arts program, but then be limited from doing so simply because of a lack of available instructional time, and/or state and district pressure to "teach to the test." The *History-Social Science Framework and Standards* are content-driven, although filled with suggestions for student activities. Teachers have more latitude for deciding how to teach history and social studies than reading. But the curriculum is so packed and backed up by state-adopted texts that it is an effort to not follow the standards.

Discussion and Implications

Given the context of California and the historic context of struggles over curriculum, how has the content standards movement re-configured codes of power and in whose interests?

Our analysis of the way the standards classify curriculum shows that they reassert disciplinary boundaries and boundaries between traditional academic knowledge in English, versus knowledge in languages other than English, as well as knowledge from home and community. In both reading/language arts and history-social science, the content standards specify a structure of knowledge and sequence for teaching it. In reading/language arts, the structure builds higher-order thinking on discrete skills, and in so doing, makes higher-order thinking more accessible to English-speaking students with average or above reading skills than to everyone else. Further, the reading/language arts documents consistently refer to California's non-White, non-English-speaking students as "these students" and "they" instead of one of "us." History-social science is structured largely as a story of European immigration and the construction of a nation around Judeo-Christian values and European political institutions. Implicitly, in an attempt to reduce the significance of the growing demographic diversity of California's students, the content standards set up a we/they perspective in which "we" are of European, Judeo-Christian heritage and English-speaking, and "they" are not. Ideologically the curriculum in both disciplines rests most comfortably on historically dominant groups' perspectives, language, and ways of seeing the world.

Framing examines the place teachers and students are expected to take within this structure and the degree of latitude they have for defining that place. Our analysis of the standards shows that, particularly in reading/language arts, teachers and students are expected to follow the state's prescription. Compliance is enforced mainly through state-wide standardized testing in English, as well as through the textbook-adoption process. Compliance is also enforced through the sheer prescriptiveness of a packed curriculum, particularly at the elementary level. Further, compliance in the way reading/language arts is taught is to be enforced mainly in schools that score low on standardized tests, and with students designated as having "special needs."

Although the content standards in both disciplines rest within a specific ideology, they are presented as if there were no serious ideological debates to consider. Both present a detailed curriculum outline, and both give enough verbal recognition to cultural, racial, and linguistic diversity that teachers without a deep understanding of diverse intellectual funds of knowledge, diverse ideological perspectives and effective pedagogy for diverse students might see the standards as fully inclusive. Use of disciplinary "experts" as curriculum document writers, and of "scientific" research about reading encourage compliance. While the documents occasionally suggest use of project-based and literature-based teaching, the prescriptiveness of the standards, limited availability of instructional time, and adoption of a mandatory scripted reading program steer teachers toward a back-to-basics curriculum. In the top-down curriculum-making structure of California, teachers and students have little recognized power. Although in California the Reading/Language Arts standards have now been reworked to be aligned with the Common Core Standards, we suspect that the logic behind the newer documents is much the same as we report here. We encourage research that explores this matter.

This standards-based curriculum-planning process harkens back to that described by Cubberley almost a century ago, when he characterized schools as "factories in which the raw products (children) are to be shaped and fashioned into products to meet the various demands of life" (cited by Beyer & Liston, 1996, p. 19). Like a century ago, curriculum has been organized scientifically for efficiency, deriving learning objectives from social and economic needs, and casting teachers as managers of the process of producing student achievement scores. But both sets of standards, and particularly those in reading/language arts, deflect attention away from their ideological underpinnings by virtue of being situated within a testing movement. Rather than asking whose knowledge, language, and points of view are most worth teaching children, teachers and administrators are pressed to ask how well children are scoring on standardized measures of achievement.

Our analysis suggests that California's curriculum standards fit within a political movement to reconfigure power relations among racial, ethnic, language, and social-class groupings. This is not simply about trying to improve student learning, but more importantly, about reasserting who has a right to define what schools are for, whose knowledge has most legitimacy, and how the next generation should think about the social order and their place within it.

Notes

1. Jamy Stillman is assistant Professor at the University of Southern California.
2. This use of science may explain why the current standards go largely unquestioned (Shannon, 2001). A growing body of research is beginning to demonstrate that *The Foorman Study* was flawed and even deliberately manipulated to attain particular results (Taylor, 1998, Coles, 2000), and that subsequent advocacy of phonological reading strategies have been overstated (Swanson, Trainin, Necoechea, & Hammill, 2003).
3. Our analysis refers to the standards that were in place as of 2004 when we conducted this analysis. Since that time, states including California have begun to align their standards with the Common Core Standards.

4

Confronting the Marginalization of Culturally Responsive Pedagogy

As argued in Chapter Two, over the past 20 years in the United States and increasingly globally, neoliberalism—or corporatocracy—has driven school reform. An economic philosophy that, as Hursh (2007) puts it, "promotes personal responsibility through individual choice within markets" (p. 496), neoliberalism emphasizes education as preparation for work, and market-based education reform. In the wake of neoliberal school reforms, many now question the value of teacher education; professional development, both for preservice teachers (see Chapter Nine of this volume) and for practicing teachers, has shrunk (Wei, Darling-Hammond, & Adamson, 2010).

In this chapter, I argue that neoliberal reforms, by negating the central importance of teacher professional learning, as well as context, culture, and racism, reverse the empowered learning that culturally responsive pedagogy has the potential to support. Research on the impact of culturally responsive pedagogy is thin, but quite promising. Advancing it requires not only a stronger research base but also political work to combat its marginalization due to persistent simplistic conceptions of what it means, and backlash prompted by fear of its potential to transform the existing social order. While my analysis of the marginalization of culturally responsive pedagogy is situated mainly in the United States, multicultural policy is in retreat in many other countries as well (Modood, 2007), and policies that use standardization and testing to tie education directly to economic productivity are in ascendance (e.g., see Comber & Nixon's, 2009, discussion of Australia).

It is helpful to begin by clarifying what culturally responsive pedagogy means. Gay (2010) defines it as teaching "to and through [students'] personal and cultural strengths, their intellectual capabilities, and their prior accomplishments" (p. 26); culturally responsive pedagogy is premised on "close interactions among ethnic identity, cultural background, and student achievement" (p. 27). She notes further that, "Students of color come to school having already mastered many cultural skills and ways of knowing. To the extent that teaching builds on these capabilities, academic success will result" (p. 213). Ladson-Billings (1995) proposed three dimensions of culturally relevant pedagogy: holding high academic expectations and offering appropriate support such as scaffolding; acting on cultural competence by reshaping curriculum, building on students' funds of knowledge, and establishing relationships with students and their homes; and cultivating students' critical consciousness regarding power relations. Later in this chapter, examples will flesh out these key ideas.

Student Learning under Standardization

Chapter Three explored how the construction of state standards-based curriculum tacitly marginalizes knowledge and languages of students and families who are not White and relatively affluent; Chapter Two illustrated how teachers attempt to resist that marginalization. How are students faring under the standards-based and test-driven teaching that has characterized schools in the U.S. for over a decade now?

The National Assessment of Education Progress (NAEP), a set of standardized tests that have changed little over the years, is a useful tool for assessing the impact of national trends on student learning. NAEP has been administered periodically since the early 1970s to national samples of students in Grades 4, 8, and 12 in various subject areas. Used to gauge how the nation's schools are doing, it is sometimes referred to as "the nation's report card."

A short view of NAEP data would seem to suggest that neoliberal school reforms that standardize teaching and learning are improving student achievement. Figure 4.1, which shows NAEP scores of eighth graders in literacy by race (Black, White), between 1992 and 2007, illustrates how NAEP data are currently reported in a way that suggests that such reforms are on the right track, improving student achievement scores (albeit very slowly), and narrowing racial achievement gaps somewhat. For those who support neoliberal reforms, such data suggest that things are moving in the right direction.

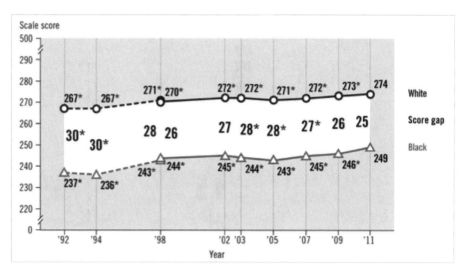

Figure 4.1: White and Black eighth-grade reading scores, 1992–2007.
Source: National Center for Education Statistics (2011)

However, if one examines NAEP scores from the early 1970s to the present, a different picture emerges. Figures 4.2, 4.3, and 4.4 show trends in reading scores for 4th, 8th, and 12th graders since 1971, disaggregated by race/ethnicity (White, Black, Hispanic). Although results for 4th graders might seem to favor standards-based reforms, results for 8th and 12th graders do not. Notably, racial achievement gaps were narrowest around 1988 and 1990, which was before the standards and testing movement. After dropping when standards-based reforms were initiated in the 1990s, scores for African American and Latino students only partially rebounded, then virtually flattened out, offering a dismally slow trajectory of improvement (Lewis, James, Hancock, & Hill-Jackson, 2008). For mathematics, the same pattern is evident but not as striking.

Education reforms that have dominated U.S. schools since the 1990s have been deliberately context blind. Although racial achievement gaps have been a focus of attention, as shown in Chapter Three of this volume, solutions have emphasized offering all students the same curriculum, taught in the same way—based on the language, worldview, and experiences of White English speakers (Gutiérrez, Asato, Santos, & Gotanda, 2002). What was happening during the 1970s and 1980s that led to jumps in the achievement of students of color, and why did policies and practices suddenly change?

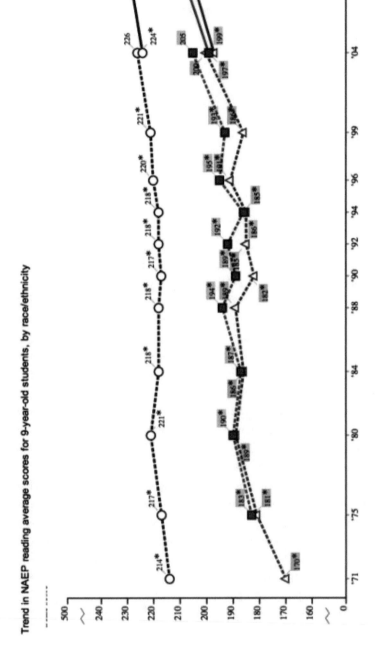

Figure 4.2: White, Hispanic and Black fourth-grade reading scores, 1971–2008.
Source: National Center for Education Statistics (2009)

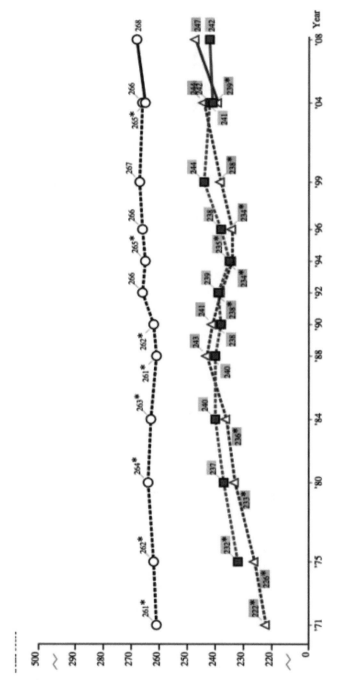

Figure 4.3: White, Hispanic and Black eighth-grade reading scores, 1971–2008.
Source: National Center for Education Statistics (2009)

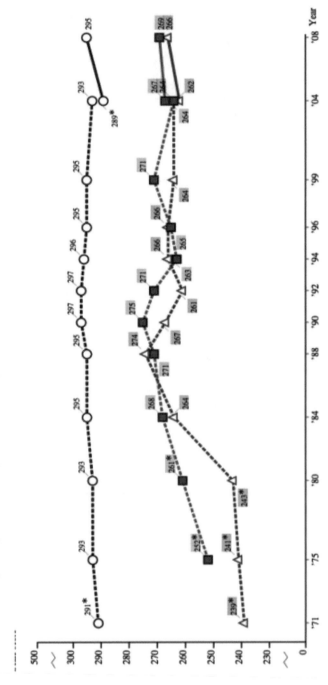

Figure 4.4: White, Hispanic and Black twelfth-grade reading scores, 1971–2008.
Source: National Center for Education Statistics (2009)

During the 1970s, schools across the United States were undergoing desegregation, and school districts were experimenting with approaches to working productively with more diverse student populations. Out of some of this work came models of bilingual education, multicultural curriculum, community control of schools, and culturally based models of instruction. Of course, the 1970s and 1980s were not a "golden age" of excellent schooling. Low teacher expectations, ethnocentric curricula, disproportionate placement of students of color in special education, disproportionate disciplinary referrals of students of color, and related problems were (and still are) common. And, it would be a mistake to attribute gains in achievement of students of color solely to growth of multicultural, bilingual, and culturally responsive teaching. Other efforts, such as desegregation and the War on Poverty, were also significant. But the significance of work seeking to help teachers respond to diverse students in schools, coupled with visible social movements for equity, should not be underestimated.

Efforts to standardize curricula and pedagogy have diminished attention to culturally responsive pedagogy. For example, based on interviews with about 200 teachers in New York City, Crocco and Costigan (2007) reported teachers' frustration with shrinking time to forge relationships with students, pressure to adhere closely to a mandated curriculum, and pressure to organize their teaching in prescribed ways that often contradicted their professional judgment. I will argue that attention to culturally responsive pedagogy has been relegated to the margins for three primary reasons: (a) persistent faulty and simplistic conceptions of what it is, (b) too little research connecting its use with student achievement, and (c) elite and White fear of losing national and global hegemony.

Simplistic Ways Culturally Responsive Pedagogy Is Often Used and Understood

Culturally responsive pedagogy is often understood in limited and simplistic ways. I will briefly discuss four simplifications: cultural celebration, trivialization, essentializing culture, and substituting cultural for political analysis of inequalities.

Culturally responsive pedagogy understood as *cultural celebration* tends to relegate attention to culture to the margins of instruction, ignore low academic expectations for students as well as the lived culture of the school and classroom, and ignore power relations altogether. For example, following a presentation in which I had specifically discussed connections between culturally responsive pedagogy and student academic learning, a participant expressed puzzlement. An advocate of multicultural education, she emphasized interest in "cultural celebration" as an end in itself and commented that linking culture and academic learning was new to her. Understanding culture in a way that disconnects it from academic learning is common.

Young (2010) studied seven teachers in an urban school who had been working to unpack the link between race and student achievement; Young wanted to find out how they understood culturally relevant pedagogy. Significantly, although all seven spoke of valuing and building on student culture, none linked this directly with improving students' academic learning. The tendency to view culturally responsive pedagogy as cultural celebration disconnected from academic learning seems to be fairly common among educators who have not examined their own expectations for the academic learning of historically underachieving students, and whose attention has become focused on learning about other cultural traditions as an end itself. Learning "about" culture then substitutes for learning to teach challenging academic knowledge and skills through the cultural processes and knowledge students bring to school with them. Writing about this limited view, Nykiel-Herbert (2010) noted, "One of the major reasons why minority students in general, and immigrant newcomers in particular, perform poorly in schools is that their home cultures, while being 'celebrated,' are not sufficiently utilized as a resource for their own learning" (p. 2). I suspect that many educators, parents, or policy makers interpret culturally responsive pedagogy as cultural celebration, *even when* it is presented as a process for building academic learning on the cultural repertoires students bring.

Trivialization of culturally relevant pedagogy involves reducing it to steps to follow rather than understanding it as a paradigm for teaching and learning. For example, during a visit to a professional development school that was connected with an urban teacher education program, I met with some student teachers who immediately told me how well prepared they were in culturally responsive pedagogy, I asked them what this meant. They showed me their textbook that was organized around 10 best practices of teaching; culturally responsive teaching was embedded in some of those practices, and they had learned to base their knowledge of students' backgrounds on a few short activities that asked students about their interests and lives outside school. When I observed student teachers working in four different classrooms, I saw only one lesson that reflected culturally responsive pedagogy (a science lesson designed around cooperative learning), and one that directly contradicted it, being pitched at an exceptionally low academic level involving content that was completely irrelevant to the students. By the end of the day, it was apparent that the student teachers' perception of themselves as knowledgeable in culturally responsive pedagogy derived from a reduction of its meaning to steps they could take to get to know their students within the walls of the classroom.

There are many ways in which culturally responsive pedagogy becomes simplified or trivialized. Patchen and Cox-Petersen (2008) found science teachers they studied to pick out strategies they could insert into teacher-directed instruction, such as occasional use of cooperative learning, rather than reconsidering their entire approach to teaching science. Thomas and Williams (2008) found mathematics teachers they worked with to define culturally relevant teaching as what they already do. Checklists that ask educators how often they engage in practices such as teaching to varied learning styles, using a culturally inclusive curriculum, and accommodating immigrant students (e.g., Nelson, Bustamante, & Onwuegbuzie, 2008; Underwoood, 2009), even if they closely reflect research on culturally responsive pedagogy, reduce complexity and allow taken-for-granted assumptions to replace inquiry. Consider, for example, a rater interpreting "Meets the needs of all students" for a checklist that asks how frequently a teacher performs certain things. Furthermore, checklists may be used as an administrative vehicle for documenting compliance with an expected change, while minimizing what is actually changed.

Essentializing culture means assuming a fairly fixed and homogeneous conception of the culture of an ethnic or racial group, assuming culture to be a fixed characteristic of individuals who belong to a group, and that students who are group members identify with that conception. For example, the teacher who equates culture with race or with a foreign country when asking her students "What are you?" and "Where are you from?" exhibits a very superficial and damaging understanding of culture (Dutro, Kazemi, Balf, & Lin, 2008).

Consider "Hispanic foods" sections of many grocery stores. This designation assumes that people from countries that speak Spanish eat much the same foods. However, when we consider the fact that "Hispanic" lumps together people who live in or have national origins that can be traced to most of South America, Central America, Spain, and parts of the Caribbean, one begins to question the sense of assuming an essentialized "Hispanic" culture. To drill down a bit deeper, in a description of diversity within Mexico, Ramos (2012) critiques the Mexican government's designation of "diversity" as meaning only the indigenous peoples of Mexico. He points out that not only did the Spanish conquer Mexico, but Mexico has also received immigrants from countries as different from each other as China, France, Ireland, Turkey, Korea, and the United States. Furthermore, indigenous Mexicans also comprise many different ethnic groups that speak different indigenous languages and are culturally distinct from each other. For a teacher to assume a homogenous Mexican culture is to engage in essentializing.

What makes more sense is for teachers to bring to the classroom an awareness of diverse cultural possibilities that might relate to their students, but then to get to know the students themselves. For example, based on her research investigating what excellent mathematics teachers of such students do, Gutiérrez (2002) argued that rather than basing pedagogy and curriculum on global and stereotypic racial and language identities that others project onto the students, excellent teachers take the time to get to know their students, then shape their pedagogy around relationships with them. Garza's (2009) interviews with White and Latino students confirm the importance of teachers building caring relationships, then scaffolding new learning in a way that builds on what is familiar to students. Gutiérrez argues that learning to support students culturally in a way that does not essentialize culture is complicated, but results in the kind of teaching in which students thrive.

Substituting cultural for political analysis involves maintaining silence about the conditions of racism and other forms of oppression that underlie achievement gaps and alienation from school, assuming that attending to culture alone will bring about equity. Lewis and colleagues (2008) point out that underlying the achievement gap is a "web of interrelated impediments"—ideologies, practices, and policies—"that are actively and passively undermining widespread academic excellence among African Americans attending urban schools. Race- and class-based inequalities create and perpetuate the unequal distribution of educational resources, which sustains the Black-White achievement gap" (p. 148). Teachers' construction of minoritized students in deficit terms, with negative consequences for their longer term academic success (Shields, Bishop, & Mazawi, 2005), results from longstanding racialized institutional policies and practices that consistently disadvantage minoritized students.

Because of the centrality of institutional racism to students' experiences, Beauboeuf-LaFontant (1999) proposed the term "politically relevant teaching," emphasizing that the central issue is often subordination rather than culture per se. Based on a review of the history of African American educators, she points out that their practice centers on a shared "understanding of systemic inequity—that is, the political, economic, and racial structures that disproportionately limit the opportunities of children of color" (p. 704); schooling is a vehicle not only for access to the mainstream but also for engaging in social change. She argued that the teachers' political clarity about the lives of their students is more central to their refusal to allow students to not learn, than is their cultural similarity with students.

Several related multicultural education discourses, elaborated in Chapter Eight, prioritize a political analysis. Antiracist education scholars, initially writing in a British context, were among the first to dismiss a culturalist emphasis as naïve and counterproductive because it simply ignores the wider structural constraints of racism, sexism, and class, that affect minoritized students' lives. Critical race theory examines the structural roots of racism and the persistence of collective White control over power and material resources. Critical pedagogy develops such concepts as voice, dialog, power, and social class that overly cultural analyses of education too often either underutilize or ignore. Critical multiculturalism prioritizes a structural analysis of unequal power relationships. A structural analysis situates culture in the context of unequal power relations, as lived out in daily interactions, examining how these power relations contribute toward the ongoing production of culture, and a fluidity of identity depending on context (May & Sleeter, 2010).

But practitioners generally struggle more with implications of structural than cultural analyses for several reasons. First, since liberalism is far more prominent in mainstream ideology than critical perspectives, educators tend not to question assumptions of liberal multiculturalism. Second, much of the theoretical work in critical multiculturalism and critical race theory is conceptually dense, with relatively few illustrations for classroom practice. Third, naming and directly challenging systemic racism through pedagogy clashes with institutionalized structures and processes teachers are expected to adhere to.

Oversimplified and distorted conceptions of culturally responsive pedagogy, which do not necessarily improve student learning, lend themselves to dismissal of the entire concept. So too does the body of empirical work that connects culturally responsive pedagogy with students learning, not because it does not document a positive impact, but because it does so mainly through small-scale case studies.

Research Connecting Culturally Responsive Pedagogy with Student Learning

Although considerable theory links culture and learning (e.g., Nasir & Hand, 2006; Rogoff, 2003), and quite a bit of research investigates culturally responsive pedagogy in the classroom, far too little systematically documents its impact on student learning.

Many case studies show what culturally responsive pedagogy looks like (variations of which go by other terms such as multicultural teaching, equity pedagogy, culturally relevant pedagogy, sociocultural teaching, and social justice teaching). Such studies may be based on interviews with minoritized students (e.g., Garza, 2009), interviews with exemplary teachers of minoritized students (e.g., Brown, 2004), or classroom observations along with interviews (e.g., Duncan-Andrade 2007; Ladson-Billings, 1994; Milner, 2011; Sleeter & Stillman, 2007; Ware, 2006). For example, Mitchell (2010) analyzes the teaching practice of three African American professors to illustrate key dimensions of culturally responsive pedagogy, noting that culturally responsive teachers are "students of their pupils' communities" (p. 626). All three situated Black life in the United States within a history of White supremacy that has ongoing effects that must be named and challenged. They recognized Black students' experiences with racism; they also recognized students' cultural assets, and they specifically sought out students' "inherent brilliance" (p. 626). Mitchell points out that the teachers who became highly skilled improvisers in the classroom were able to set the right tone for open discussions of racism in a way that prompted rather than hindered students' academic learning. Portraits such as this serve as helpful tools that can move teachers beyond simplified notions of culturally responsive pedagogy discussed earlier.

Several small-scale studies connect culturally responsive pedagogy with student engagement, reasonably suggesting that academic learning follows engagement (e.g., Copenhaver, 2001; Hill, 2009; Nykiel-Herbert, 2010; Rodriguez, Jones, Pang, & Park, 2004; Thomas & Williams, 2008). For example, using observations and interviews, Howard (2001) studied the impact on African American students of four elementary teachers who used culturally responsive pedagogy. The students described the teachers as caring about them, creating community and family-like environments in the classroom, and making learning fun. As a result, they wanted to participate. In one of the very few large-scale studies on culturally responsive pedagogy (see Chapter Thirteen of this volume), Savage and colleagues (2011), who investigated 23 secondary schools in New Zealand, found Maori students to describe with enthusiasm their responses to and engagement with teachers who had been trained in culturally responsive pedagogy. Specifically, students appreciated that teachers acknowledged their identity as Maori learners, and teachers' attempts to know the students and incorporate things Maori into the classroom.

The relatively few studies that directly connect culturally responsive pedagogy with its impact on student academic learning, although very helpful, also consist of small-scale case studies (e.g., Camangian, 2010; Cammarota & Romero, 2009; Krater & Zeni, 1995; Lipka et al., 2005; Rickford, 2001; Sheets, 2005; see also reviews by Brayboy & Castagno, 2009; Gay, 2010). For example, Lee's (2006) Cultural Modeling Project "is a framework for the design of curriculum and learning environments that links everyday knowledge with learning academic subject matter, with a particular focus on racial/ethnic minority groups, especially youth of African descent" (p. 308). The curriculum leverages the ability of speakers of African American English to interpret symbolism, a skill students use routinely in rap and Hip Hop, but do not necessarily apply to analysis of literature in school. Cultural Modeling moves from analysis of specific language data sets students are familiar with and that draw on elements of Black cultural life such as Black media or the Black church, to more general strategies of literary analysis and application to canonical literary works. Lee has assessed its impact both quantitatively and qualitatively, often by having students write an analysis of a short story they have not seen before. In a study comparing four English classes taught using Cultural Modeling with two taught traditionally, she found that, from pretest to posttest, the Cultural Modeling students gained over twice as much as the traditionally taught students (Lee, 1995). Lee's (2006) qualitative research shows students gradually learning to direct discussions interpreting and analyzing texts through the Cultural Modeling process, which traditional English achievement tests often do not capture (Lee, 2007).

Research on the preparation of teachers for culturally responsive pedagogy is also thin and consists mainly of case studies. Case studies of teachers learning culturally responsive pedagogy illuminate problems and barriers teachers experience, sometimes showing how those problems can be addressed (e.g., Bondy, Ross, Gallingane, & Hambacher, 2007; Milner, 2010; Patchen & Cox-Petersen, 2008; Sleeter, 2005; Thomas & Williams, 2008). For example, in their case study of two mathematics teachers, Leonard, Napp, and Adeleke (2009) found teachers to make inaccurate assumptions about what might be relevant to their students. Because the authors were working with the teachers on an ongoing basis, they were able to prompt the teachers to question and think beyond their assumptions. Most case studies of teachers learning culturally responsive pedagogy explore the impact of specific kinds of preservice and professional development programs, including school–university partnerships (e.g., Bales & Saffold, 2011), inquiry-based courses (Jennings & Smith, 2002), teacher networks (El-Haj, 2003), community-based learning (Fickel, 2005; Moll & González, 1994), and sustained workshops combined with classroom-based coaching (Zozakiewicz & Rodriguez, 2007).

Connecting professional development of practicing teachers, their implementation of culturally responsive pedagogy, and its subsequent impact on students is challenging because teachers do not necessarily enact a robust conception of culturally responsive pedagogy as a result of professional development. There is some such research; but much more is needed. Research on Te Kotahitanga, a professional development model focusing on culturally responsive teaching of Māori students, is elaborated on in Chapter Thirteen. Bishop, Berryman, Cavanagh, and Teddy (2009) studied its impact on 422 teachers in 12 schools, finding a shift in teachers' pedagogy from didactic to discursive and relationship-based teaching, which was accompanied by an increase in Maori students' literacy and numeracy test scores. An external evaluation of the program using quasi-experimental methodology found Te Kotahitanga schools to retain Māori students at a higher rate than comparison schools, prepare students for university entrance at a much higher rate, and yield higher results in some academic areas. In addition, they found Māori students in Te Kotahitanga Schools to describe teachers respecting them as Māori, which was quite different from how Māori students described teachers in non-Te Kotahitanga schools (Meyer et al., 2010; Sleeter, 2011). Phillips, McNaughton, and MacDonald (2004) studied the impact on 73 teachers in 12 schools of a professional development project focusing on a sociocultural approach to teaching literacy to Māori and Pasifika young children. Using an experimental research design, they found children being taught by the teachers participating in the intervention to outperform the students of teachers in the non-intervention group on all measures of literacy achievement.

There is clearly a need for much more systematic research that links culturally responsive pedagogy with its impact on students, and also research that links teacher professional development in culturally responsive pedagogy with improved student learning. At the same time, such research needs to attend to two related issues. The first is describing and clarifying what culturally responsive pedagogy means and looks like in any given study. In an attempt to operationalize culturally responsive pedagogy by synthesizing 45 classroom-based studies, Morrison, Robbins, and Rose (2008) found a wide variation of loosely related actions teachers might take. They classified 12 kinds of actions into three broad categories, following Ladson-Billings' (1995) theoretical framework: high academic expectations with appropriate support such as scaffolding; cultural competence reflected in work with curriculum and students' funds of knowledge; establishing relationships with students and families; and cultivating students' critical consciousness regarding power relations. Significantly, none of the 45 studies depicted all 12 key actions although each study depicted several of them.

The second related issue that warrants attention is the cultural context(s) of students, and how a given conception of culturally responsive pedagogy derives from or fits that context. Ladson-Billings' (1995) articulation of culturally relevant pedagogy, for example, although frequently applied to other contexts, was based on her study of effective teachers of African American students in the United States. Bishop and colleagues' (2009) articulation was based on narratives of Māori students in New Zealand. While both conceptions overlap, they are not identical. Because of the centrality of context to culturally responsive pedagogy, researchers cannot skip over the task of grounding what it means in the context being studied. At the same time, while maintaining context specificity, it is important to also show what principles of culturally responsive pedagogy apply across groups and across national boundaries. There is a tendency in the United States, for example, to ignore research outside the United States based on the assumption that such research is about "them over there," and therefore has no direct application to "us over here."

Political Backlash

Culturally responsive pedagogy is not only about teaching, but is also a political endeavor. This book situates schooling within neoliberalism and its reforms based on standardization and decontextualization, reforms that frame education as both a commodity for individual economic advancement and a tool to shape workers for the global economy. Although there is considerable variation among nations in the extent to which school practice is being shaped by such reforms, they are increasingly pervasive.

As the work of teachers is standardized and pressurized, attempts to work with culturally responsive pedagogy become increasingly difficult. Teachers have less time to research and develop curriculum that students can relate to, non-tested curriculum disappears under pressure to raise test scores, and teachers are increasingly patrolled to make sure they are teaching the required curriculum, at the required pace (Achinstein & Ogawa, 2006; Comber & Nixon, 2009; Crocco & Costigan, 2007; Gillborn & Youdell, 2000; Sleeter & Stillman, 2007). For example, in a study of new teachers whose preparation had been from a critical multicultural perspective, Flores (2007) found that the schools in which they were hired pressured them away from it in various ways: what veteran teacher colleagues modeled and espoused, the standardization of curricula and testing, and the institutionalized model of a "good student." While teachers can learn to navigate accountability pressures, as illustrated in Chapter Two of this volume, and while principals can buffer demands on teachers (Bergeron, 2008; Stillman, 2011), teachers in schools where students are underachieving tend to be pressured toward standardization rather than responsiveness to their diverse students.

Describing neoliberal reforms as "backlash pedagogy," Gutiérrez and colleagues (2002) note that they make it "professionally and, in some cases legally, risky" to use culturally responsive practices that conflict with mandated "sameness" masquerading as equality for all (p. 345). Indeed, one should anticipate backlash as historically oppressed communities make gains. As Gutiérrez and colleagues argue,

> Backlash pedagogies do not just happen: they are rooted in backlash politics, products of ideological and institutional structures that legitimize and thus maintain privilege, access, and control of the sociopolitical and economic terrain. Backlash politics are counterassaults against real or perceived shifts in power. (p. 337)

NAEP data show clearly that in the United States, during the 1970s and 1980, while students of color were making dramatic gains in achievement, White students were not. Achievement gains of students of color were accompanied by other political, social, and economic gains communities of color were making. Ultimately, culturally responsive pedagogy represents a paradigm of education that challenges, and in turn is being challenged by, neoliberal school reforms. Nowhere is political backlash against culturally responsive pedagogy clearer than in Arizona, where the state recently banned ethnic studies. At issue is what many White Arizonans regard as an un-American curriculum (Kossan, 2009; see also Bunch, 2010).

Recommendations

In light of connections among politics, research, and perceptions of culturally responsive pedagogy, I offer three recommendations. First, there is a clear need for evidence-based research that documents connections between culturally responsive pedagogy and student outcomes that include, but are not necessarily limited to, academic achievement. Politically, it is difficult to build a case to change approaches to teaching without strong evidence. Small-scale case studies illustrate what is possible, but we also need research on the impact of scaled-up work in culturally responsive pedagogy, including research showing how teachers can learn to use it in their classrooms. Research that documents the impact of culturally responsive pedagogical practices on White students would also be helpful. The Te Kotahitanga work in New Zealand, for example, has evidence that White students also benefit when teachers learn to teach Indigenous students better because teachers become better with all of their students (Meyer et al., 2010). Such evidence can help to counter White fears that somehow culturally responsive pedagogy will harm White children.

Second, there is a need to educate parents, teachers, and education leaders about what culturally responsive pedagogy means and looks like in the classroom. Although presently there are many helpful descriptions in the professional literature, widely accessible portraits that include video would be very useful. Researchers might work to create such portraits with organizations that already have a sizable audience. For example, the Southern Poverty Law Center has been collaborating with the American Association of Colleges of Teacher Education to develop an online resource for teaching about culturally responsive pedagogy, including video portraits of classroom teaching. Such a resource can be very helpful for guiding teachers, parents, and other members of the public beyond simplistic conceptions of what culturally responsive teaching means.

Third, there is a need to reframe public debate about teaching, especially teaching in diverse and historically underserved communities. Nurturing intellectual development in complex classrooms is a complex process (Ball, 2009). It might be relatively cheap to impose standardized and scripted curricula on teachers, and doing so might seem logical when students from underserved communities are viewed through a deficiency lens. However, I believe that a public case must be made that it is in the interest of society as a whole to nurture the intellectual talent of its highly diverse population and that investing in developing quality professional teaching that is culturally responsive to today's students is one necessary factor.

PART II

Teaching Back to Power

5

Transgressing Boundaries for Socially Just Teaching

As a student teacher in 1972, I remember hearing about a time in the "dark ages" when teachers were all expected to be on the same page of the same text, at the same time. I was aghast! How stifling that would be! But these days when I go into schools, I feel as if I am in a time warp as I see teachers expected to march their students all toward the same page of the same text at the same time, regardless of students' interests. I am told that this approach guards against teaching to low expectations. I see things quite differently, however. I will show how and why by sharing stories about the power of connecting academics with real issues of concern to young people. When done well, such connection not only prompts academic growth, but also enables young people to see themselves as active agents who can appropriate academics for their own purposes.

Teaching Boldly: My Roots

Many of my childhood teachers used creative, student-centered approaches in which they embedded college-preparatory academic skills in interesting projects. I saw my task as a student teacher in the early 1970s as figuring out how to replicate that kind of inspiring, student-centered teaching in an inner-city high school, where I found that teaching meant covering the textbook. As I helped students, I could see that textbook-driven teaching bored them. So, when it came time for me to take the class, I rather spontaneously invited the students to help me organize a unit around a topic of interest to them (they chose "Women's Liberation"), then collaborate with me in planning their learning activities for that unit. Students who had previously slept through class came alive.

At the time, I did not know how to embed academic skills in such teaching, and it took me a couple of years to shed what I later realized were low academic expectations for students from low-income homes. However, through this early experience, I saw clearly the power of engaging students' questions and interests, a lesson that has guided my teaching ever since. During the late 1990s, I began to document what academically strong multicultural teaching looks like in practice by following teachers who had completed my multicultural curriculum design course into the classroom. By 2001, this documentation had shifted to focus on how teachers who are committed to such teaching navigate controls over their work in standards-based and test-driven contexts (Sleeter, 2005). Below, I will describe two of the teachers I became acquainted with in California, then a project with a similar focus in Arizona.

Kathy: Teaching Boldly in First Grade[1]

"If I refuse to take a position on something I consider to be harmful to children, I am contributing to that harm." (Kathy, in Sleeter, 2005, p. 111)

Kathy had been teaching for over twenty years in California when I met her. Kathy's students were all of Mexican descent, many having recently emigrated; all were from low-income homes. As a bilingual teacher, Kathy taught much of the day in Spanish so her students would have access to grade-level curriculum; she also explicitly taught students English. Kathy is White and had grown up mainly on a farm in Ohio, but had lived several years in Mexico where she became fluent in Spanish. Her current residence was near the school in which she taught. She was involved with the community her students came from and welcomed parents into her classroom. Like that of the students' parents, who strongly desired that their children gain a good education in order to have a better future, Kathy's vision for students' learning was ambitious. She wanted them to become "hungry for books. I don't want them to think of reading as using the…text and workbooks. I want them to be able to apply their abilities to analyze, to question, to figure out meanings in text…to be able to draw parallels between nature and their lives, and between one book and another" (Sleeter, 2005, p.111).

Three features of Kathy's teaching caught my attention: her use of class meetings as a tool for teaching students to work on real problems, her ability to build academic learning on students' everyday knowledge, and her interest in raising their political awareness about social issues. Class meetings regularly provided a space in which student concerns led the agenda, and students took charge of problem-solving. Kathy explained, "I figure if kids learn to resolve problems at this level, they're a lot more likely to resolve them later. And I've been amazed at their problem solving abilities and their compassion" (Sleeter, 2005, p. 112). Many problems students brought to class were interpersonal, but some were political. Kathy explained that children regularly hear adults discuss political issues at home and want to know more:

> Last fall when on the ballot there was the tax to keep [the county hospital] open, one of my children brought that up in class and we talked about it. . . . This one little girl said, Yeah, everybody has to go vote or they're going to close the hospital, and there won't be any place left to go. We talked about that. She's heard her parents, and aunts and uncles discussing it. The war in Iraq. A year ago one of the kids brought in a picture of the soldiers from Salinas that had appeared in the paper, soldiers from Salinas that were serving in Iraq. And so we talked about it. (Sleeter, 2005, p. 113)

Class meetings served as a basis for student-centered teaching Kathy used during the rest of the day, and as a venue for getting to know her students' interests and concerns.

Kathy designed and taught an interdisciplinary thematic unit on Monterey County agriculture, which she mapped carefully against the first-grade curriculum standards for reading/language arts, math and science, and her English Language Development text. She credited her principal for giving her freedom to construct a thematic curriculum as long as it met state standards. She showed me a copy of the first grade standards on which she annotated how various portions of the unit addressed specific standards, so that she would be able to explain the relationship if called on to do so.

Kathy developed this unit because "agriculture directly affects the lives of my students. Out of my twenty students, most have at least one parent who is employed in agriculture or an agriculture-related industry such as vegetable packing. The parents' income and work schedules are determined by the crops and the large companies which grow them" (Sleeter, 2005, p.112). She wanted the children to learn more about their parents' work, not to become agricultural workers themselves, but to respect the work their parents do. Having grown up on a farm herself, she believed that everyone should know where food comes from, and situate that knowledge within a vision of environmentally sustainable farms that ordinary people can afford. She was deeply concerned about "the conflict between what agriculture has become in this country and what it can be." Increasingly, large corporations control agriculture, and thereby also dominate "land use, water use and availability, pesticide use, and economic and political power." She commented, "So many of my students' parents work in agriculture, yet so few can be farmers" (Sleeter, 2005, p. 113).

Kathy creatively connected grade-level academic skills with students' knowledge. For example, the unit addressed several math concepts in the first-grade curriculum standards: numbers to 100, the concept more than/less than, units and tens, and graphing. To teach graphing, she had the class construct a bar graph representing how many parents worked with various crops. Across the bottom of the graph were the names and drawings of vegetables indicating crops in which parents worked. Students placed 3 x 3" cards above the vegetable of their parents' work site which, when arranged vertically, became bars. After the graph was made, Kathy engaged students in quantitative reasoning with questions such as: *¿Cuántas personas trabajan en la lechuga?* (How many people work in lettuce?) *¿Trabaja más gente en la casa o en un empaque?* (Do more people work at home or in packing?) As she helped students use the graph to reason numerically, focusing particularly on more than/less than, Kathy prompted students to think in terms of not just isolated numbers, but also what the numbers mean, such as how many students are in the class, and how many of their parents do what kind of work. Linking the abstract concept to what student knew already helped them "get it."

For social studies, Kathy taught critical analysis of the political context in which students' families lived and worked, and a vision anchored in memories and possibilities. Since most of the children's parents worked in agriculture, and since Kathy believed firmly that agribusiness is not the only (or best) way to construct farming systems, she wanted students to explore agricultural economic systems and worker politics. To compare large-scale corporate farms and small family farms, she invited a parent with experience working in agriculture in both the U.S. and Mexico to come and describe the nature of work in both places. Using slides she had taken in rural Mexico, Kathy had students compare the small farm system there with agribusiness students see locally. The class also studied the history and struggles of the United Farm Workers, particularly the work of local organizers, and immigration issues connected with agriculture.

To teach boldly, Kathy identified a rich theme that was significant to the lives of her students and their families, and in which subject matter content could be anchored, and then carefully wove the required curriculum standards around this theme. When I asked how her students were doing on the district's tests, Kathy explained that while first graders do not participate in the mandated testing program, they were doing well on benchmark assessments. As long as they did so, Kathy's principal would continue to support her.

Christi: Teaching Boldly in High School

"Are [students] developing in their knowledge of the subject, and also their heart knowledge? Do they have insights?" (Christi, in Sleeter, 2005, p. 76).

Christi, a tall blond with blue eyes, had been teaching high school English for seven years. She grew up in a working-class, racially diverse community where she had become very interested in cultural differences. Going through school, she hung out with different groups; she commented to me that, "You could start a conversation with somebody or a friendship with somebody that just changes your whole point of view" (Sleeter, 2005, p. 52). The school in which she was teaching served the community where she grew up, as well as an adjacent affluent, White community.

What caught my attention was Christi's efforts, as a White teacher, to engage a diverse class of students in probing issues related to racism, ethnocentrism, and exclusion in the context of standards-based English. She told me that she "couldn't tolerate the racism" she found in the White community, and was concerned about its impact on young people. Since California is experiencing large waves of immigration, Christi cared passionately that her students develop empathy rather than hostility toward newcomers as well as people who are already here, commenting that her "passion is contagious" (Sleeter, 2005, p. 146).

Christi designed and taught a unit on West Coast immigration. As she described it, the unit's main themes included:

> respect for other cultures, understanding of our multicultural region, historical perspectives of our immigrant nation, family bonds, identity and culture and the American high school experience. I see the entire unit as a vehicle to assist students in gaining a better grasp of our immigrant nation, to search for connection and commonalities among immigrants, and to forge a sense of what makes cultures unique (Sleeter, 2005, p. 53).

As Kathy had done, Christi figured out how to connect the unit with the state's English Language Arts curriculum standards, which focused largely on reading comprehension of grade-level text, and skill in writing in various genres, using English language conventions appropriately. She was equally interested in both developing students' writing and the substance of what they wrote about. She explained: "I think that if you ponder and research any book/topic/lesson long enough you can teach it from a multicultural/activist perspective" (Sleeter, 2005, p. 51).

Her West Coast immigration unit included three major writing assignments: a narrative written from the point of view of a fictitious adolescent immigrant, a fictitious diary the immigrant might write about four days of school, and a poem in which the fictitious immigrant expresses feelings. Christi had students analyze samples of writing to identify mood and tone, point of view, and sensory detail and imagery, then practice expanding their own use of detail words in descriptions. The unit also included a research project in which small groups of students collaboratively wrote short research papers about West Coast immigrant groups to provide background for the other writing assignments. As a culminating project, students created a webpage that synthesized their work. Christi posted her entire unit on the Internet to make it available to students. There she described its overall rationale, mapped the learning outcomes against state content standards, described the various assignments students would be doing and evaluation rubrics for each, and posted notes for each day that included handouts, homework, and readings.

Christi drew from her textbook to the extent that it fit the unit, but she also actively sought additional resources. She extensively used short stories and videos, such as *El Norte* (featuring Mexican and Central American immigrants) and *A Dollar a Day, Ten Cents a Dance* (featuring Filipino immigrants). When asked where she found her rich pool of resources, Christi explained that she had become very good at scavenging.

> Sometimes things just drop into my lap, and like, Wow!....I've actually been collecting over the last seven years, because, you know, I've always wanted to do something like this....So, I dedicated myself to just grabbing everything that I could, you know....I ended up with a lot of stuff, a lot of stuff! I mean, (pointing to a corner) these are just some of the huge file cabinets full of things. (Sleeter, 2005, p. 164)

I visited one day when the class was reading "On the Other Side of the War" by Elizabeth Gordon (1990), who was born in Vietnam to a Vietnamese mother and an Anglo American father, then grew up in Tennessee after the Vietnam War. Christi led a discussion about the story that focused on both the author's experiences and bi-racial identity, as well as how she constructed the narrative and used figurative language. Some of the White students were puzzled by Gordon's struggles around a bi-racial identity, asking questions such as why schools have students check a box indicating race. This discussion was followed by a clip from the film *Lakota Woman* that focused on Mary Crow Dog's experiences in a mission school, particularly the school's efforts to strip Indian youth of their identities, and various ways the youth resisted. Students rearranged their chairs so they could see clearly; they seemed very engrossed. The bell rang signaling the end of class before students were able to discuss the video that day, but later Christi commented that narrative stories, and particularly film, drew in students who were struggling with concepts like racism.

To teach boldly, Christi structured a unit around experiences of ethnically and culturally diverse adolescents, then designed various writing and discussion activities to engage students with ideas related to immigration, race, and ethnicity. She carefully connected the entire unit to the grade-level English Language Arts standards to make sure it was as academically sound as it was intellectually and emotionally engaging. Speaking about how one of the White male students reacted to the stories and videos, she remarked, "It seems like it engages them, it pulls them in, even if they don't want to be pulled in. And he doesn't want to be pulled in, and it's still, it sort of grabs him once in a while" (Sleeter, 2005, p 77).

"Critically Compassionate Intellectualism": Teaching Boldly for Social Justice

> "It is in our best interest to transform the education of our people so that our blood is no longer used to grease the wheels of global capitalist greed." (Cammarota & Romero, 2006, p. 23)

In 1996 in Tucson, Arizona, a group of concerned Mexican American citizens petitioned the district's governing board for a Mexican American studies curriculum. Two years later, the board approved funding for it, and Tucson Unified School District (TUSD) Mexican American/Raza Studies was launched. I became acquainted with the work of the department in 2005, when I was invited to address the annual Raza Studies Summer Institute. What continued to catch my attention has been its unwavering vision of education reform, and its powerful impact on students. Readers may be aware that the state of Arizona's ban on ethnic studies was directed specifically at this program. As of this writing, the program has been disbanded and its teachers and students distributed among other programs; for this reason, I describe it here in the past tense. But the legitimacy of the state law banning ethnic studies, as well as of the district's decision to dismantle the program, is still being actively contested.

Since 1998 when it was first created, the Mexican American/Raza Studies Department worked with schools to strengthen teaching and learning, using Chicano studies' intellectual frameworks. Over time, the department developed a rich array of curriculum resources for classroom use from kindergarten through high school, which align with the state curriculum standards.

In 2003, a Social Justice Education Project (SJEP) was begun in one of the Raza Studies high schools. Initially, three Latino educators (a high school teacher, the director of the TUSD Mexican American/Raza Studies Department, and an assistant professor from the University of Arizona) collaborated to develop a four-semester social studies curriculum that met the state's eleventh- and twelfth-grade social studies standards (see Cammarota, 2007; Cammarota & Romero, 2009; Romero, Arce & Cammarota, 2009). This curriculum is based on a model of "critically conscious intellectualism" for strengthening teaching and learning of Chicano students in a school district where over 40% of its Chicano students leave school during the high school years (Cammarota & Romero, 2009). The model has three components: 1) curriculum that is culturally and historically relevant to the students, focuses on social justice issues, is aligned with state standards but designed through Chicano intellectual knowledge, and is academically rigorous; 2) critical pedagogy in which students develop critical thinking and critical consciousness, creating rather than consuming knowledge, and 3) authentic caring in which teachers demonstrate deep respect for students as intellectual and full human beings.

The curriculum teaches about racial and economic issues, immersing students in university-level theoretical readings. It includes a community-based research project in which students gather data about manifestations of racism in their school and community and use social science theory to analyze why patterns in the data exist and how they can be challenged. Students give formal presentations of results of their research to the community, as well as to academic and youth conferences. Cammarota and Romero (2006) noted that, "the standard educational system treats them as empty slates ready to be carved and etched on by teachers" but this project had offered students "an opportunity to see themselves as knowledgeable Subjects" (p. 20). Students were able to learn to do advanced level academic work when it directly addressed realities of their lives. As Cammarota (2007) pointed out, remedial work does not engage students because it is not about changing their lives; a challenging, socially relevant curriculum like the one in this project helps students see how to use academics as a tool for changing their lives.

A considerable amount of data has been compiled on the academic impact of the Mexican American/Raza Studies Department's courses on students; patterns in those data are presented in Chapter Six of this volume. Consistent with those data, Cammarota and Romero (2009) report that Chicano students in the SJEP outscored Anglo students in the same school on the state's exams: 34 out of 36 passed the reading exam, 35 out of 36 passed the writing exam, and 27 out of 35 passed the math exam, which was a considerably higher pass rate than the Anglo students attained. Importantly, in interviews SJEP students consistently credit the program for their academic success. Students who participated in the broader array of Mexican American/Raza Studies courses in middle school and high school demonstrate remarkable achievement gains on Arizona's high stakes high school graduation exam.

Teaching Boldly in Real Classrooms

In over 30 years in which I have been an educator, I do not recall meeting a student who truly does not want to learn anything. However, I have met many, many students who find textbook-driven teaching incredibly boring and irrelevant; when that is all they are offered, they often appear disinterested in and incapable of learning. I have also met many teachers who can think creatively about students' interests and important social issues, but have little idea how to embed demanding intellectual work in a relevant thematic curriculum. As a result, a good number of school administrators these days are highly suspicious of attempts to be "relevant" and "student centered." Add to this the number of educators who fear opening up examination of racial, ethnic, and social class inequalities—or anything remotely political—and the result is systemic exclusion from academics of that which is meaningful to the lives of many young people.

Ironically, when we use student-centered rather than textbook-centered teaching, embed preparation for college in rich thematic units that have meaning to one's own students, and engage students in critically questioning society and learning to act for justice, then students from communities that had not been achieving well in school blossom in ways that show up even on standardized tests. Doesn't this make more sense than the current approach that consists of marching everyone lock-step through the same pre-packaged curriculum materials?

Note

1. Kathy has written about the unit described here in more detail in Sleeter and Cornbleth (2011).

6

The Academic and Social Value of Ethnic Studies

A Research Review

Carlos entered my office to find out more about the graduate program in Education that I was directing in order to decide whether to apply to it.[1] I asked him to tell me about himself, which is how I usually began such conversations. He said that he had graduated from a local high school. While not a good student, the fact that he graduated mattered since most of his friends had not. But he found school very boring, so he decided to enter the military rather than college. After completing a tour of duty, he returned to his hometown and got a minimum wage job. One day he ran into a friend from high school who was attending a local community college. The friend was taking Chicano studies courses and encouraged Carlos to come check them out. At first Carlos had no interest in more school, but his friend was so enthusiastic that Carlos finally decided to go see what Chicano studies was all about. That hooked him on education. For the first time in his life, the curriculum was centered on his reality. Carlos completed two years of community college, taking as many Chicano studies courses as possible, then went on to complete a BA degree in Spanish. In the process, he became an avid reader about Mexican vaquero (cowboy) culture and accumulated a mini-library at home on this subject. He wanted to continue his education in order to teach, which to my knowledge, he is still doing today.

The impact that Chicano studies had on Carlos is not unique. Informally, for many years I have witnessed similar impacts on students, especially, but not exclusively, students of color. This chapter synthesizes research on the social and academic value of ethnic studies curricula. Since ethnic studies can be understood as a counter to the traditional mainstream curriculum, I begin by framing the mainstream curriculum as "Euro-American Studies." Then, after briefly defining ethnic studies, I review research on its impact, first as designed specifically for students of color who are members of the group under study, and second as designed for diverse student groups that include White students. While there is some overlap between these kinds of curricula, there are also some differences.

Mainstream Curricula as Euro-American Studies

Beginning in the late 1960s, educators and scholars of color pressed schools, school districts, and textbook companies to produce and offer curricula that reflected the diversity of the U.S. population. Through the 1970s and early 1980s, textbook publishers addressed the most glaring omissions and stereotypes, but as national concern shifted toward establishing curriculum standards and systems of accountability, with a few exceptions, efforts to make texts and other curricula multicultural gradually subsided. Educators, particularly those who are White, often assume that publishers "took care" of most forms of bias.

Systematic analyses, however, consistently find the opposite. While content related to African Americans, Latinos, and Native Americans has been added, deeper patterns and narratives that reflect Euro-American experiences and worldviews, and that have traditionally structured K-12 textbooks—particularly history and social studies texts—remain intact (Foster, 1999; Hickman & Porfolio, 2012a, 2012b; Loewen, 1995; Sanchez, 2007; Sleeter & Grant, 1991). Whites continue receive the most attention and appear in the widest variety of roles, dominating story lines and lists of accomplishments. African Americans, the next most represented racial group, appear in a more limited range of roles and usually receive only a sketchy account historically, being featured mainly in relationship to slavery. Asian Americans and Latinos appear mainly as figures on the landscape with virtually no history or contemporary ethnic experience. Native Americans appear mainly in the past, but also occasionally in contemporary stories in reading books. Immigration is represented as a distinct historical period that happened mainly in the Northeast, rather than as an ongoing phenomenon (Vecchio, 2004). Texts say little to nothing about contemporary race relations, racism or racial issues, usually sanitizing greatly what they mention (Hughes, 2007).

In other words, racial and ethnic minorities are added consistently in a "contributions" fashion to the predominantly Euro-American narrative of textbooks. Scholarship by and about African Americans, Latino/as, Native Americans, and Asian Americans continues not to be used to frame academic content. Even texts published recently, while having added content that previously was absent (such as depictions of racial violence directed against African Americans during slavery), continue to disconnect racism in the past from racism today, and to frame perpetrators of racism as a few bad individuals rather than a system of oppression, and challenges to racism as actions of heroic individuals rather than organized struggle (Alridge, 2006; Brown & Brown, 2010). Additional recognition of communities of color usually takes the form of Black History Month and Cinco de Mayo, rather than substantive curriculum revision (El-Haj, 2006; Lewis, 2001). As Hughes (2007) explains, the result of continuing to minimize attention to racism and White complicity,

> is that students perceive racism as a tragedy of the past divorced from other historical issues…and the contemporary realities of power in American society. When textbook authors bury the history of American racism within a larger narrative of inevitable American progress, students perceive race relations as a linear trajectory of improvement rather than a messy and continual struggle over power that encompasses both progress and, in the case of the decades after Reconstruction, significant steps backward in terms of racial justice. (p. 203)

Ethnic studies scholarship by and about racial minority groups presents a different narrative that is shaped partially by histories of oppression in the U.S. as well as by the intellectual and cultural resources and traditions of those communities. In an analysis of ethnic studies scholarship, I identified the following consistent themes that differentiate it from Euro-American mainstream school knowledge: 1) explicit identification of the point of view from which knowledge emanates, and the relationship between social location and perspective; 2) examination of U.S. colonialism historically, as well as how relations of colonialism continue to play out; 3) examination of the historical construction of race and institutional racism, how people navigate racism, and struggles for liberation; 4) probing meanings of collective or communal identities that people hold; and 5) studying one's community's creative and intellectual products, both historic and contemporary (Sleeter, 2002). Juxtaposing textbooks against these themes reveals a wide chasm that students of color become aware of as they go through school.

Beginning as early as elementary school, students have been found to respond to curricula based partly on what they learn and experience in their homes and communities. Epstein (2001, 2009) reports interviews with Black and White children in grades 5, 8 and 11 regarding their perspectives about topics taught in social studies. While perspectives of White fifth graders tended to resonate with the mainstream school curriculum, perspectives of many Black fifth graders diverged. For example, although White fifth graders believed that the Bill of Rights gives rights to everyone, about half of the Black children pointed out that not everyone has rights. While Black children were beginning to articulate a sense of racial oppression, White children described the U.S. as being built on progress, democracy and opportunity for all. What teachers taught added detail to what the children knew but did not change their overall interpretive framework, which derived from their experiences outside school.

Middle school students of color, when asked, are able to articulate frustrations with Eurocentric curricula. Like the eighth graders Epstein interviewed, 43 gifted Black middle-school students Ford and Harris (2000) interviewed all expressed a desire to learn more about Black people in school; most agreed that this would make school more interesting, and almost half agreed that they got tired of learning about White people all the time. Similarly, in a study of a professional-class White middle school that had recruited a significant number of students of color (mainly African American), El-Haj (2006) found that the students felt marginalized and "angry that African American history was rarely discussed outside Black History month and was almost always portrayed in terms of victimization" (p. 54). Students posited that teachers avoided in depth discussions of race and racism out of fear that the Black students would react violently. A few teachers did try to create curricula that represented multiple social groups, but most of the students of color "framed their desire for a more representative curriculum in terms of learning about one's 'own' cultural history and literature" first, before going on to study other groups (p. 156).

By the time they reach high school, students of color are not only aware of a Euro-American bias in curriculum, but they can describe it in some detail, and view it as contributing to their disengagement (Wiggan, 2007). Epstein (2000, 2009) found African American students to bring a fairly sophisticated analysis of racism to their understanding of U.S. history. Although their perspectives varied, rather than discussing the U.S. in terms of individual rights, they interpreted its history in terms of systemic racism, from which African Americans continue to struggle for emancipation. Epstein points out that the academic perspectives offered in social studies frameworks did not address the perspectives of African American adolescents, and only partially addressed perspectives of White students, some of whom expressed interest in learning more about diverse peoples. As a result, she concluded that African American students "learned to distrust the historical knowledge taught in schools and turned to family, community members, and black oriented texts" for their education (2009, p. 115).

University students also notice and react to whose knowledge is represented in curriculum. Based on a survey of 544 university students, Mayhew, Grunwald and Dey (2005) found that students, and especially students of color, judge the extent to which their university values diversity primarily based on willingness to integrate diverse racial and ethnic perspectives into curriculum. While students also saw extracurricular activities as important, whose perspectives are in the university curriculum was the most important factor they used to assess the campus's commitment to diverse students.

White adults generally do not recognize the extent to which traditional mainstream curricula marginalize perspectives of communities of color and teach students of color to distrust or not take school knowledge seriously. Epstein (2009) found that while White teachers were willing to include knowledge about diverse groups, they did so intermittently and within a Eurocentric narrative. She found that White parents, like their children, "thought only of Europeans and white Americans as nation builders, portrayed blacks as victims and one-time freedom fighters, and Native Americans as first survivors and later as victims of government policies. They never mentioned whites (other than Southerners) as perpetrators or beneficiaries of racism and 80 percent believed that blacks had achieved equal rights today" (p. 93). White parents Lewis (2001) interviewed believed that talking about race would be divisive, even in the context of Black History Month; many dismissed ethnic diversity with statements such as "We should all be Americans" (p. 788). My own informal discussions with White adults suggest that they base their evaluations of textbooks on comparisons with those they used when they were in school, rather than on comparisons with ethnic studies literature (which most White people have not studied).

In sum, it is important to recognize that ethnic studies grew from a desire to counterbalance both inaccuracies and the predominance of Euro-American perspectives that underlie mainstream curricula. Because of this bias, mainstream curricula contribute to the academic disengagement of students of color. Ethnic studies can reverse that disengagement.

Ethnic Studies and the Scope of this Review

Ethnic studies arose as a counter to "Euro-American studies" curricula. Ethnic studies curricula and programs are often traced to their beginnings in 1968 at San Francisco State University, then other campuses in California; from there, ethnic studies spread across the country. Ethnic studies has a much longer history, however, building on pioneering works such as the writings of Carter G. Woodson (1933) and W. E. B. Du Bois (1903), freedom schools of the 1960s, Black independent schools and Afrocentric public schools (e.g., Durdin, 2007; Lee, 1992; Span, 2002), tribal schools (e.g., Begay, et al., 1995), and language immersion schools.

Before briefly describing what ethnic studies is, I will note what it is not. First, although commonly described as "divisive," un-American, and teaching racial separatism and even overthrow of the U.S. government, ethnic studies curricula very intentionally include historically marginalized communities and students in a multicultural American curriculum and narrative, often supporting and developing cross-group communication. Second, although commonly perceived as touchy-feely and non-academic, even as lowering academic standards, as examples will illustrate, ethnic studies curricula are academically-based, usually designed to improve students' academic performance, and sometimes explicitly focus on university preparation. Third, although sometimes characterized as cheating students of color by substituting ethnic pride for knowledge and skills needed to succeed in the mainstream society, well-designed ethnic studies curricula do, in fact, prepare students to succeed while embracing their ethnic identity at the same time; indeed, these are linked rather than competing goals.

It is highly significant that ethnic studies came about because students of color demanded, and have continued to demand, an education that is relevant and meaningful, affirms their identities and selfhoods, and works toward human liberation (Hu-DeHart, 2004; Rangel, 2007). Mainstream Euro-American studies deny all students—both White and of color—an education that takes seriously the realities of institutionalized racism that people of color live everyday, and knowledge that arises from within communities of color. Ethnic studies, by allowing for multiple voices to enter dialog constructing the narrative of this country, is critical to development of a democracy that actually includes everyone.

Whether one is referring to Black studies, Chicano/a studies, American Indian Studies, or Asian American studies, ethnic studies have similar foci that center around "their objective of systematically examining and dismantling institutional racism" (Hu-DeHart, 2004, p. 874). For example, King (2005) explains that, given the "inherent liberatory potential of Black education, the ultimate object…is the universal problem of human freedom. That is, a goal of transformative education and research practice in Black education is the production of knowledge and understanding people need to rehumanize the world by dismantling hegemonic structures that impede such knowledge" (p. 5). Similarly, in a discussion of American Indian studies, Riding In and colleagues (2005) explain that the main objective is decolonization, empowerment, and sovereignty: "We have been cast as peoples who do not have the moral authority of non-Indians. And so we have to establish ourselves as humans with a moral situation equal to all others" (p. 177).

As ethnic studies matured, epistemologies have been developed around the most significant ways to understand and address the concerns of historically marginalized communities. For example, Macías explains that the issue is not curricular separatism, but rather reorganizing knowledge and research processes around questions that are central to the well-being of communities of color:

> We're not talking about Chicana/o history, Chicano sociology, Chicano education, Chicano political science, Chicano literature, etc. We are talking about different topical, thematic, problem, situational sets within the studies of Chicana/o studies communities, in the United States and throughout the Americas, that has to be driven by its own visions, its own view of itself in the future, and its own methodologies, including approaches to its scholarship. (in Rangel, 2007, p. 198)

Duncan-Andrade and Morrell (2008) propose "pan-ethnic studies," which connects related fields of ethnic studies, critical pedagogy, postcolonial studies, critical race theory, multicultural education, and youth popular culture. Pan-ethnic studies begin "with the relationship between racialization in U.S. society and dehumanization of students of color" (p. 134). In agreement with Macías above, Duncan-Andrade and Morrell show how pan-ethnic studies can intersect with the K-12 curriculum across the disciplines. Significantly, their model includes students as producers rather than only consumers of knowledge: students learn to become public intellectuals engaging in research and collective agency to address problems in their own communities. Also, Duncan-Andrade and Morrell specifically prioritize the importance of cariño—relationships between teacher and students that are based on reciprocity and commitment to improving the welfare of the community students live in.

For this review, I sought published studies and reviews of research that systematically document the impact of ethnic studies curricula, Pre-K through higher education, on students. I specifically focused on academic outcomes (such as test scores) as well as attitudinal outcomes. Currently in education, the "gold standard" for program evaluation consists of experimental research using randomized assignment to control and experimental groups, with pre- and post-assessments that include standardized achievement tests. While some research on ethnic studies takes this form, much of it consists of small-scale qualitative studies that use outcome measures (such as descriptions of student engagement) that were meaningful to the context and time in which the study was conducted. Ironically, what counts as program evaluation data shifted toward experimental research using test scores at the same time that education policy made it more difficult to develop and sustain K-12 ethnic studies curricula.

Much of the work in ethnic studies has been developmental in nature—researching subjugated and often forgotten knowledge, creating curriculum, developing pedagogies that link ethnic studies content with core academic concepts, preparing ethnic studies teachers, locating resources, navigating school district administrative and hiring policies, and so forth. And, because of their challenge to race relations, ethnic studies programs are always engaged in defending their existence. As Hu-DeHart (2004) explains,

> As long as ethnic studies and multicultural education in general remain within the confines of 'sensitivity training' and 'celebrating diversity,' it is safe and uncontested. But the minute ethnic studies and multicultural educators take seriously the edict that education's highest purpose is to liberate and empower (as opposed to socialize), then it becomes controversial and, frankly, threatening to the status quo. (p. 880)

In many cases, energy to develop high-quality programs and courses has simply taken precedence over efforts to systematically document their impact on students.

Nonetheless, I was able to locate a sizable body of research on the impact of ethnic studies on students. I have organized this review into two main sections: first, ethnic studies curricula as designed specifically for students of color who are members of the group under study, and second, ethnic studies curricula as designed for diverse student groups that include White students.

Impact of Ethnic Studies Designed Primarily for Members of the Group under Study

Ethnic studies curricula include units of study, courses, or programs that are centered around the knowledge and perspectives of an ethnic or racial group, reflecting narratives and points of view rooted in lived experiences and intellectual scholarship of that group. Although usually open to students from all backgrounds, curriculum reviewed in this section is pitched primarily toward students who are members of the focal ethnic group, usually as part of a broader effort to improve the quality of education afforded to them. Although this chapter focuses primarily on the impact of curriculum, it is important to note that well-designed ethnic studies courses and programs include other related features, including interactive and culturally responsive pedagogy, teachers who are members of the ethnic group and well-versed in ethnic studies, and connections with the community.

Ethnic studies curricula are supported by a body of research documenting the relationship between racial/ethnic identity of students of color and academic achievement. Studies using different research methodologies, investigating students at middle school through university levels, in different regions of the U.S. consistently find a relationship between academic achievement, high level of awareness of race and racism, and positive identification with one's own racial group. For example, Altschul, Oyserman and Bybee (2006) surveyed 98 African American and 41 Latino students in three low-income Detroit middle schools periodically over a two-year period. Although students' grades dropped as they moved from middle school to high school, grades of students with the highest racial-ethnic identity dropped the least. Chavous and colleagues (2003) surveyed 606 African American students from four predominantly Black high schools during twelfth grade, then again two years later. The students most likely to graduate and go on to college expressed high awareness of race and racism and high regard for being Black. Those least likely to stay in school expressed low awareness of race and racism, low personal regard for being Black and a perception that other people do not value Blacks (see also Miller & MacIntosh, 1999; Sanders, 1997). Altschul, Oyserman and Bybee (2008) surveyed 185 Latino/a eighth graders in three low-income middle schools where students ranged from being recent immigrants to second and third generation; most were of Mexican descent. Students with higher grades tended to have bicultural identities, identifying with their ethnic origin as well as focusing on overcoming obstacles within mainstream society. Students who identified little with their ethnic origin tended to achieve poorly, as did the relatively fewer students who identified exclusively with their culture of origin and not at all with the mainstream society (see Sellers, Chavous & Cooke, 1997, for similar findings with African American students). The researchers also found that from the time of immigration through subsequent generations, Latino students identify progressively less with their ethnic community, often resulting in a downward spiral of achievement.

Carter (2008) and O'Connor (1997) each conducted in-depth interviews with small numbers of high-achieving African American adolescents, both researchers finding that students' critical consciousness of race and racism helped them develop an achievement ideology to navigate a racially hostile environment, and that a strong Black identity contributed to their sense of agency. O'Connor (1997) noted that the students' familiarity with individual and collective struggle did not curtail their academic success, but rather contributed to their sense of agency and facilitated their academic motivation.

Ethnic studies teachers may not be aware of this research. What they are aware of, however, is the negative set of experiences that many students of color have in school, the relative absence of their ethnic group in the curriculum, and the lack of effort in many schools to help them develop an academic ethnic identity that connects school learning with their ethnic self, and helps them to see how education can serve as a tool for their own advancement as well as for serving their community. Students of color experience racism; ethnic studies does not introduce them to that concept. Rather, by taking racism and culture seriously, ethnic studies curricula attempt to give students the tools to navigate racially hostile systems—tools that many high-achieving students of color acquire in their communities.

Ethnic studies curricula have been studied in relationship to three overlapping effects on students: academic engagement, academic achievement, and personal empowerment. Because these areas have been studied somewhat differently according to academic subject area, the discussion below is organized mainly by subject area, beginning with literacy.

Several studies have examined the relationship between using a culturally relevant literacy curriculum, student engagement, and in some cases, student academic achievement.[2] Three qualitative studies with middle school students documented high levels of student engagement when literature by authors of the students' ethnic background is used. Brozo and Valerio (1996) described responses of eighth grade Mexican-American students to high-quality literature by Mexican-American authors such as Rudolfo Anaya, as the teacher introduced works over the year. It was "immediately apparent" to the authors that students connected with the literature, as formerly passive students become highly engaged in reading (see also Bean, Valerio, Senior & White, 1999). Copenhaver (2001) analyzed 12 African American elementary school children's responses to reading *Malcolm X: A Fire* in small groups. She found the children brought a good deal more knowledge of the life of Malcolm X than their teachers were aware they had, and in groups composed of only African Americans, they drew readily on their shared knowledge of African American media, civil rights leaders, and everyday racial issues, to follow the plot, make connections, and interpret the story.

Studies have assessed the impact of five ethnic studies literacy curricula on students' achievement: three involving low-achieving African American secondary students in high-poverty schools, and two involving Native American students.

In the Webster Groves Writing Project (Krater, Zeni & Cason, 1994), 14 middle and high school English teachers in school districts adjacent to St. Louis used action research to improve writing achievement of their African American students; the project was then extended to all students (Black and White) performing below grade level. The project gradually developed several principles based on what was working, which included using various literary works by African American authors, and a process approach to teaching writing in which some direct instruction was embedded. Over time the teachers realized that they needed to "acknowledge [students'] culture—not just by incorporating their cultural heroes into the curriculum, but by weaving the threads of their culture into the tapestry of our classroom" (Krater & Zeni, 1995, p. 35), which included recognizing how teachers' cultural biases got in the way. A significant realization was that dialect was a problem only when teachers focused on correcting grammar rather than on helping students communicate ideas; as students' ability to communicate ideas developed, students began to address their own grammar. Over the years of the project's existence, participating students made greater gains in writing than non-participating students on the local writing assessment, then later on the state writing test (see Gay, 2010, p. 160–161).

In a qualitative study, Rickford (2001) studied the impact of culturally relevant texts (African American folk tales and contemporary narratives), coupled with emphasis on higher-order thinking, on 25 low-achieving African American middle school students' enjoyment and comprehension of literature. She found that the students became very engaged because they were able to identify with "deep structure" themes such as struggle, perseverance, and family tensions, as well as with surface structure features such as African American vernacular. In assessment of their comprehension, she found that the students excelled on the higher-order comprehension questions, while they missed many of the lower-order questions. Rickford concluded that familiarity with situations and people in stories increased students' motivation, and that even while missing many lower-order comprehension questions, students were able to analyze and interpret the stories well. Research on Lee's Cultural Modeling Project (Lee, 1995, 2001, 2006, 2007), described in Chapter Four of this volume, concurs with findings of these studies. Lee (2006) posits that African American life affords young people a wealth of cultural scripts and contexts that can be used in the classroom to develop literary analysis strategies students can then apply to unfamiliar texts, and that a curriculum that enables students to use their cultural frames of reference immediately engages them in much higher levels of cognition than is usually the case with a traditional curriculum (Lee, 2006).

Two bilingual/bicultural indigenous literacy curricula have been examined in relationship to their impact on student achievement. The Rough Rock English-Navajo Language Arts Program (RRENLAP), originally funded by Title VII of the Bilingual Education Act, was designed to develop biliteracy skills of K-6 students, the majority of whom spoke Navajo as their primary language. Because a written Navajo literacy curriculum did not exist, the teachers needed to develop materials written in Navajo and relevant to the lives of the children. An example of a thematic unit the teachers created was Wind, "an ever-present force at Rough Rock"

(McCarty, 1993, p. 184). McCarty (1993) reports that after four years in the program, the students' achievement on locally developed measures of comprehending spoken English had increased from 51% to 91%, and their reading scores on standardized reading tests rose steadily after the second year, although students were still below national norms. Those who participated in the bilingual/bicultural program three to five years made the greatest gains. Similarly, Lomawaima and McCarty (2006) explain that in Peach Springs, Arizona, teachers worked with parents, elders, and linguists to develop a writing system for the Hualapai language, then developed culturally relevant teaching units and materials across the academic subject areas, in Hualapai. While initially non-Indian teachers objected to this curriculum, they relented when they saw children's positive responses, improved academic learning, ability to work in English, and 100% high school graduation rate. In both of these related projects, Indigenous students responded well to a curriculum designed around their culture and language. Even if, as in the case of the Navajo students, they were not yet performing at grade level on standardized tests in English, they were doing much better academically than they had been prior to the curriculum's development and implementation; they were also thriving psychologically. Lomawaima and McCarty suggest that these programs have not survived, not because they were not serving students well, but rather because they require teachers who speak the indigenous languages, thereby posing a threat to non-indigenous teachers who did not speak the language, and because Indigenous control over curriculum challenges federal power over the tribes.

I located studies of the impact of two ethnic studies math/science curricula on student learning,[3] both focusing on Native American students. Math in a Cultural Context (MCC) grew from collaboration between Alaska Yup'ik Native elders, teachers, and math educators to develop an elementary level curriculum that connects Yup'ik culture and knowledge with mathematics as outlined in the National Council of Teachers of Mathematics standards. Lipka and his colleagues (2005a) describe it as offering a "third space" that weaves together math content and local cultural knowledge. The curriculum has ten modules that link mathematics with community culture; for example, "Parkas and Patterns" focuses on geometry. The curriculum also supports traditional ways of communicating and learning, such as collaborative learning and cognitive apprenticeship. The modules and assessment materials, as well as papers reporting research on the project, can be found on the project's website (Math in a Cultural Context, 2010). For about two decades, Lipka and colleagues have been documenting the curriculum's development, use and impact (e.g., Lipka, 1991; Lipka et al., 2005a; Lipka et al., 2005b). Most of the publications describe in detail how teachers and students work with the curriculum (e.g.,

Lipka, 1991; Lipka et al., 2005b). Some also report experimental studies that use a pretest-posttest control group design, assessing students' learning based on the state's benchmarks or achievement tests. These studies find that students in classrooms using the MCC curriculum make more progress toward the state mathematics standards than students in classrooms not using it (Lipka & Adams, 2004; Lipka et al., 2005b). Not only does the curriculum help make mathematical concepts comprehensible for the Yup'ik children, studies also find it to improve Yup'ik teachers' practice by drawing on what is culturally familiar to them, thereby giving them confidence and authority over what they are teaching, as well as helping them to structure their math curriculum (Lipka et al., 2005a).

Matthews and Smith (1994) reported an experimental study (pretest-posttest control group design) investigating the impact of a much more modest project—using Native American science materials—on Native American students' attitudes toward science, attitudes towards Native people, and understanding of science concepts. The study investigated fourth through eighth graders in nine schools administered by the Bureau of Indian Affairs. The intervention, which lasted 10 weeks, involved use of biographies of Native Americans using science (such as a silversmith or a water quality technician) and other activities that related science to Native communities. The experimental group made greater gains in achievement than the control group, and expressed more positive attitudes toward science and toward Native Americans in the posttest. The findings suggest that the materials, limited in scope as they were, made a positive impact on students.

Research investigates the impact of five ethnic studies curricula (three in social studies, one in literature, and one in "life skills") on students' achievement and empowerment, which in these studies refers to students' sense of agency and ability to take positive action on problems in their communities.

Tyson's (2002) case study examined the use of literature about social issues in an African American urban middle school social studies class of 20 students. Literature was linked with social studies to enable students to begin to think about how to participate in social life. The literature included five adolescent novels: three were African American, one was multiethnic, and one was set in Japan; all featured social justice concepts and characters acting in world around them, such as working with neighbors to transform a vacant lot into a community garden, or taking a stand on behalf of one's community. The researcher documented students' developing understanding of complexities of social action, as well as their ability to use text to derive meaning; most of the students demonstrated growth in both areas over the semester.

Lewis, Sullivan and Bybee (2006) reported an experimental study of a one-semester African American emancipatory curriculum for eighth graders in a predominantly Black inner-city public middle school. Students were randomly assigned to the experimental course or the control course (Life Skills). The experimental course focused on African and African American history and culture, African rituals and practices, building communalism, student leadership and activism, and school-community partnerships. It included considerable attention to racism, oppression, discrimination, White privilege, need for Black empowerment, and self-reliance. Youth in the experimental curriculum scored higher than those in the control group on communal orientation, school connectedness, motivation to achieve, overall social change involvement, and (contrary to the study hypothesis) individualism and competitiveness. The authors point out that by giving considerable sustained curricular space to African American heritage rather than bringing it out only at certain times (Black History Month, study of slavery in history), students could see that their own heritage has worth.

Vasquez's (2005) case study examined the responses of 18 college students to a Chicano literature course, in which all of the selections were authored by Chicana/os and dealt with topics such as immigration, migrant labor, poverty, and Catholicism. Eleven of the 18 students were Latino/a. The Latino/a students all said that they identified with the texts, and that the texts filled in blanks in their understandings of their families' biographies. They reported developing a sense of community based on recognition of similar experiences and hardships. Realizing there is an abundance of Chicano literature prompted feelings of ethnic and personal affirmation, confidence, empowerment, finally occupying the place of "insider" in an academic institution. For one student, recognition that there is strong Latino American culture strengthened his identification as American. The non-Latinos found shared human issues in the texts to identify with; they had to wrestle with recognition of differences while also seeing cross-group human similarities. They also had to deal with lacking the authority of shared experiences with the authors and characters, and not being able to direct where discussions went; for the White students, not being "insiders" to the content was a new experience.

Halagao (2004, 2010) examined the impact of *Pinoy Teach* on Filipino American college students. *Pinoy Teach* is a curriculum she co-developed that focuses on Philippine and Filipino American history and culture, using a problem-posing pedagogy that encourages students to think critically through multiple perspectives on history. Halagao explains that *Pinoy Teach* offers a different perspective about history than students learned before, and some of it is uncomfortable; the pedagogical issue is not replacing one master narrative with another, but rather helping students grapple with and think their way through diverse and conflicting perspectives, then considering what to do with their new knowledge. As part of the learning process, the college students mentor and teach what they are learning to younger students. Through a series of interviews, Halagao (2004) examined the curriculum's impact on six Filipino American college students at the end of the course. As in Vasquez' study, she found that since none of them had learned about their own ethnic history in school, they described this curriculum as "filling in the blanks." Students also described collisions between their prior knowledge of Philippine history, learned mainly from their parents, and that in the curriculum, particularly around the experiences of Spanish, then U.S. colonization. The students expressed interest in learning about their own history in relationship to that of other groups. As in Vasquez' study, they moved from seeing other Filipinos through learned stereotypes to building shared sense of community, and they developed a sense of confidence and empowerment to stand up to oppression and to work for their own communities. Several years later, Halagao (2010) reported a follow-up survey of 35 who had participated in the curriculum about 10 years earlier; 30 were Filipino American and 5 were Euro-American; all had completed college and were working in various professions. Students reported that what remained with them was a "deeper love and appreciation of ethnic history, culture, identity, and community" (p. 505). The curriculum, through its process of decolonization, had helped them to develop a sense of empowerment and self-efficacy that persisted, as well as a life commitment to diversity and multiculturalism. They also developed ongoing activism in their work as teachers, in other professions, and/or through civic engagement where they lived. The two Euro-American respondents had learned to work as allies; for example, one became an editor for a textbook publisher so she could influence textbook content in a positive way.

The Mexican American/Raza Studies program in Tucson, Arizona, was described in some detail in Chapter Five. Cambium Learning and National Academic Educational Partners (2011) were commissioned by the state superintendent of education to conduct an external evaluation of the program, including its academic impact on students. In their examination of high school graduation data, the auditors found that students enrolled in the high school courses "graduate in the very least at a rage of 5% more than their counterparts in 2005, and at the most, at a rate of 11% in 2010" (p. 47). On the state's academic achievement tests, students who had failed the reading and writing portions earlier, then completed a Mexican American Studies class, were more likely to pass by the end of their junior year than students who did not take the class. Importantly, in interviews students consistently credited the program for their academic success. Cammarota (2007) has noted that many students credit the Raza Studies project with saving their lives, and showing them how to stand up and fight racism for themselves; many have gone on to college and credit the project as motivating them to do so (Cammarota, 2007).

I located one study of an ethnic studies curriculum project that did not achieve the intended outcomes. Ginwright (2004) documented an initiative to transform an urban high school that served mainly Black youth from low-income families, for the purpose of increasing students' academic performance and preparing them for higher education. To formulate a plan, school district leaders consulted with several prominent African American scholars whose work focused on Afrocentric curriculum and pedagogy, who subsequently persuaded them to base reform in "African precepts, axioms, philosophy" (p. 80) and to structure the curriculum around themes in African knowledge. As the reform was implemented, however, the Black students rejected it because it ignored their needs, which pragmatically began with the need for employment. Ginwright argues that what became an unsuccessful reform pitted two conceptions of Blackness against each other: that of middle-class Black reformers who connected African and African American knowledge systems with origins in Egypt, and low-income urban Black youth whose central concerns revolved around needs such as housing, employment, and health care, and whose identity was formed through urban youth cultural forms and local experiences with racism and poverty. This study shows how problems arise when culture, which is highly complex and dynamic, is operationalized in curriculum in a way that conflicts with culture students know and live daily.

In sum, all but one study that was located investigating the impact of ethnic studies curricula designed for members of the group under study found a positive impact on students. We can understand why the impact of these projects was so positive. Since all but one (Ginwright, 2004) centered curriculum on students' cultural reality, students became classroom "insiders" whose prior knowledge was valued and useful to academic learning. In that context, students' thinking and problem-solving abilities were evident; they became intellectually engaged. By reflecting the realities of students' lives, including racism and poverty, and providing students with tools to understand and act on those realities, curricula helped them develop a sense of constructive participation and hope about their lives. By being treated as intellectually capable, which many of these projects emphasized, students began to acquire an academic identity linked with rather than conflicting with their ethnic identity. Finally, by seeing depth and richness of their own American ethnic history and culture, some students who had questioned their identity began to affirm and claim an American identity.

Ethnic Studies Curricula for Diverse Student Groups that Include White Students

Most of the research on ethnic studies curricula designed for diverse student groups that include White students has investigated its impact on students' knowledge about and attitudes toward race and people who differ from themselves. This body of research is reviewed first, followed by the smaller body of research on the academic impact of such curriculum.

Several studies, mostly with children, reveal features of curricula that make the most difference. Simply infusing representation of racially and ethnically diverse people into curriculum, based on the assumption that students will develop positive attitudes by seeing diversity, makes only a marginal impact. Bigler (1999) reviewed a large number of research studies on the impact of multicultural curricula and materials on children's attitudes about race. She found most of the research weak, consisting mainly of small-scale case studies that lacked processes for determining whether change had occurred, and if so, whether changes could be attributed to the curriculum. More significantly, she noted that racial attitudes are acquired actively rather than passively. Curricula that simply depict or label groups or group members (for example, pointing out a person's race, ethnicity, or gender) may draw students' attention to group markers and differences and invite stereotyping, without engaging them in questioning their own thinking (Bigler, Brown & Markell, 2001). In addition, she noted that most curricula did not take account of children's age-specific cognitive development. She suggested that effective approaches would focus explicitly on stereotyping and bias, present strong counter-stereotypic models, and engage students in thinking about multiple features of individuals (such as race and occupation), within-group differences, and cross-group similarities.

In subsequent experimental studies, Hughes, Bigler, and Levy (2007) and Hughes and Bigler (2007) documented the impact on African American and White elementary children of a few short lessons that include information about Black and White historical figures and (in the treatment condition) about racism. Both studies found that lessons teaching about racism and successful challenges to it improve racial attitudes of White children, allowing them to see how racism affects everybody, and offering them a vision for addressing it. They posited that children's valuing of racial fairness accounts for much of the positive impact. Lessons about racism made less impact on the African American children (probably because it duplicated what they already knew), but the information about historical figures improved their regard for African Americans.

Aboud and Fenwick's (1999) studies offer further clues as to how curricula affect racial attitudes. They reported two studies building on previous research that found that a great majority of White parents do not talk with their children about race, and those that do, usually do not do so at a developmentally appropriate level. Aboud and Fenwick investigated two curricular inventions designed to help elementary children talk about race. Both studies used a pretest-posttest design, one with a control group and the other without. Both studies documented the kind of talk that reduces prejudice, especially among high-prejudiced children: talk that directs attention toward individual qualities rather than group membership only, or talk that offers positive information about a group, and talk that directly addresses a listener's concerns rather than general talk that does not.

A sizable body of survey research in higher education supports and extends the research findings on curricula for children. Much of the higher education research examines development of democracy outcomes, which Gurin, Dey, Gurin and Hurtado (2003) define as including "commitment to promoting racial understanding, perspective taking, sense of commonality in values with students from different racial/ethnic backgrounds, agreement that diversity and democracy can be congenial, involvement in political affairs and community service during college as well as commitment to civic affairs after college" (p. 25). This research examines the impact of various diversity experiences, with a focus on course-taking and interracial interaction. For the most part, the courses students took in these studies were required diversity courses on their campuses, lists of which include ethnic studies courses, women's studies courses, and courses that focus broadly on a range of forms of diversity.

The overwhelming and most consistent finding is that, in most studies, such courses have a positive impact on students' development of democracy outcomes (Astin, 1993; Denson, 2009; Gurin, Dey, Hurtado & Gurin, 2002; Lopez, 2004). Engberg's (2004) review of 73 studies of the impact of a diversity course, a diversity workshop, a peer-facilitated invention, or a service intervention found that 52 of the studies reported positive gains, 14 reported mixed gains, and only 7 reported no change. Although most studies had methodological weaknesses (such as use of convenience samples and limitations stemming from wording of some of the survey questions), there was still a consistent pattern of finding a positive impact of diversity coursework on reducing students' biases.

The impact of such courses is considerably stronger when they include cross-group interaction (Astin, 1993; Bowman, 2010b; Chang, 2002; Denson, 2009; Gurin, Dey, Hurtado & Gurin, 2002; Lopez, 2004), or as Nagda, Kim and Truelove (2004) put it, "enlightenment and encounter." Because of the importance of cross-group interaction (encounter), some research focuses specifically on its nature. Gurin and Nagda (2006) found that participation in structured intergroup dialogs:

> fosters active thinking about causes of social behavior and knowledge of institutional and other structural features of society that produce and maintain group-based inequalities,…increases perception of both commonalities and differences between and within groups and helps students to normalize conflict and build skills to work with conflicts,…[and it] enhances interest in political issues and develops a sense of citizenship through college and community activities. (p. 220)

In an experimental study, Antonio and colleagues (2004) found that small group discussions in which students vary by race or by opinion produce greater cognitive complexity than when participants are homogeneous (see also Hurtado, Engberg, Ponjuan, & Landreman, 2002).

The higher education studies found that required diversity courses have a greater positive impact on White students than on students of color (Denson, 2009; Engberg, 2004; Bowman, 2010a; Lopez, 2004). This is probably because exposure to a systematic analysis of power is newer to White students than it is to students of color, and because while most students of color have engaged in cross-racial interaction previously, a large proportion of White students have not. In addition, although the researchers do not note this, my experience is that introductory diversity courses are often pitched toward a White audience; students of color may appreciate White students being taught about racism, but often do not find their own understanding stretched. Blackwell (2010), an African American woman who had been on the receiving end of such curricula, points out that students of color frequently feel marginalized in diversity curricula that focus on raising consciousness among White students by being positioned as cultural expert, teacher's aid, and witness of race and racism; she argues that "home spaces" where students of color can learn about race, ethnicity, and culture at a deeper level are also needed.

The studies also found that for many students—particularly White students—the first diversity course is emotionally challenging (Hogan & Mallot, 2005). In a large survey study of students in 19 colleges and universities, Bowman (2010a) examined the impact of taking one or more diversity courses on students' well-being, and comfort with and appreciation of differences. He found that many students who take a single diversity course experienced a reduced sense of well-being due to having to grapple with issues they have not been exposed to before. However, students who took more than one diversity course experienced significant gains, with gains being greatest for White male students from economically privileged backgrounds (who had the farthest to go). Completing a diversity course also appears to mitigate what is otherwise an escalation of intolerance in the university experience. In a pre-post survey study of students at the University of Michigan, Henderson-King and Kaleta (2000) found that while the students (majority White) who completed a one-semester race and ethnicity course did not shift in their attitudes about various groups (such as African Americans and Latinos), students who did not complete such a course became less tolerant.

Research on the academic impact of ethnic studies curricula designed for diverse student groups, while not voluminous, shows that such curricula, when designed to help students grapple with multiple perspectives, produces higher levels of thinking.

In the Multicultural Reading and Thinking Project (McRAT), which was developed in Arkansas for grades 4–6 (Arkansas Department of Education, 1992), lessons that used multicultural content across the curriculum were designed to develop both higher-order thinking and cultural awareness. By the end of the second year of the project, which was being used in seven school districts, Quellmalz and Hoskyn (1988) found "substantial increases" in student achievement percentile rankings across social class and student achievement levels (p. 54). They also reported qualitative data that showed an increase in students' writing ability, and parent reports that children were reading more at home. In a subsequent experimental evaluation of the project (30% of the students were of color), students using the McRAT curriculum outperformed the control group in analysis, inference, comparison, and evaluation (Arkansas Department of Education, 1992; see also Fashola & Slavin, 1997). The multicultural curriculum, with its multiple perspectives, complemented teaching of higher-order thinking.

At the higher education level, Bowman (2010b) reported a meta-analysis of 23 statistical studies of the relationship between college student participation in diversity experiences (courses, workshops, and/or interactions), and cognitive development (such as critical thinking, moral reasoning, problem-solving). He found that participation in diversity experiences is "significantly and positively related to cognitive development" (p. 20). While the magnitude was small, the effects were consistent across the studies. Diversity experiences that include interpersonal interaction related to racial diversity had the strongest positive impact because interaction across diverse perspectives forces students to think.

There is also indication that classes of diverse students find well-planned multicultural curricula to be interesting and engaging. Qualitative studies of two literature projects at the elementary level bear this out. The Multicultural Literacy Program (Diamond & Moore, 1995, cited by Gay, 2010) entailed use of multiethnic literature with students in grades K-8 in Ypsilanti, Michigan, taught through a whole-language approach, learning centers, and cooperative learning. Qualitative data based on classroom observations and analysis of student work showed increased enjoyment of reading and writing, increased knowledge of various forms and structures of written language, expanded vocabulary and reading strategies, improved comprehension and reading fluency, longer and clearer written stories. Grice and Vaughn (1992) reported an interview study of responses of nine Black and four White low-achieving third-graders from working class urban community, to 20 "culturally conscious" books (set in inner-city and some middle-class Black neighborhoods, with Black protagonists and storyline that did not involve trying to gain white approval) and four "melting pot" books (middle-class setting, no reference to racial identity) books. The children responded most positively to books with characters and situations they could identify with, and that had a positive message.

To summarize, research on ethnic studies curricula designed for diverse student groups that include White students reports that just infusing representation of racially and ethnically diverse people into curriculum, without doing anything else, makes only a marginal impact on students' attitudes, in contrast with curricula that teach directly about racism. The large body of research in higher education that examines the impact of various diversity experiences, particularly course-taking and interracial interaction, on "democracy outcomes" reports quite consistently that such courses have a positive impact, particularly when they include cross-group interaction, and particularly on White students. Research on the academic impact ethnic studies curricula designed for diverse student groups, while not voluminous, shows that such curricula, when designed to help students grapple with multiple perspectives, produces higher levels of thinking.

Conclusion

Considerable research evidence shows that well-designed and well-taught ethnic studies curricula have positive academic and social outcomes for students, and that curricula are designed and taught somewhat differently depending on the ethnic composition of the students and the subsequent experiences they bring. These positive findings should not be interpreted, however, as meaning that schools can assign any teacher an ethnic studies curriculum to teach, or that students of color will automatically achieve more if ethnic content is added to the curriculum. As noted above and in conjunction with Chapters Four and Eleven in this volume), well-planned and well-taught ethnic studies includes related components. Ethnic studies teachers must be able to relate well with their students, believe in students' academic abilities, and know ethnic studies content and perspectives well; often (but not always) they are members of the same ethnic background of most of their students. Pedagogical strategies need to engage students in active thinking. Culture, rather than being conceptualized as something static from the past, is viewed as complex and dynamic, and students' everyday lived culture and language is part of the ethnic studies curriculum. Finally, particularly at the Pre-K through 12 level, ethnic studies is not a separate subject but rather a reconceptualization of subject matter that takes into account state standards and assessments for which students will be held accountable.

Both students of color and White students have been found to benefit academically as well as socially from ethnic studies. Indeed, rather than being non-academic, well-planned ethnic studies curricula are often very academically rigorous. Rather than being divisive, ethnic studies helps students to bridge differences that already exist in experiences and perspectives. In these ways, ethnic studies plays an important role in building a truly inclusive multicultural democracy and system of education.

Notes

1. This account, which actually happened with a student whose name I changed here, represents several similar conversations I have had with students over the years.
2. To keep this review manageable, although I recognized that language is central to literacy of students for whom English is not the primary language, I excluded research on native-language immersion/bilingual education unless the project included ethnic culture in the curriculum.
3. While many articles discuss culturally relevant pedagogy broadly in math and science, only a few specifically examine the impact of curriculum on students.

7

Working an Academically Rigorous, Multicultural Program

With Bob Hughes,[1] Elizabeth Meador,[2] Patricia Whang,[3] Linda Rogers,[4] Ka-ni Blackwell,[5] Peggy Laughlin,[6] & Claudia Peralta-Nash[7]

It is too often the case that programs disrupting the status quo have short lives and are then forgotten. As higher education faculty members who collaborated on curriculum development and teaching, we write so that our work is not forgotten, but rather chronicles what is possible. We consider our work in an academically rigorous, post-credential master's degree program that is framed by theoretical perspectives about the relationship between education and society, the political and ethical nature of teaching, and research on transforming higher education.

Education can be viewed as either domesticating or liberating (Freire, 1970; Macedo, 1994). A domesticating education prepares students to acquiesce reflexively to the dictates of authority figures, uncritically consume information, and feel no compulsion to question or to act. This might not be problematic if the world were harmonious and just. But because it is not, we found post-colonial, critical, anti-racist, and feminist theories to provide essential insights into ways of achieving an education that frees students from blind obedience, ignorant bliss, and complacent inaction. Post-colonial theorists, for example, draw attention to how dominant groups use research and knowledge to colonize those constructed as "others" (Smith, 1999). Defining "what counts as valued knowledge, skills, and traditions," as well as determining "who gets to ask," ask "what," and "to whom" affords great power to structure the world in a way that maintains power and privilege.

Hence, first-generation college students tend to go to state schools that are less well-funded than many private and research-focused universities and that are structured around a "knowledge transmission" factory model more so than a "knowledge production" model (Aronowitz, 2000). This means that students from historically underserved communities, such as our students, are likely to attend a university that is structured to enable them to consume knowledge produced by those from more affluent institutions.

We worked to disrupt this institutionalized domesticating system by intentionally orienting the Master of Arts in Education program at California State University Monterey Bay (CSUMB) around knowledge production in which educators from local communities, working with knowledge frameworks and theoretical traditions that have arisen within historically oppressed communities, create knowledge that is of, by, for, and about the community and its own empowerment. We embraced the concept of transformative knowledge that "is based on different epistemological assumptions about the nature of knowledge, about the influence of human interests and values on knowledge construction, and about the purpose of knowledge" (Banks, 1993, p. 9). Transformative knowledge offers "an alternative narration of the arrangement of social space" (Gallegos, 1998, p. 236), providing conceptual tools to address conditions that have historically oppressed and excluded.

One such tool, our concept of social justice collaboration, involves students using knowledge to enhance the collective condition. We use the term social justice from a Freirean perspective that focuses on transforming the structures that perpetuate the unequal distribution of social power. Freire (1970) contends that changing the status quo involves naming injustices that oppress and then taking action with other people through dialogue and work. Naming injustice is critical, since so much of it is taken for granted as "commonsense" (Kumashiro, 2004a).

Teaching is inherently political and ethical because teachers have direct influence on the lives of others. That is, as a social institution, education affords or denies access to resources that directly impact one's life chances. Because we see teaching as a process of empowerment and engagement with knowledge that arises in part from lived experience, we value engaged pedagogy that facilitates honest, critical dialogues that allow consideration of significant issues among people who share experiences of oppression, as well as with those who do not. We see this process as enabling collective claiming of power. Understanding teaching as political and ethical substantiates the need to prepare teachers who are able to act as committed transformative intellectuals (Giroux, 1988)—who have confidence to use their knowledge, skills, and position to work toward positive change in classrooms, schools, and communities. The transformative intellectual must grasp the precondition of a collective process of liberation through participation in a community that values the need to change the social condition of oppression (Freire, 1970; hooks, 1994; Huiskamp, 2002). This is why many of our core program learning outcomes, described later, reflect the knowledge, skills, and dispositions necessary to work as a change agent.

Essentially, just as we believe that education should be decolonized, so too should teaching. Education is decolonized as students claim a political identity, which is facilitated within the context of a politically engaged community of practice (Huiskamp, 2002; Lave & Wenger, 1991). Claiming a political identity entails claiming rights as citizens, not only in a legal sense but also in a cultural sense (Flores & Benmayor, 1997). This socio-historical perspective explicitly recognizes the importance of more established learning community members in affording access to experiences, knowledge, and dispositions. Fuller participation signifies and requires adoption of the values of a particular community of practice as one claims membership while maintaining sufficient reflective distance to create productive change.

We came to see our students as formulating "layered" identities, as accepting the challenge of forming an identity within the academic community, maintaining the integrity of their community affiliations, and working toward the possibility of altering historically constructed injustices (Gandhi, 1998). Many of our students first experienced the idea of higher education as a dream of their parents and their community. They had worked alongside their parents in the fields nearby or had taken care of family members while other family members worked long and difficult hours. Part of their childhood revolved upon stories that created narratives of possibility—"one day you will" or "I came here so that you could"—that operate as a secondary consciousness for the perceiver (Bakhtin, Holquist, & Emerson, 1986). The student's drive to finish his or her studies is not only the "I" voice of achieving an individual goal but also the vibrant collaborative "I" (Visweswaren, 1994) of all of those who struggled.

As traditionally structured, higher education does not support the vision sketched above. Further, on-going systemic racism persistently privileges the academic success of students who are White, native English speaking, and from affluent backgrounds. To discover how institutions of higher education might equalize degree completion rates across diverse groups, we drew on research that investigated what factors help and hinder first-generation students of color. Based on interviews with baccalaureate recipients of color, Richardson and Skinner (1992) identified three kinds of barriers. Firstly, the most widely reported barrier was preparation for higher education. Unpreparedness had several components: students felt that they were academically unprepared for the rigorous curriculum they discovered in college; for the racial isolation they felt when surrounded by a largely white campus, and for coping with the time demands that school life placed upon them, especially since most had external pressures (such as working and family responsibilities) to consider. Secondly, most structures and schedules were created with traditional students in mind: most first-generation students attended in non-traditional modes as they worked jobs away from campus and supported themselves and dependents; they stayed away from on-campus enrichment activities and had to maintain strict schedules to keep up with their schoolwork while juggling competing responsibilities. Lastly, students felt that some faculty members and students in their classes held lower expectations for them than for their white peers. Coupled with feelings of isolation, this led them to remain in small cliques of people similar to themselves, further isolated from the larger campus culture and possible new communities of practice they might join (see also Allen, 1992; Warburton, Bugarin, & Nuñez, 2003).

Living the Vision

Between 1997 and 2005, we enacted a post-credential master's degree program to support students with complex lives and widely varying degrees of preparedness for academic rigor. We have organized this discussion of it around four broad themes through which the core values of the CSUMB vision were given form in the campus's strategic plan: 1) a pluralistic academic community, 2) student learning, 3) support for student learning, and 4) engaged campus community (California State University Monterey Bay, 2002).

A pluralistic academic community

Building a pluralistic academic community reflects the assumption that, "Diversity enriches the learning and life experience of all" (CSUMB, 2002, p. 5). Our commitments to decolonizing minds from the subjugation and dehumanization of a domesticating education would make no sense if we were not committed to attracting and graduating a diverse student body.

We recruited students through various methods that included advertising through County Offices of Education, the school mail system, the university's advertising systems, and the Master of Arts in Education (MAE) website, but the strongest recruitment came from word of mouth, on and off campus. As educators who were interested in bilingual and multicultural education heard about the focus of our program, its diverse faculty, and successful experiences of those who had graduated, they came. We admitted students using criteria that included: 1) our expectation of their ability to do graduate work (as reflected in letters of recommendation and their strong GPA) and 2) a match between the applicant's purpose for seeking an advanced degree at our university (as reflected in a professional goal statement) and the focus and resources of the program. An important section in the application addressed applicants' cultural and experiential strengths and desire for becoming education leaders with a passion to transform culturally and linguistically diverse schools.

An unanticipated benefit of our location is its close proximity to the Naval Postgraduate School in Monterey, which provided a pool of international students who are local teachers or spouses of naval officers who are visiting from their home countries. Varied perspectives and life experiences of students from the People's Republic of China, Greece, Chad, Japan, Kenya, Korea, Sudan, and Brazil enriched our program. For example, the success of the first students from Greece (whose valued input helped us make the program more inclusive) became known to subsequent Greek families who moved to the area and followed in their footsteps. One student, Maria Vasilaki (2002), wrote in the introduction of her thesis, "As I'm looking back in time, I now understand that I had to travel abroad, beyond the borders of my country to understand and appreciate both my country's culture and history as well as the whole world's" (p. 6).

By July 2003, the program had graduated 49 students. Table 7.1 shows their racial and ethnic composition, with some oversimplification of categories, since many were of mixed backgrounds (such as Mexican/Indian). The graduates mirrored the racial and ethnic composition of California, unlike the proportion of master's degrees awarded in California at large, as the column on the right indicates (U.S. Department of Education, 2002), showing the program's efficacy in reaching the people it was intended to serve.

As of 2004, about half of the program's 49 graduates taught at the K-12 level in local schools; many had remained actively engaged in school transformation efforts. One was vice president of a statewide K-12 school improvement consulting agency. Four international students returned to their home countries. Several graduates (mostly people of color) were working toward doctorates: one had completed a doctorate and was an assistant professor, and seven were either in or had been accepted to doctoral programs. Three had used their master's degree to obtain teaching positions in higher education. We lost track of a few, mainly those who moved out of the area.[8]

Table 7.1: Master's Degrees, by Race/Ethnicity: CSUMB and California

	Number of degrees awarded, CSUMB Master of Arts in Education	% Degrees awarded, CSUMB Master of Arts in Education	% Masters degrees awarded in California	% Population in California in 2004
White American	20	41	70	47
African American	3	6	8	7
Latino	15: 12 Mexican, 1 Puerto Rican, 1 Colombian, 1 Portuguese	30	4	32
Asian, Pacific Islander*	6: 2 Chinese, 1 Japanese, 1 Korean, 1 Hmong, 1 Fiji Indian	12	5	11
American Indian/Alaska Native	0	0	0.5	1
Other	5: 4 Greek international, 1 Assyrian American	10	13**	2

* For our program and the state of California, a distinction is not made between those born inside versus outside the U.S. Data on master's degrees awarded in California, however, distinguish between U.S. citizens and resident aliens.

** There is some lack of parallelism in this category. In our program, the Greek international students do not identify with White Americans, so we classified them separately, along with an Assyrian American who identifies partially with the Latino community. For population statistics on California, "other" includes any who checked a box that does not fit the above categories. For data on master's degrees awarded in California, this box means "resident alien."

From the beginning, faculty members who chose to work in the program were racially and ethnically diverse. We use the word "chose" because the majority of faculty committing time and energy to this program were hired in positions that largely served the teacher credential programs. Of this article's eight authors, we are African American (1), Native American (1), Asian American (1), Latina (1), Australian (1), and Euro-American (3); 1 male and 7 females. We grew up in diverse socio-economic contexts, in places as diverse as Oregon, California, Kentucky, Ethiopia, Uruguay, and Australia. Our background experiences allowed us to relate closely with the diverse students the program attracted. For example, students were often amazed when they discovered that one of us, a person of color, was raised in an orphanage, often confronted with marginalizing experiences, and possessed deep scars of discrimination. Students often expressed feeling that we as faculty were "real," understanding, and approachable. Students also stated that they could feel our passion for equity, social responsibility, and multicultural ideologies.

Student learning

Our curriculum was built around interdisciplinary learning that is cross-cultural, technologically sophisticated, and academically challenging. We structured it around eight core learning outcomes. They include: 1) critical questioner, 2) scholar, 3) action researcher, 4) educator, 5) bilingual communicator, 6) technological navigator, 7) communicator, and 8) social justice collaborator. As explicit statements of valued and desired skills, knowledge, and dispositions, they guided the development of coursework and program exit requirements that intentionally reflect a knowledge production model that upholds the rigor expected in more elite institutions.

We developed a definition for each learning outcome, as well as rubrics that detail criteria and standards for evaluating student work. For example, Table 7.2 explicates the criteria by which we evaluate students' work as scholars and the standards we use, distinguishing among work that is "exemplary," "developing," and "emerging." Although most courses integrate these criteria to some degree, this outcome was most directly addressed in the Professional Literature Seminar course, described later.

The learning outcome "social justice collaborator" reflected our mission to engender activism for liberation. Its criteria include coalition-building, quality of coalition participation, and action taken on behalf of social justice. As was true of all eight core learning outcomes, its standards and criteria were integrated throughout courses. However, the idea of a "social justice collaborator," introduced at the beginning of the program, was attended to most strongly through action students planned or undertook as part of their thesis.

Students completed eight courses: four core research courses and four electives. A core of research coursework grounded much of their work from the program's beginning to end. The first course, Proseminar on Multicultural and Bilingual Education, explored the sociopolitical context of schools, helping students to locate their work, interests, and goals in larger discourses about social justice and education. The students were introduced to various epistemological stances toward research. What many assumed counts as knowledge was critically questioned and analyzed, beginning with the dominant paradigm—positivism. Students then

Table 7.2 Learning Outcome Scholar

Scholar: Students will search, navigate, and critically consume (read, analyze, and use) educational research.

Criteria and standards for evaluation

	Rigor	Appropriateness
Exemplary	Conducts thorough and extensive review and synthesis, uses significant multiple resources, uses broad range of considerations for critiquing and evaluating sources, includes primary research.	Uses and critiques major contributors to field related to focus of action thesis; uses relevant search processes; uses research from multiple perspectives pertinent to the question.
Developing	Conducts review and synthesis, uses some significant resources, uses range of considerations for critiquing and evaluating sources, includes primary research.	Finds material related to the focus, and uses and critiques some of the major contributors to that field; uses relevant search processes; uses research from limited perspectives pertinent to the question.
Emerging	Just reviews, does not synthesize; limited range of resources, limited critique and evaluation, minimal primary research.	Finds some material related to the action thesis, but recognizes and uses few of the major contributors; ineffectively uses search processes; uses research from narrow perspectives; does not recognize the perspectives of research.

explored phenomenological, narrative, and participatory (emancipatory) research grounded in critical analysis of problems that are experienced within historically marginalized communities. Our intent, beginning in Proseminar, was to help students claim validity of knowledge based in lived experience, situating it within intentionally selected epistemological stances. Students were required to identify an important issue in their work context, articulate and defend a position on the issue, and act on their position. If, for example, a student was convinced that standardized testing is negatively impacting teaching and learning in his or her classroom, using both the established research literature and research done at his or her school, the student advocated for this position, executing and reflecting upon an appropriate "reACTion." For many, this initial effort launched the culminating requirement of the program, the action thesis.

Three subsequent core courses helped students develop the conceptual and academic tools necessary to complete the action thesis. Professional Literature Seminar (developed after realizing that most students needed to complete independent studies to ground themselves in literature related to their thesis topic) guided students through activities that helped scaffold analysis of literature relevant to their topic, develop a theoretical context,

and write a coherent and informed literature review. In the process, it provided an oppor-
tunity for students to critically develop their position more systematically and in depth.
In Qualitative Research Methods, students conducted mini-qualitative studies to bet-
ter understand methods they may use in their own research. This course also provided
the forum for developing a methodologically sound research proposal for review by a fac-
ulty committee and preparation of an application to the Committee for the Protection
of Human Subjects. The final core research course, Capstone Seminar, supported stu-
dents in writing the thesis, offering opportunities for peer review along with periodic
review of drafts by two faculty readers, and opportunities to present their work to the
broader MAE program community.

Students also completed four elective courses. Course titles reflect our curricu-
lum's explicit focuses on transformative education (such as Arts as Culturally
Responsive Pedagogy, Biliteracy, Multicultural Curriculum Design, Literacy for
Linguistically Diverse Learners, and Technology as a Tool for Inclusion in
Multicultural Classrooms). All courses featured content and readings based heavily on research and theory produced by scholars of color and scholars who examine education through the lens of multicultural social justice. For example,
Multicultural Curriculum Design featured a curriculum planning process that
included considerable attention to teacher ideology (Macedo, 1994), selection
and use of transformative knowledge to design and plan a unit, and voices of critical multicultural teachers analyzing their own approaches to multicultural curriculum planning and teaching (Sleeter, 2005). Chapter Twelve of this volume presents
a case study of a student when she was in this particular course.

The culminating action thesis connected five learning outcomes: critical questioner, scholar, communicator, action researcher, and social justice collaborator. We
conceptualized the action thesis as a process through which students learn to use
research to transform their environments, collaborating with their communities.
Examples included building a parent-school partnership to support literacy development in a bilingual school, working with young adult students to transform curriculum so that it responds to them, and collaborating with colleagues in a
low-income school to bring computers into classroom instruction. Through this
work, students developed cohesion and coherence between their multifaceted
experiential lives and their emerging professional lives. Often, the disjuncture
between student as family/cultural group member clashes with an emerging professional identity (Rastier, 1997). We do not believe that the student needs to be
transformed by knowledge as much as making it a part of his/her operational
"within-ness" (Ricoeur, 1988), by layering possibilities of other visions within
their existing frames of reference.

Thus, rather than writing a traditional knowledge production thesis, our students learned to use research and personal experience to renegotiate their environment and in that process, themselves. Their action theses took varied forms that reflected that renegotiation. All included a written narrative connecting the purpose of the thesis with the student's life experiences and commitments, a literature review and theoretical grounding, a description of methodology, and a concluding reflection on action planned or taken. In addition, while most collected and analyzed data, some developed new curriculum, websites, film, or CD-ROMs for classroom use.

Support for student learning

Since our students brought rich and varied experiences and levels of preparation for graduate work, intentionally supporting their learning was critical. Our support attended to the academic, motivational, and social factors found important for first-generation students of color (Richardson & Skinner, 1992). These include scaffolding students' learning, building trusting relationships through community, supporting learning culturally, and flexibly responding to complex needs.

Scaffolded instruction is "the systematic sequencing of prompted content, materials, tasks and teacher and peer support to optimize learning" (Dickson, Chard, & Simmons, 1993, p. 12). Under the watchful guidance of professors (who serve as more skilled others or old-timers) the required coursework, beginning with the Proseminar and ending with the Capstone seminar, provided students with opportunities to engage in the steps necessary to successfully complete their action thesis. Systematically using coursework in this way assured faculty availability to monitor student frustration, give feedback, and provide assistance. This support is further complemented by each student's action thesis advisor. Furthermore, this structure provides multiple perspectives and critiques on each student's evolving action research, thus increasing the rigor, sophistication, and potency of resultant projects.

We intentionally built trust and community in a variety of ways. Instructional activities that require interaction, risk-taking, and performance, through role-playing, debates, or arts-based activities allowed students to be fully present, revealing, and participatory. Such activities also invited modes of expression that are not primarily dependent on verbal-linguistic ability, thus expanding what can be expressed as well as who can express it. Group projects and course-based writing groups (both online and face-to-face) built community. In addition, classes frequently provided a forum to work through interpersonal conflicts that may arise because of the dynamics within groups, thus decreasing the likelihood that resentments fester or factions develop.

Community also developed in unintentional ways. Because all courses met in the late afternoon and evening, many involved potluck dinners. This contributed to a sense of community as students and instructors generously and proudly shared food representative of their racial or ethnic groups, thus providing an opportunity for the chef to talk about him/herself and his/her culture. These meals additionally provide an informal opportunity to talk about life, to discuss common issues or interests, and to share frustrations and struggles.

Developing trust was critical because of the range of issues explored and the diversity of experiences, backgrounds, and perspectives represented in a typical class. Trust is essential if members of the dominant group are to hear critiques of their power and privilege and if members of non-dominant groups are to voice their experiences or desires. Similarly, members of dominant groups must trust that they can voice perspectives that may not be politically correct and not be condemned or ostracized. This requires vigilance and a willingness to be open and learn on the part of students and faculty. Consider a class in which a Black male student objected to an author's work because he perceived her to be a lesbian. His comments surprised the instructor into silence. This was a good thing, as the class was given opportunity to react. Immediate reactions related to the prejudicial nature of the comment. As questions were asked and stories shared, the most powerful were those insights shared by a woman who revealed herself to be a lesbian and told what those comments meant to her in the context of her experiences. If either of these students had not felt supported or safe to voice their opinions or stories, then the class would have been much more sanitized and more about domestication than liberation.

The cultural relevance of our curriculum and practices supported our students. Understanding that learning is inherently a cultural endeavor (Gay, 2010), students of color found themselves well represented in readings. Elective courses, such as Culture, Cognition, and Development, also made explicit the importance of culture to teaching and learning. The varied experiences and perspectives of international students also unintentionally stretched and prodded our thinking about cultural relevance (e.g., Whose culture?) and our American-centric assumptions about schools and schooling.

We worked in additional ways to respond to students' needs, such as keeping reading lists affordable and accessible, providing support for students who lacked a computer at home, and re-thinking assignments that presuppose easy access to a computer or the Internet. Because most students were employed full-time, we had to schedule courses in the evenings, on weekends, and online. To support Spanish-speaking teachers, we included a course taught in Spanish. As students or prospective students communicated their needs to us, we tried to address as many barriers to students' success as possible within the constraints of the institution.

Engaged campus community

An engaged campus community prepares citizens and community builders. This aim is consistent with programmatic practices and perspectives that facilitate knowledge production and the education of transformative intellectuals.

Darder (1991) advocates integrating students' lived experiences into the classroom environment in order to link culture, community, and power. In her view, cultural democracy must allow "bicultural students to develop their bicultural voice and experience a process of empowerment in the classroom" (p. 47). This is a dialectical process in which students bring as much knowledge to the situation as professors. As professors, we do not have the experiences of our students and, often in our desire to present formal curriculum, can fail to connect to student experience. We can also forget to invite students to consider how concepts would affect, interact, disrupt, or change situations in their lives. For example, in one course, one of us learned that a student's attempts to replace square dancing with Mexican dances in her school's curriculum was not simply a matter of learning who controlled access to the gym and how to change classroom activities. It also meant that she had to learn who in the community was appropriate to contact for discussion about which region of Mexican dance, who was the acknowledged leader of each dance community, and what happened when people with expertise chose not to communicate. Although such questions begin as practical problems, they are embedded within social and political relationships regarding who has power to name reality. Thus, class time enables voice—where students (whose normal mode of survival in schools has often been a profound silence) learn to articulate their concerns and questions and eventually conceive of actions that addressed their issues (Visweswaren, 1994).

Throughout this process, all of our courses examined social and political issues with power implications in the context of schooling. Since most of our students were practicing teachers who chose to make change in their own classrooms or schools, critical discussions often centered on conditions in schools and how transformation is not only difficult but necessary if any difference is to be made for students from historically marginalized backgrounds. For example, a bilingual teacher in a school that was resistant to bilingual education asked her peers in class for help in thinking through how to educate her fellow teachers about the benefits of teaching children two languages simultaneously. She had been ostracized from the rest of the staff and needed a place where she could vent her frustrations. While this took considerable class time, it allowed the entire class to deepen their understanding of bilingual education and to problem-solve with her about ways she could speak up for her beliefs. Other students requested time to describe their dilemmas about working toward change within their settings. Since the course focused on qualitative research methods, these critical dialogues created perfect examples of social justice collaboration.

Exploring their stories within the safe environment of the classroom helped students understand how their support network—parents, community, and individual academic prowess—helped them survive in often-hostile environments. Students of color felt empowered and found their voices to speak out. The following was shared by one of the graduates:

> I was able to reflect on my tracking experience growing up in the Oakland Public School System, and how standardized testing took a toll on my self esteem....I was also able to recall experiences of being a mom in a system not set up for married middle-class families....This research has provided me with the foundation necessary to make changes to my own preschool program. It gave me an in-depth view of what our preschool program looks like from multiple perspectives, and provided the vehicle necessary to advocate for change on a campus-wide level. (Chavarin, 2002, pp. 64–65)

A program that critically engages students in local concerns can also have a tremendous impact on White students.

> On the first day of ED 620...[professor] asked the class if discrimination still existed in U.S. schools. I remember thinking that, of course, there were still problems, but that things have gotten a lot better recently. Three years later, through exposure to research and literature written by minorities, I now realize that I am a White teacher who wanted what was best for all my students, but was unaware or in denial of how the United States educational system marginalizes people of color. (Pipes, 2002, p. 6)

Tensions arise, however, when some students who are White and native English speaking persistently perceive themselves as entitled to frame and to dominate discussions in terms of their experiences. For example, in Paradigms of Assessment, students reviewed the fairtest.org website to critically examine the SAT test. A White male, who attested to having benefited from bias in the test, staunchly maintained his position that the test was the only way to measure achievement across race, class, and gender lines. Other students attempted to provide counter examples but did not appear to pierce his awareness of the power and privileges inherent in his being White. Fortunately there were multiple opportunities to engage in discussion about issues related to white privilege throughout the program.

In addition to creating intra-program communities, we reached out to communities where students live and work, thus, modeling community engagement by being active change agents within the region. This was accomplished through community projects, faculty scholarship, and students' action thesis projects, which afforded opportunities for students to function as transformative intellectuals in their particular communities. In addition, we took the program itself into the community.

For example, a highly successful collaboration came as faculty worked with Starlight Elementary School in Watsonville to develop a cohort there. The distance between Watsonville and the campus made it difficult for teachers to attend evening classes during the week. Starlight was already providing professional development for teachers, and the school's administrators supported the goals of the MAE program. Watsonville serves mostly farm workers' children, requiring teachers to be proficient in teaching English-language learners. Teachers brought defined needs that they wished to address in their classroom, their school, and their community. We co-planned some of the courses with them, and taught six of the eight MAE courses at Starlight. The resulting cohort generated projects that ranged from reaching out to linguistically diverse students to the development of community-based arts projects. Working closely with teachers at a school site also allowed us as faculty to deepen our own understanding of teachers' experiences, furthering the symbiotic nature of learning.

Sustaining the Vision

A graduate described her thesis as a cycle of empowerment through educating oneself and then helping the next generation to cultivate tools for community uplift:

> This project has been a whole hearted attempt to give form to all…I have been given by way of all my mentors and teachers who not only taught me about history, cultures, languages but most importantly how to think. This project for me is an attempt to honor and give back a little of the great gift that the work of dedicated educators, theorists and researchers…have given me as a second language learner as well as an educator of second language learners. Their works have given a voice to the silenced. Their works have given power to the oppressed. Their words have lifted the fallen….What is most important though is what has been provided for all those in the arena of life who are here to serve others. They have been given the strength and tools to not only give fish to the hungry man, as an old Chinese proverb goes, but to teach the hungry man to fish. (Díaz, 2002, p. 90)

Programs such as ours that resist the grain of institutional racism require continued advocacy, vigilance, resistance, and support. Several factors seem critical to sustaining such a program.

A faculty is more than the sum of its members; universities need to recognize the interactive culture faculty members create that is integral to programs. State institutions tend to conceptualize people as interchangeable parts. The relationship between schools of education and state credentialing agencies solidifies that conception, since faculty members are hired mainly to teach prescribed credentialing courses, rather than "against the grain" coursework we have examined here. Programs such as ours require a core of educators who are supported sufficiently to create a shared culture, feel valued for that work, and do not burn out. As of the 2005–2006 academic year, only four of the 11 faculty who had shaped this program as core faculty were still teaching in it. Many had left the university altogether, due largely to its unsustainable workload and fragmented support.

A program rests not only on a vision but also on "nuts and bolts" practices that support that vision, requiring leadership that can anticipate and sustain everyday policies and practices. For example, mentoring and supporting students academically is labor intensive, requiring creative thinking about faculty workload. Leaders who are not a part of the learning community of a particular school or program tend to treat it as if it were similar to any other, rather than supporting what distinguishes and sustains it.

We can build a program like the one we have described, but sustaining it requires sustained financial support. Currently mass public higher education is being "downsized" (Aronowitz, 2000), while large numbers of students from historically marginalized communities are seeking higher education. We believe there is a clear social benefit to investing in first-generation college students. For example, Vernez, Krop and Rydell (1999) quantified costs and benefits of closing the achievement gap, arguing that in the long run investing in education pays off by producing a better-educated workforce

We have maintained that education is political, but not everything can be explained by politics. Although being political is often associated with passion, political passion does not explain the hope our students bring nor the care that has driven us. The experiences we have gained from working with our students has shown us that programs like this can work and can bring new solutions to the educational community—it is more than a narrative of possibility. The commitment and flexibility that working in such a program demands goes beyond the political into the personal and acknowledges the personal as part of Cixous' (1988) extending and evolving conversation of love.

Notes

1. Bob Hughes is associate professor at Seattle University.
2. Elizabeth Meador is an independent scholar in Boulder, CO.
3. Patricia Whang is professor at California State University Monterey Bay.
4. Linda Rogers is professor Emerita, California State University Monterey Bay.
5. Ka-ni Blackwell is professor emerita, University of Hawaii at Manoa.

6. Peggy Laughlin is assistant professor at Brandman University.
7. Claudia Peralta is associate professor at Boise State University.
8. I maintained contact with many of the program's graduates long after they had finished the program. Two patterns stood out in these contacts. First, those who were classroom teachers commented on how much they used the pedagogy we modeled in their own classrooms; visits I made to a few of these classrooms supported those comments. Second, a significant proportion of graduates, and particularly people of color, went on to complete doctorates at several different universities, reporting back how well the MA program had prepared them for successful doctoral study.

8

Critical Pedagogy, Critical Race Theory, and Antiracist Education

Their Implications for Multicultural Education

With Dolores Delgado Bernal[1]

Multicultural education grew out of social protest movements of the 1960s, particularly challenges to racism in education and the ethnic studies movement (see Chapter Six). During the 1960s, in the context of social activism addressing a range of manifestations of racism, community groups, students, and ethnic studies scholars pressed for the inclusion of ethnic content in the curriculum in order to bring intellectual counter-narratives to the dominant Eurocentric narratives. Multicultural education, thus, began as a scholarly and activist movement to transform schools and their contexts. Over time, as more and more people took up and used multicultural education, it came to have a wider and wider array of meanings. In the process, ironically (given its historical roots), a good deal of what occurs within the arena of multicultural education today does not address power relations critically, particularly racism. This chapter will review some of today's critical discourses for their implications for multicultural education. Our intent is not to move multicultural education away from its core conceptual moorings, but rather to anchor the field more firmly in those moorings.

Many contemporary renderings of multicultural education examine difference without connecting it to power or a critical analysis of racism. This is probably because the great majority of classroom teachers and school administrators are White and bring a worldview that tacitly condones existing race and class relations.

For example, Sleeter (1992) studied a group of teachers who had volunteered to participate in a staff development project in multicultural education. Of twenty-six who discussed what multicultural education meant to them by the second year of the project, seven White teachers saw it as irrelevant to their work and six White teachers saw its main purpose as helping students learn to get along with each other. Eight teachers (one African American and the rest White ESL or special education teachers) saw multicultural education as building students' self esteem in response to exclusion some students experience in school and the wider society. Five (two African American and three White) had more complex conceptions, but only one of these directly connected multicultural education with social activism. In short, almost all of these educators filtered their understanding of multicultural education through conceptual discourses of individualism and psychology, and took for granted as neutral the existing structures and processes of school and its relationship to communities.

At the same time that multicultural education has been acquiring a range of meanings, many theorists and educators (both inside and outside multicultural education) who are concerned about racism, oppression, and how to build democracy in historically racist and hierarchical multicultural societies, have advanced perspectives that explicitly address social justice. To distinguish these perspectives from non-critical orientations toward multicultural education, some use the term "critical multiculturalism" (e.g., Kanpol & McLaren, 1995; May & Sleeter, 2010; Obidah, 2000) or increasingly, "social justice" (e.g., North, 2008).

Some conceptions of critical multiculturalism foreground racism. Based on an analysis of teacher education student responses to a discussion of race, Berlak and Moyenda (2001) argued that liberal conceptions of multiculturalism support "white privilege by rendering institutional racism invisible," leading to the belief that injustices will disappear if people simply learn to get along (p. 94). They stated that "central to critical multiculturalism is naming and actively challenging racism and other forms of injustice, not simply recognizing and celebrating differences and reducing prejudice" (p. 92). McCarthy (1995) argued that various models of multicultural education rest far too heavily on attitude change as a means of social transformation, and take for granted essentialized racial identities, failing to situate racial inequality within global relations. Critical multiculturalism "links the microdynamics of the school curriculum to larger issues of social relations outside the school" (p. 43). Similarly, in an effort to join anti-racism with multicultural education, May (1999a) stated that critical multiculturalism "incorporates postmodern conceptions and analyses of culture and identity, while holding onto the possibility of an emancipatory politics" (pp. 7–8).

Other conceptions link multiculturalism with critical pedagogy (e.g., Kincheloe & Steinberg, 1997). Kanpol and McLaren (1995) used the term "critical multiculturalism" to emphasize that "justice is not evenly distributed and cannot be so without a radical and profound change in social structures and in terms of a development of historical agency and a praxis of possibility" (p. 13). Obidah (2000) described herself as a critical multiculturalist because the tools of both critical pedagogy and multicultural education have helped her to link a dynamic conception of culture, identity and lived experience with an analysis of power structures and pedagogy.

This chapter explores the implications of critical traditions for multicultural education in order to connect it more firmly to its transformative roots and to encourage dialogue across contemporary critical traditions. To keep the chapter manageable, we could only focus on three traditions. We selected critical pedagogy, critical race theory, and anti-racist education. The chapter, therefore, omits groundbreaking work in multicultural feminism (e.g., Collins, 1990), critical cultural studies (e.g., Hall, 1993), and disability studies (e.g., Linton, 1998), which also have implications for multicultural education. Each section that follows provides a brief genealogy, implications, and limitations for each of the three bodies of literature as they relate to multicultural education. The final section of the chapter sketches out a synthesis of this analysis, and in the process suggests the need to expand the dialogue between critical pedagogy, critical race theory, anti-racist education, and multicultural education.

Critical Pedagogy and Multicultural Education

Critical pedagogy can be defined as "an entry point in the contradictory nature of schooling, a chance to force it toward creating conditions for a new public sphere" (Giroux, 1983, p. 116). According to Giroux (1992), critical pedagogy should "explore how pedagogy functions as a cultural practice to *produce* rather than merely *transmit* knowledge within the asymmetrical relations of power that structure teacher-student relations" (p. 98). Theorists of critical pedagogy view schools as "contradictory social sites" (Giroux, 1983, p. 115) in which class relations are not simply reproduced but also contested through the actions students and educators construct everyday. As such, youth could learn collectively to construct a new democratic public sphere. Critical pedagogy, then, offers a language of both "analysis and hope" (McLaren, 1991, p. 30).

Critical pedagogy can be traced to at least two different genealogical roots: critical theory and the Frankfurt School, and the work of Paulo Freire and Latin American liberation movements. The Frankfurt School, which began in Germany prior to World War II, connected a Marxist analysis of class structure with psychological theories of the unconscious to understand how oppressive class relations are produced and reproduced. The culturalist paradigm of the Frankfurt School emphasized human agency, focusing on the lived experiences of people and how consciousness is formed within class struggles. The structuralist paradigm analyzed how oppressive political and economic structures are reproduced, but tended to ignore or deny personal agency (Giroux, 1983). The rise of Nazism in Germany caused many members of the Frankfurt School to flee to the U.S., where theorists in many disciplines took up critical theory. Critical theorists do not necessarily practice or write about critical pedagogy. In the 1980s, theorists such as Henry Giroux and Peter McLaren applied critical theory's analytical tools to pedagogy, creating a "pedagogy of critical theory" (Pruyn, 1994, p. 38). According to Giroux (1983), critical pedagogy seeks to "bridge the agency-structural dualism" of the Frankfurt School by viewing youth culture as a site of cultural production, social struggle, and social transformation (p. 139).

A second genealogical root of critical pedagogy is the work of Paulo Freire (1970, 1973, 1976) and Latin American liberation movements. Freire, who began writing while in exile in Chile, had promoted popular literacy in Brazil, connecting the act of reading with the development of critical consciousness. Freire argued throughout his life that oppressed people need to develop a critical consciousness that will enable them to denounce dehumanizing social structures, and announce social transformation. In the process of teaching literacy to adults, he created culture circles in which students took up topics of concern to them, discussed and debated in order to clarify and develop their thinking, and developed strategies for action. Freire did not call these culture circles "schools" because of the passivity traditionally associated with school learning. A fundamental task in culture circles was to distinguish between what humans have created and what nature created, in order to examine what role humans can play in bringing about change. Freire's connection between critical education and political work for liberation took up similar questions to those being asked by critical theorists.

Potential implications of critical pedagogy for multicultural education

Critical pedagogy has four main implications for multicultural education: 1) conceptual tools for critical reflexivity; 2) an analysis of class, corporate power, and globalization; 3) an analysis of empowering pedagogical practices within the classroom; and 4) a deeper analysis of language and literacy than one finds generally in the multicultural education literature.

Critical pedagogy as a theoretical space develops several concepts that relate to multicultural education, including voice, power, culture, and ideology. In so doing, it offers tools for critical reflexivity on those concepts. "Voice" is grounded in Freire's notion of dialogical communication, which rejects both the authoritarian imposition of knowledge and also the idea that everyone's beliefs are equal. To Freire (1998), the development of democratic life requires critical engagement with ideas through dialogue. Dialogue demands engagement; it occurs neither when some parties opt out silently, nor when those with the most power simply impose their views. Voice is rooted in experience that is examined for its interests, principles, values, and historical remembrances (Darder, 1995; Giroux, 1988; hooks, 1994). The concepts of voice and dialogue act as tools for uncovering whose ideas are represented and whose ideas have been submerged, marginalized, or left out entirely.

Critical pedagogy offers tools for examining the concept of "culture." Simplistic conceptions of culture are common in multicultural education, although many multiculturalists also critique them. McCarthy (1998) noted that too often "culture, identity, and community are narrowly read as the final property of particular groups based on ethnic origins" (p. 148); for example, teachers commonly conflate ethnicity and culture, seeing them as synonymous. Within this conception of culture, "Multiculturalism is generally about Otherness" in a way that makes whiteness and racial struggle invisible, and takes for granted boundaries of race, ethnicity and power (Giroux, 1992, p. 117). Whose conceptions of culture tend to predominate, and what gets left out of those conceptions? For example, hybrid cultural identities defy fixed and essentialized definitions of culture (e.g., Darder, 1995; McCarthy, 1998). Dominant cultures can be examined with much greater depth when contextualized within relations of colonialism and power than when they are decontextualized (McLaren & Mayo, 1999). Popular culture as a form of collective meaning-making also "counts" as culture (Giroux & Simon, 1989; Livingstone, 1987; Shor, 1980).

"Power" is yet another concept within multicultural education that critical pedagogy helps to examine (Kincheloe & Steinberg, 1997). Giroux (1985) pointed out that some progressive and multicultural education discourses "quietly ignore the complexity and sweat of social change," and reduce power and domination to misunderstandings that can be corrected by providing accurate information (p. 31). Challenging power relations is central to critical pedagogy (Freire, 1970), which is based on an analysis of structural as well as cultural power. It is the centrality of interrogating how power works and how power relations can be challenged that led McLaren (2000) to focus on revolution rather than reform. Multicultural education in its inception challenged power relations, particularly racism, and for some multicultural educators power remains a central concept. However, power is often displaced by more comfortable concepts such as tolerance. Critical pedagogy offers an important critique of that displacement and continues to ask the question: comfortable for whom?

"Ideology" is a concept that is central to critical pedagogy, but used surprisingly little in multicultural education. Ideology refers to the formation of the consciousness of the individuals in a society, particularly their consciousness about how the society works (Apple, 2004). Within multicultural education, curriculum is often discussed in terms of bias, a concept that does not necessarily lead to an analysis of power and consciousness. Similarly, examining teachers in terms of attitudes focuses on individual psychology rather than collective power. "Ideology" offers a much more powerful conceptual tool, connecting meanings with structures of power, on the one hand, and with individuals, on the other. Ideology as a tool of analysis "helps to locate the structuring principles and ideas that mediate between the dominant society and the everyday experiences of teachers and students" (Giroux, 1983, p. 161). It helps us to examine who produces what kinds of ideologies, why some ideologies prevail, and whose interests they serve (see also Apple, 2000). Ideology can also serve as a reflexive tool of critique when multicultural education itself is conceived as a field of discourse.

A second potential implication of critical pedagogy is its analysis of social class, class power, corporate power, and global corporate control. While multicultural education grew primarily out of racial and ethnic struggle, critical pedagogy grew primarily out of class struggle. In the U.S., connections between race and class tend to be under-theorized partially because of the myth that the U.S. is a "classless" society, which leads to a general refusal to examine class relations critically. Yet, the forms and persistence of racism can be understood more clearly when racism is connected historically with capitalism (Marable, 2000; Roediger, 1991; Sleeter, 2001a). Freire (1973) specifically located his work in a history of colonialism and class struggle: "It was upon this vast lack of democratic experience, characterized by feudal mentality and sustained by a colonial economic and social structure, that we attempted to inaugurate a formal democracy" (p. 28).

Connections between racism and global capitalism lend urgency to the significance of class. Over the past two decades, a small corporate elite has extended global control markedly and consolidated means for wealth accumulation. At the same time, however, even critical pedagogues have retreated from concern with class and capitalism. McLaren (1998) argued that the "growing diasporic movements of immigrants in search of employment across national boundaries" has led to an increased discourse around ethnicity, but domesticated ways of thinking about it have displaced critiques of capitalist expansion. Given the rampant and unchecked expansion of global capitalism, critical pedagogy and multicultural education need to "address themselves to the adaptive persistence of capitalism and to issues of capitalist imperialism and its specific manifestations of accumulative capacities through conquest." Multicultural education could benefit from a trenchant analysis of capitalist expansion and global capitalism. Increased poverty, racial strife, incarceration of youth of color, movements of people around the globe, and corporate-driven school reforms can be understood more clearly when class is part of the analysis. That is not to imply that class be given primacy over race or gender, but rather that these concepts be developed as connected structures of oppression, lenses of analysis, and sites of struggle.

A third potential implication of critical pedagogy for multicultural education is its examination of how power plays out in the classroom, and its connection of pedagogical processes with empowerment. In this regard, critical pedagogy and feminist pedagogy share similar concerns (hooks, 1994; Lather, 1991). Multicultural education as a field has extensively examined school knowledge and developed insights for transformative curricula, usually discussing pedagogy mainly in relationship to strategies that support high achievement for all students (e.g., Banks, 2007; Bennett, 1998). Critical pedagogy complements this work by conceptualizing students as creators of knowledge and by connecting student-generated knowledge with student empowerment. Freire (1970) explicitly rejected a "banking" form of pedagogy "in which students are the depositories and the teacher is the depositor" (p. 53), viewing it as an instrument of control over the masses. Instead, he viewed empowering pedagogy as a dialogical process in which the teacher acts as a partner with students, helping them to examine the world critically, using a problem-posing process that begins with their own experience and historical location.

Several critical pedagogy theorists have written about the use of this form of pedagogy in their own classrooms. Most of these discussions focus on adult students (e.g., Ada, 1988; Mayo, 1999; Shor, 1980; 1992; Simon, 1992; Sleeter, 1995a; Solorzano, 1989), although a few focus on the K-12 level (Bigelow, 1990; Duncan-Andrade & Morrell, 2008; Goldstein, 1995; Peterson, 1991). In all of these discussions, pedagogy starts with students' lived experience, and involves students in analysis of that experience. Students are treated as active agents of knowledge creation, and classrooms as democratic public spheres. Class materials are used as tools for expanding students' analyses, rather than as content that is simply deposited into the students. This view of pedagogy complements multicultural education well.

A fourth potential implication of critical pedagogy for multicultural education is its analysis of language and literacy, which connects to concerns of bilingual educators. Multicultural education and bilingual education have emerged as distinct fields, with only some overlap; critical pedagogy can serve as one bridge. Drawing from his experience teaching literacy to adults, Freire distinguished between a technical and a critical approach to literacy. A technical approach focuses on language as a subject distinct from the world of students, or "words emptied of the reality they are meant to represent" (Freire, 1973, p. 37). Critical literacy begins with words within students' experience, then situates them historically, helping students learn to question their world with language serving as a tool of critical analysis. Language, then, is a key tool to development of consciousness and voice. Macedo and Bartolome (1999) challenged the notion that multicultural education can take place in English only, noting that "one cannot celebrate different cultural values through the very dominant language that devalues, in many ways, the cultural experiences of different cultural groups," and that "language is the only means through which one comes to consciousness" (p. 34). Identity, values, experiences, interpretations, and ideologies are encoded linguistically; one knows the world and oneself through language. Because consciousness is shaped through language, language can serve as a means of control as well as means of liberation (Giroux & McLaren, 1992; Macedo, 1994).

Many second-language teachers and bilingual educators who are conscious of oppression resonate with these ideas. For example, based on his work as an ESL (English as a Second Language) teacher to adult farmworkers, Graman (1988) explained that when language was treated as a subject abstracted from everyday life, students lost interest. Drawing language from life, then examining students' problems and dreams politically in the context of second-language instruction engaged them in learning, and helped them to use education to act on their own behalf. In short, critical pedagogy can enrich analysis of language within multicultural education.

Limitations of critical pedagogy and its implications for multicultural education

Critical pedagogy has two major limitations that need to be acknowledged. First, although it developed through practice in Latin America, within the U.S. it has been developed mainly at a theoretical level, often leaving practitioners unclear about what to do. Its theoretical writings tend to be conceptually dense, which many practitioners find difficult to understand, although one can find literature that shows what critical pedagogy "looks like" in practice (e.g., Bromley, 1989; Duncan-

Andrade & Morrell, 2008; Pruyn, 1994, 1999; Students for Cultural and Linguistic Democracy, 1996; Wink, 1997). In this, a strength and limitation of critical pedagogy are joined. Critical pedagogues argue that the ideology of the teacher is of central importance; critical pedagogy cannot be reduced to method or technique. At the same time, teachers need guidance translating ideological clarity into practice; radical teachers can still teach in very traditional ways (Pruyn, 1999). This translation needs to go far beyond learning steps or seeing lesson plans, since critical pedagogy directly opens up very difficult and painful issues in the classroom (Ellsworth, 1989; Obidah, 2000). We have worked with many teachers who, even when they are drawn to ideas of critical pedagogy, end up dismissing it because they do not know what to do with it in their classrooms. Particularly given the standards-based reforms teachers now experience, critical pedagogy suggests a very different paradigm from that institutionalized in most schools. There is a need for practical guidance that does not, in the process, sacrifice conceptual grounding.

Second, most of the literature in critical pedagogy does not directly address race, ethnicity, or gender, and as such has a White bias. Since much of it grows from a class analysis, with some exceptions it foregrounds social class. Critical pedagogy may well appeal to radical White educators who see class as the main axis of oppression, but doing so can marginalize race, and have the effect of elevating the power of largely White radical theorists over theorists of color, even if this is not intended. Further, White theorists taking on race and racism does not resolve the problem of Whites having the power to define how race and racism are theorized. In a discussion of Chicana/o border pedagogy, Elenes (1997) argued that people of color must articulate theory for themselves. However helpful writings of White critical pedagogues might be, White writers still produce silences and assumptions that arise from lived experiences. She writes, "Much of the problematic of this discussion over differences is that until recently only those who were marked as different were considered in the theorization of difference. If differences are going to be constituted in nonessentialist ways, it is necessary to mark, deconstruct, and decenter whiteness and privilege" (p. 371).

Grande (2000) took this argument further, pointing out ideas and assumptions that are central to critical pedagogy that clash with indigenous perspectives. Critical pedagogues question essentialized identities and value border crossing, while the history of border crossing and blending cultures has meant "Whitestream America…appropriating Native lands, culture, spiritual practices, history and literature" (p. 481). Further, the "seemingly liberatory constructs of fluidity, mobility, and transgression" are part of "the fundamental lexicon of Western imperialism" (p. 483). Thus, although the insights of critical pedagogy and their implications for multicultural education are valuable, one also needs to be concerned with how the power to name the issues affects both which issues get addressed, and whose interests are served in the process.

Critical Race Theory and Multicultural Education

Critical race theory is an analytical framework developed initially by legal scholars of color to address social justice and racial oppression in U.S. society. According to Delgado and Stefancic (2001), "The critical race theory (CRT) movement is a collection of activists and scholars interested in studying and transforming the relationship among race, racism, and power" (p. 2). Among CRT's basic theoretical themes is that of privileging contextual and historical descriptions over abstract or ahistorical ones. It is therefore important to understand the genealogy of CRT in education based on its contextual and historical relations to critical legal studies, the Civil Rights movement, radical/U.S. third world feminisms, and the other theoretical traditions from which it borrows (Matsuda, Lawrence, Delgado, & Crenshaw, 1993). Its conception can be located in the mid-1970s with the work of legal scholars such as Derrick Bell and Alan Freeman, who were frustrated with the slow pace of racial reform within the liberal civil rights tradition in the United States. They were joined by other legal scholars, students, and activists who felt that the advances of the civil rights movement had been stalled and in fact were being rolled back (Delgado & Stefancic, 2000).

During the 1980s CRT responded to critical legal studies (CLS), which originated with a predominantly White male group of leftist law professors who challenged the traditional legal scholarship that creates, supports, and legitimates social power in US society (Matsuda et al., 1993). As Wing (1997) pointed out, "People of color, white women, and others were attracted by CLS because it challenged orthodox ideas about the inviolability and objectivity of laws that oppressed minorities and white women for centuries" (p. 2). However, some of these scholars also felt that CLS excluded the perspectives of people of color and that the CLS movement was inattentive to racism's role in both the U.S. legal system and US society. As a result, legal scholars of color began articulating a theory of race and racism that "allows us to better understand how racial power can be produced even from within a liberal discourse that is relatively autonomous from organized vectors of racial power" (Crenshaw, Gotanda, Peller, & Thomas, 1995, p. xxv).

Just as CRT builds on the insights and weaknesses of CLS, it also draws on the work of ethnic studies and U.S. third world feminisms. Most recently critical race theory has borrowed much from the postmodern cultural revolution in the humanities and from postcolonialism and poststructuralism (Roithmayr, 1999). Indeed, CRT has expanded to include complementary branches such as Latina/o Critical Race Theory (LatCrits), Critical Race Feminists (FemCrits), and Tribal Crits (Brayboy, 2005). These branches continue to influence and reshape a growing CRT movement that by the year 2005 included over four hundred CRT law review articles and dozens of books (Solorzano & Yosso, 2001).

Although CRT began in legal studies, it has spread to other disciplines, including education. One might think of CRT in education as a developing theoretical, conceptual, methodological, and pedagogical strategy that accounts for the role of race and racism in U.S. education and works toward the elimination of racism as part of a larger goal of eliminating other forms of subordination (Solorzano, 1998). Since 1994 scholars of color in the field of education have been increasingly employing it in their research and practice. Tate's (1994) autobiographical article in *Urban Education* was the first explicit use of CRT in education. A year later Ladson-Billings and Tate (1995) laid the conceptual background for much of the applied CRT work done shortly thereafter. Today a growing body of scholarship in education uses CRT as a framework to examine a variety of educational issues at both the K-12 and post-secondary levels (e.g., Aguirre, 2000; Gonzalez, 1998; Ladson-Billings, 1998, 1999, 2000; Lynn, 1999; Parker, Deyhle, & Villenas 1999; Solorzano, 1997, 1998; Solorzano & Delgado Bernal, 2001; Solorzano & Villalpando, 1998; Solorzano & Yosso, 2002; Tate, 1997). Special journal issues on CRT in education have also appeared (such as *Qualitative Inquiry*, 2002 and *Equity and Excellence in Education*, 2002), and journals such as *Race, Ethnicity and Education* now feature mainly work that uses CRT.

Potential implications of critical race theory for multicultural education

Critical race theory has at least three important implications for multicultural education: 1) it theorizes about race while also addressing the intersectionality of racism, classism, sexism, and other forms of oppression; 2) it challenges Eurocentric epistemologies and dominant ideologies such as meritocracy, objectivity, and neutrality; and 3) it utilizes counterstorytelling as a methodological and pedagogical tool.

Although multicultural education emerged as a challenge to racism in schools, its writings tend to focus on classroom practices without necessarily contextualizing classrooms within an analysis of racism. Teacher training in multicultural education often takes the form of offering solutions to problems connected to race and ethnicity without digging very deeply into the nature of the problem. CRT in education is similar to anti-racist education (discussed in the next section) because it is a social justice paradigm that seeks to combat racism as part of a larger goal of ending all forms of subordination. Education scholars using CRT theorize about "raced" education in ways found too little in multicultural education. As Ladson-Billings and Tate (1995) pointed out, there is a need to do this because race remains untheorized as a topic of scholarly inquiry in education. Although scholars have examined race as a tool for understanding social inequities, "the intellectual salience of this theorizing has not been systematically employed in the analysis of educational inequality" (p. 50). CRT scholars believe that race as an analytical tool, rather than a biological or socially constructed category used to compare and contrast social conditions, can deepen the analysis of educational barriers for people of color, as well as illuminate how they resist and overcome these barriers.

One example of using race as an analytical tool is found within what Ladson-Billings and Tate (1995) called the "property issue." Critical race legal scholars introduced the property issue by examining the historical construction of whiteness as the most valued type of property and how the concept of individual rights has been linked to property rights in the U.S. since the writing of the US Constitution (Bell, 1987, Harris, 1993). Ladson-Billings and Tate demonstrated that property relates to education in explicit and implicit ways. One of the more obvious examples is how property owners largely reap the highest educational benefits—those with the best property are entitled to the best schools. They write, "Recurring discussions about property tax relief indicate that more affluent communities (which have higher property values, hence higher tax assessments) resent paying for a public school system whose clientele is largely non-white and poor" (p. 53). An implicit way in which property relates to education is the way in which curriculum represents a form of "intellectual property" that is interconnected to race. The quality and quantity of the curriculum varies with the "property values" of the school so that intellectual property is directly connected to "real" property in the form of course offerings, classroom resources, science labs, technology, and certified and prepared teachers (Ladson-Billings & Tate, 1995).

In addition to using race as an analytical tool, critical race theorists challenge the separate discourses on race, class, and gender and focus on the intersectionality of subordination (Solorzano & Yosso, 2002). Crenshaw (1993) saw intersectionality as a concept that links various forms of oppression (racism, classism, sexism) with their political consequences (e.g., global capitalism, growing poverty, large numbers of incarcerated youth of color). The property issue is an example of how the intersection of race and class interests offers a more complete understanding of the current inequities in schools and districts in which the majority of students are poor and of color.

Latina/o critical race theory (LatCrit) has added layers of complexity to the concept of intersectionality by analyzing Latinas/os' identities and positionalities in relation to race, class, and gender, as well as language (Romany, 1996), immigration (Garcia, 1995, Johnson, 1996–97), culture (Montoya, 1994, 1997), religion/spirituality (Iglesias & Valdes, 1998; Sanchez, 1998), and sexuality (Iglesias & Valdes, 1998). For example, Villalpando (2003) used a CRT and LatCrit framework to examine how Chicana/o college students draw from their language, religion/spirituality, and culture as tools in their struggle for success in higher education. He uses a counterstory methodology and an intersectional analysis to highlight cultural practices and beliefs of the peer group that function as empowering and nourishing cultural resources for Chicana/o students. One of the more important cultural practices is how the peer group adopts roles and characteristics of a student's family of origin. In other words, Chicana/o peers often offer support, understanding, or admonishment similar to what they receive at home. This cultural practice helped Chicana/o students cope with the marginalization they experienced via racist structures, practices, and discourses in higher education.

These types of analyses could contribute to multicultural education by interrogating the racialized context of teaching and connecting race with multiple forms of oppression. Multicultural research conducted within a CRT framework might offer a way to understand and analyze the multiple identities and knowledges of people of color without essentializing their various experiences.

A second potential contribution of CRT is the way that it challenges Eurocentric epistemology and questions dominant discursive notions of meritocracy, objectivity, knowledge, and individualism. The concept of epistemology is more than just a "way of knowing" and can be defined as a "system of knowing" that is linked to worldviews based on the conditions under which people live and learn (Ladson-Billings, 2000). Ladson-Billings argues that "there are well-developed systems of knowledge, or epistemologies, that stand in contrast to the dominant Euro-American epistemology" (p. 258). Critical race theorists ground their research in these systems of knowledge and "…integrate their experiential knowledge, drawn from a shared history as 'other' with their ongoing struggles to transform . . ." (Barnes, 1990, pp. 1864–1865). For example, in his study of socially active African American teachers, Lynn (1999) drew from African-centered epistemological paradigms and critical race theory to theorize about a critical race pedagogy that is in part based on a system of knowledge that counters the dominant Euro-American epistemology. He defined critical race pedagogy as "an analysis of racial, ethnic, and gender subordination in education that relies mostly on the perceptions, experiences, and counterhegemonic practices of educators of color" (p. 615). Based on the reflections of African American educators he argued that critical race peda-gogues are concerned with the following issues: the endemic nature of racism in the United States; the importance of cultural identity; the necessary interaction of race, class, gender; and the practice of liberatory pedagogy. Practicing a liberatory peda-gogy was in some ways similar to the Freirean notion of critical pedagogy that encourages inquiry, dialogue, and participation in the classroom. However, Lynn demonstrated two key differences between a critical pedagogy and a critical race ped-agogy: 1) the daily struggle against racist discursive practices provided African American teachers with a unique position from which to build their curricula, and 2) there was a strong emphasis on developing and maintaining a sense of cultural identity by teaching children about Africa and African American cultural experiences.

By grounding itself in systems of knowledge that counter a dominant Eurocentric epistemology, critical race theory in education offers a tool for disman-tling prevailing notions of fairness, meritocracy, colorblindness, and neutrality (Parker, Deyhle, & Villenas, 1999). "Raced" and "gendered" epistemologies allow CRT scholars to deconstruct master narratives and illustrate the way in which dis-cursive and cultural sites "may be a form of colonialism, a way of imparting white, Westernized conceptions of enlightened thinking" (Roithmayr, 1999, p.5). For example, Gutiérrez (2000) examined Walt Disney's ideological shift from conser-vatism (1930s–1970s) to present-day liberal multiculturalism particularly within its Spanish-speaking market. He argued that the discursive notions promoted by Disney continue to be based on dominant Eurocentric ideologies that maintain a form of cultural hegemony. He offered critical race theory as one of several ways to examine the master narratives (capitalist, racist and heterosexist ideals) exposed specifically to Latina/o children and believed Disney movies provide "numerous opportunities for children and adults to engage in critical discussions regarding power, domination, and repression" (p. 31). These types of critical discussions that challenge the insidious nature of a Eurocentric epistemological perspective and dis-mantle master narratives can and should take place more frequently in multicul-tural classrooms. As this example shows, by engaging teachers and students in a critical analysis of epistemologies that underlie curriculum and other school processes, critical race theory offers tools that dig deeply into issues and problems that concern multicultural education.

A third and potentially the greatest contribution of CRT is its justification and use of storytelling in legal analysis and scholarship. CRT work in storytelling provides a rich way of conceptualizing multicultural curriculum. Because critical race schol-ars view experiential knowledge as a strength, they draw explicitly on the lived expe-riences of people of color by including such methods as storytelling, family history, biographies, parables, *testimonios, cuentos, consejos,* chronicles, and narratives. Storytelling has a rich legacy and continuing tradition in African American, Chicana/o, Asian American, and American Indian communities. Indeed, Delgado (1995) asserted that many of the "early tellers of tales used stories to test and challenge reality, to construct a counter-reality, to hearten and support each other and to probe, mock, displace, jar, or reconstruct the dominant tale or narrative . . ." (p. xviii).

Counterstorytelling is a methodological tool that allows one to tell the story of those experiences that are not often told (i.e., those on the margins of society) and to analyze and challenge the stories of those in power (Delgado, 1989). The stories people of color tell often counter the majoritarian or stock story that is a natural part of the dominant discourse. Building on the work of Delgado (1989), some education scholars argue that these counterstories serve multiple methodological and pedagogical functions such as building community among those at the margins of society, putting a human and familiar face on educational theory and practice, and challenging perceived wisdom about the schooling of students of color (Solorzano & Delgado Bernal, 2001; Solorzano & Yosso, 2002).

One way education scholars are attempting to put a "human and familiar face to educational theory and practice" is through the development of composite characters that are based on interviews, focus groups, and biographical narratives in the humanities and social science literature. This work builds on the scholarship of Bell (1985, 1987), who told stories of society's treatment of race through his protagonist and alter ego, Geneva Crenshaw, and Delgado (1995, 1999) who addresses race, class, and gender issues through Rodrigo Crenshaw, the half-brother of Geneva. The web of composite characters that have recently appeared represent very real life experiences and are created to illuminate the educational system's role in racial, gender, and class oppression, as well as the myriad of responses by people of color (Delgado Bernal, 1999; Solorzano & Delgado Bernal, 2001; Solorzano and Villalpando, 1998; Solorzano & Yosso, 2002; Villalpando, 2003). In addition these composite characters allow students and educators of color to relate to or empathize with the experiences described in the counterstories, through which they can better understand that they are not alone in their position. Solorzano (1998) writes:

> In that space or moment when one connects with these experiences, these stories can be the catalyst for one's own coming to voice, of not feeling alone, and knowing that someone has gone before them, had similar experiences, and succeeded…(pp. 131).

Counterstorytelling can serve as a pedagogical tool by allowing multicultural educators to better understand and appreciate the unique experiences and responses of students of color through a deliberate, conscious, and open type of listening. In other words, an important component of using counterstories includes not simply telling non-majoritarian stories, but learning how to listen and hear the messages in them (Delgado Bernal, 2002). Legal scholar Robert Williams (1997) believes that counterstorytelling and critical race practice are "mostly about learning to listen to other people's stories and then finding ways to make those stories matter in the legal system" (p. 765). Likewise, learning to listen to counterstories and then making those stories matter in the educational system is an important pedagogical practice for teachers and students.

Indeed, Gay (1995a) asserted that the foundation of multicultural curriculum should be counterstories, but much of what ends up passing for multicultural curriculum is the dominant story with "Others" incorporated into it. Yosso (2002) proposed a critical race curriculum that is based on counterstories, thereby providing "students with an oppositional language to challenge the deficit societal discourses with which they are daily bombarded" (p. 15). Rather than adding on the experiences of "Others" or pushing students toward "discovering" a monolithic people of color, her understanding of a critical race curriculum "explores and utilizes shared and individual experiences of race, class, gender, immigration status, language, and sexuality in education" (p. 16). As such, a multicultural curriculum that grounds itself in the counterstorytelling of critical race theory has the potential to move a watered-down multicultural curriculum away from simply celebrating difference and reducing prejudice to a "critical race curriculum" that actively names and challenges racism and other forms of injustice.

Limitations of critical race theory and its implications for multicultural education

Critical race theory has received numerous critiques within legal studies, but few within education. We will address two of these critiques: the essentialist critique and the personal stories and narratives critique. We will also address the problems associated with being a relatively new area of study in education.

Within legal studies, some critics argue that CRT is an essentialist paradigm based on race. In general, essentialism is rooted in an identity politics that is based on a unidimensional characteristic, such as race, ethnicity, or gender. Critics argue that an essentialist notion of identity is simplistic and does not allow for the myriad experiences that shape who we are and what we know. Crenshaw and colleagues write, "To be sure, some of the foundational essays of CRT could be vulnerable to such a critique, particularly when read apart from the context and conditions of their production" (Crenshaw, Gotanda, Peller, Thomas, 1995, p. xxv). However, what many critics do not understand is that despite the name critical *race* theory, most critical race scholars argue against an analysis based solely on race or some other unitary essentialized defining characteristic. For example, Harris (2000) points to the inherent problem of race and gender essentialism in fragmenting people's identities and experiences:

> In this essay I use the term "gender essentialism" to describe the notion that there is a monolithic "women's experience" that can be described independently of other facets of experience like race, class, and sexual orientation. A corollary to gender essentialism is "racial essentialism"—the belief that there is a monolithic "black experience" or "Chicano experience." The effect of gender and racial essentialism (and all other essentialisms, for the list of categories could be infinite) is to reduce the lives of people who experience multiple forms of oppression to addition problems: "racism + sexism = straight black women's experience," or "racism + sexism + homophobia = black lesbian experience." (p. 263)

With increased transnational labor and communication, many critical race scholars argue to move beyond essentialist notions of identity and of what counts as knowledge. Although race is forefronted in CRT, it is viewed as a fluid and dynamic concept and as one of the many components that are woven together to form one's positionality in a shifting set of social relationships.

There are numerous critiques of critical race scholars' use of stories and narratives in legal scholarship (e.g., Farber & Sherry, 1993, 1997; Posner, 1997). Many critical race scholars have responded in more detail than we can within the scope of this chapter. The critiques are grounded in a debate over alternative ways of knowing and understanding, subjectivity versus objectivity, and different conceptions of truth. Briefly stated, critics believe that CRT theorists:

> . . . relentlessly replace traditional scholarship with personal stories, which hardly represent common experiences. The proliferation of stories makes it impossible for others to debate....An infatuation with narrative infects and distorts [their] attempts at analysis. Instead of scientifically investigating whether rewarding individuals according to merit has any objective basis, [they] insist on telling stories about their personal struggles...(Simon, 1999, p. 3)

Farber and Sherry (1993) argued against the pedagogical and methodological use of stories in legal scholarship, stating that "storytellers need to take greater steps to ensure that their stories are accurate and typical, to articulate the legal relevance of the stories, and to include an analytic dimension in their work" (p. 809). They also argued that just because counterstories draw explicitly on the lived experiences of people of color does not prove the existence of a new perspective based on "a voice of color." They, in fact, disagreed that people of color write in a different voice or offer a new perspective that differs from traditional scholarship.

Interestingly, most critics do not acknowledge that Eurocentrism has become the dominant mindset that directly affects the mainstream stories told about race. Because Eurocentrism and White privilege appear to be the norm, many people continue to believe that education in the United States is a meritocratic, unbiased, and fair process. Delgado (1993) points out that "majoritarians tell stories too. But the ones they tell—about merit, causation, blame, responsibility, and social justice—do not seem to them like stories at all, but the truth" (p. 666). At the same time, critics argue that critical race scholars' stories, narratives, and autobiographies are unreliable sources of truth (Posner, 1997). At issue is the question of what counts as truth and who gets to decide. Also at issue is the matter of how to generalize. Counterstories derive generalization through their resonance with lived experiences of oppressed peoples, rather than through parametric statistics, but some empirical researchers do not see this as a valid way of making claims that generalize.

Finally, critical race theory is a relatively new area of study in education with a limited amount of literature utilizing it as an analytical framework, and with few specific connections to multicultural education. Although education scholars are reshaping and extending critical race theory in ways very different from legal scholars, they need more time to study and understand the legal literature from which it emerges (Ladson-Billings, 1998; Roithmayr, 1999). Most education scholars who use CRT make a sharp distinction between CRT and multicultural education based on the popular manifestations of multicultural education that pay little attention to racism and its intersections with other forms of subordination. With a few exceptions (Ladson-Billings & Tate, 1995; Ladson-Billings, 1999), education theorists have not offered direct implications of CRT for multicultural education. The future of critical race theory in education and in multicultural education depends on the efforts of educators to explore its possible connections to racism in schools and communities of color (Parker, 1998; Tate, 1997).

As a relatively new area of study, CRT may face a problem that multicultural education has experienced: transmutation into a depoliticized discourse in schools. Ladson-Billings (1998) warns that CRT in education may continue to generate scholarly papers and debate, but she doubts that it will ever penetrate the classrooms and daily experiences of students of color. If it does, she worries that it may become a very different innovation similar to the transmutation of multicultural education theory. She points out that many scholars such as James Banks, Carl Grant, and Geneva Gay began a "scholarly path designed to change schools as institutions so that students might be prepared to reconstruct the society" (p. 22). Yet, in its current practice multicultural education is often superficial and based on holidays and food. In order to remain true to its principles of social justice and advocacy, critical race scholars will need to be attentive to the possibility of the transmutation of CRT into depoliticized discourses and practices in schools.

Anti-racist Education

Anti-racist education emerged largely in opposition to multicultural education, particularly in Britain (Brandt, 1986), where it challenged "the apolitical and folksy orientation of multicultural education" (Bonnett & Carrington, 1996). Contexts in which multicultural and anti-racist education emerged have differed across national borders, so national debates have differed (Bonnett & Carrington, 1996; May, 1999); but debates have been vigorous, particularly in Canada and Britain (Modgil, et al., 1986). In both countries during the late 1970s and 1980s, multicultural education was codified into national policy and school programs, drawing "its inspiration and rationale from white middle-class professional understandings of how the educational system might best respond to the perceived 'needs' and 'interests' of black students and their parents" (Troyna, 1987, p. 308). Its critics saw multicultural education as a way for White educators to "manage" the "problems" brought about by ethnic minority students (e.g., James, 2001; Troyna, 1987). Anti-racist education grew mainly in urban areas out of community activism addressing racism in various dimensions of public life (Steiner-Khamsi, 1990). Anti-racist education "can be defined as an action-oriented strategy for institutional, systemic change to address racism and the interlocking systems of social oppression (Dei, 1996, p. 25).

In Britain, anti-racist education was severely attacked by the New Right in the late 1980s. After 1988, national educational policy was "deracialized," in that references to race and ethnicity were replaced by references to authority and national identity. Anti-racist education was also criticized by its allies who argued that it had marginalized culture and overly essentialized racial categories (Gillborn, 1995). Anti-racism as a movement declined in Britain, and subsequently re-emerged by making connections with critical versions of multicultural education (Bonnett & Carrington, 1996; May, 1994; Gillborn, 1995). In Canada, Australia, and elsewhere, distinctions between anti-racism and multicultural education were less sharply drawn (May, 1999). Anti-racist education in Canada, for example, made connections with critical pedagogy and African-centered pedagogy (Dei, 1993; 1996).

In the U.S., multicultural education initially grew out of the Black struggle in the context of the Civil Rights movement, rather than out of national policy debates. Therefore, it did not prompt an activist counter-discourse until, over time, it had taken on watered-down and apolitical meanings. For some, multicultural education and anti-racism are or should be interchangeable (e.g., Nieto & Bode, 2007; Perry & Fraser, 1993; Sleeter & Grant, 2009; Thompson, 1997). Others, however, do not ground multicultural education in an analysis of structural racism, but rather in interpersonal prejudice, cultural difference, and cross-cultural misunderstandings. For example, Tiedt and Tiedt (1999) emphasize individual uniqueness, unity with diversity, and community building; the word "racism" does not appear in their book.

There have been a number of efforts to bring anti-racist education and multicultural education together (e.g., May, 1999). However, because multicultural education often takes forms that avoid racism, and because, like critical race theory, anti-racism foregrounds race as a site of struggle, it has significant implications for multicultural education.

Potential implications of anti-racist education for multicultural education

Anti-racist education has five main implications for multicultural education. It 1) directs attention specifically to challenging racism in education; 2) addresses racist school structures such as tracking which are often not addressed in multicultural education; 3) situates culture within power relations, 4) connects school with community; and 5) problematizes Whiteness. As noted above, some multicultural educators also address these issues.

Anti-racist education challenges systemic racism. Despite the work of many of its leading theorists, multicultural education is often enacted in schools by adding in contributions, advocating "let's all get along," or promoting individual upward mobility within hierarchical structures rather than critiquing the structures themselves (Kailin, 1998/99). Too often it takes the form of telling "white children about the lifestyles and cultural achievements of ethnic minorities" (Short & Carrington, 1996). The term itself—multicultural—suggests starting with the idea of "many cultures." For Whites, this idea can fit within the taken-for-grantedness of White dominance, the assumed normality and superiority of European and Euro American cultures, and the assumption that society is already structured fairly.

Troyna's (1987) critique of four assumptions of multicultural education in Britain is relevant to the discussion here. First, the assumption that "Britain is a multicultural society" (p. 313)—which can also be said of Canada, the U.S., and most other countries—assumption correctly describes what is, but not what should happen as a result. Beginning with the premise of diversity rather than justice and solidarity leads to addressing only diversity and not necessarily justice. Second, "the curriculum should reflect that substantive fact [of multiculturalism]," and third, "learning about other cultures will benefit all students" (p. 313). Troyna did not dispute the desirability of making the curriculum multicultural, but questioned whether learning about "other cultures" is actually a corrective for racism. For members of oppressed groups, this proposition suggests that learning about diverse lifestyles enhances their life chances, which is fallacious. Assuming that White students will adopt anti-racist behavior simply by learning about lifestyles of "others" is also questionable, and "increased knowledge of other groups might in fact enhance feelings of 'differentness'" (p. 313). Flecha (1999) agreed, pointing out that neo-Nazis also "use the concept of difference to support their programs of hate" (p. 152). Also, adding into the curriculum "other" cultures does not necessarily lead to a critical examination of the dominant culture. The problem here is not learning about others, but rather doing so within a conceptual framework that does not question relationships between dominant and subordinate groups. The fourth assumption, that "cultural relativism is a desirable and tenable position" (p. 313), leads to "anything goes" rather than dialogue across groups about how to work through differences. In addition, the entire formulation following this line of reasoning assumes the state and its institutions to be culturally neutral.

Anti-racist education, in contrast, focuses on "the racist underpinnings and operation of white dominated institutions...rather than ethnic minority cultures and lifestyles" (Troyna, 1987, p. 310). In so doing, it directs attention to White supremacy, and to needs articulated by communities who are oppressed on the basis of race (Dei, 1996; Thompson, 1997). Anti-racist education begins not with a description of changing demographics, which suggests a new problem stemming from immigration, but with an analysis of historic and contemporary imperialism and racism (Blumer & Tatum, 1999; Brandt, 1986; Derman-Sparks & Phillips, 1997; Walker, 1989). It examines how a racist system is maintained, roles of individuals in maintaining it, and how racism can be challenged both collectively and individually. Anti-racist teaching entails helping students identify manifestations of racism, learn how racism works, and learn to interrupt it. Anti-racism gives tools to not only talk about racism, but also do something about it (James, 2001; Lee et al., 1998).

A second implication of anti-racist education is that it questions various ways in which schools structure unequal access to education (Brandt, 1986; James, 1995; Lee, 1985; Perry & Fraser, 1993). Racist structures and processes can include institutionalizing better instruction for White children than children of color; using tracking, special education and gifted programs to differentiate instruction along racial lines; using racially biased tests and other assessment processes; employing mainly White professionals; and so forth. In other words, anti-racism critiques the supposed neutrality of institutions such as schools; this does not necessarily happen in some versions of multicultural education (May, 1999).

For example, the anthology *Rethinking Schools: An Agenda for Change* (Levine, et al., 1995) includes a section critiquing tracking, that examines race and class biases in tracking systems, class and race biases in standardized testing, biases in access to algebra, and teaching in untracked secondary-level classrooms. Similarly, Lee (1985) examined racism in academic expectations, career counseling, assessment, and placement. Although many multicultural educators also address racism in the structure and operations of schools, those who focus entirely on what teachers can do in the classroom usually miss this important contextualization.

A third implication of anti-racist education is that it situates culture within relations of power (Dei, 1996). As mentioned earlier, multicultural education enacted in schools often assumes culture to be fixed and bounded, groups to be relatively homogeneous, and culture to be separate from its material and relational contexts. Anti-racist educators point out that the experience of subjugation itself acts on cultures of both those who are subjugated and those who dominate (May, 1999). People take up and adapt cultural forms in response to experiences; rap music, for example, is a form of popular Black youth culture that often speaks to racial subjugation (Rattansi, 1999). Further, global movements of peoples produce complex cultural identities that cannot be reduced to essentialist portrayals. Anti-racist education is similar to critical pedagogy in conceptualizing culture within a nexus of power relations, overlapping histories, and complex identities (Dei, 1996).

A fourth implication of anti-racist education is that it situates schooling in the broader community, viewing parents and community members as necessary parts of the education process (Perry & Fraser, 1993). Again, while many multicultural educators also do this, many do not. Part of the issue involves how one views race, power-sharing and professionalism. If one views teaching as "a series of technical decisions made by experts who have a claim to authority" (Sleeter & Montecinos, 1999, p. 116), then professionally trained educators should not share authority with parents. However, "for oppressed groups, framing teaching as a series of technical decisions made by experts constitutes cultural invasion—the dominant society renders as illegitimate systems of meaning and reality originating in oppressed communities" (p. 117). Anti-racism directs attention toward relationships between historically oppressed communities and professionals who are complicit in perpetuating racism. Anti-racist educators argue that transformation initiatives need to come at least in part from communities that are usually excluded from decision-making, particularly communities of color (Dei, 1996; Lee, 1985). One reason why anti-racist education makes sense to First Nations people in Canada is that it advocates stronger community control of education for their own children (Young, 1995).

A fifth implication of anti-racist education is that it problematizes Whiteness and White dominance (Stanley, 1998)—anti-racism helps to locate White people within multicultural education, and to critique depoliticized White identities. Whiteness tends to be normalized in traditional discourse, and very often in multicultural education as well (Dei, 1996; Lee, 1995). While White ethnic identities might be named, Whiteness usually is not. When teachers teach what they believe are universals, they draw too often from European and Euro-American culture and experience. Multicultural becomes, then, the "Other," implicitly exoticized and still deficient. By shifting the gaze, anti-racism names and critiques dominance (Stanley, 1998). Teaching about racism, however, can place White students in the position of being the named oppressor, thus alienating them from dialogue and engagement (Gillborn, 1995). This presents a pedagogical dilemma for anti-racist educators who embrace a student-centered pedagogy (Thompson, 2002). A goal of anti-racist education is to help students make significant political shifts in their thinking around racism and privilege, and this "sits uneasily with the aims of student-centered education, which is meant to be open-ended and emergent" (p. 443). In Chapter Ten of this volume, I illustrate a student-centered process for anti-racist teaching of a White student.

Limitations of anti-racist education and its implications for multi-cultural education

Anti-racist education has three limitations. First, the term itself, with its oppositional stance toward multicultural education, suggests a binary with two opposing agendas, each of which supposedly has an internally consistent body of ideas and practices. This assumed binary has been problematic on a number of fronts. Banks (1984) pointed out that "the critics [of multicultural education] have chosen some of the worst practices that are masquerading as multicultural education and defined these practices as multicultural education" (p. 60). In fact, a fair amount of literature in anti-racist education and multicultural education is virtually interchangeable.

Binaries assume that people within each camp think alike, and define one camp as "good" and the other as "bad," which closes off rather than encouraging dialogue (Bonnett, 1990; Bonnett & Carrington, 1996; Green, 1982; Rattansi, 1999). Further, the terms themselves do not have the same meanings across national borders, which also confuses or greatly truncates discussion.

Second, anti-racism has been criticized for giving too little attention to culture and too much attention to race, and in the process, essentializing race as a construct (Gillborn, 1995; Mansfield & Kehoe, 1994). Briefly, critics argue that many groups see race as a construct that is used against non-Anglos and would rather give serious attention to culture, language, and religion instead. Anti-racism is often too reductive, painting the world in black and white, and leaving too little space for diverse ethnic minorities, which in Britain has alienated Asian Muslims. Further, anti-racism reduces even the experiences of Black people solely to race, giving too little credence to culture. Gillborn (1995, p. 76) argued that rather than privileging either race or culture, we need to connect both, situating culture within in a sociopolitical context. Similarly, Flecha (1999) pointed out that the older racial categories do not work well today, yet racist movements aimed toward exclusion are gathering momentum. Anti-racism needs to develop a dialogic approach "emphasizing the need for equal rights among ethnicities" (p. 164). This means that an essential agenda for anti-racist education is to work toward dialogue among diverse groups "that is oriented toward creating conditions for people from different cultures and ethnicities to live together" (p. 165).

A third limitation is that anti-racist education can end up subsuming multiple forms of oppression (such as gender and class) under racism. Some educators who are trying to connect multiple forms of oppression, and who enter the dialogue through an interest in sexism or class oppression do not see anti-racist education as a venue for addressing anything except racism. For example, the focus on racism to the exclusion of other forms of oppression has alienated many White working-class youth who find it difficult to develop a sense of solidarity with oppressed people when the only identity they see for themselves is as the oppressor (Bonnett & Carrington, 1996). At the same time, in Canada, anti-racist educators have been making connections with multiple forms of oppression (e.g., Dei, 1999; James, 2001; Ng, Staton & Scane, 1995), and offer ways of framing anti-racism that address multiple oppressions without losing focus on racism, similar to the work of critical race theorists.

Discussion

Like the other three fields discussed in this chapter, multicultural education emerged as an intellectual and activist movement to transform social institutions. In its inception, its primary focus was challenging racism, but it became transmuted as it filtered through schools and mainstream discourses. Although multicultural education today has taken on a wide range of meanings and practices, many within the field have continued to develop it consistently with its original conceptual moorings. This chapter has attempted to act as a corrective to superficial and depoliticized versions of multicultural education by connecting the field to critical intellectual work. This chapter has also sought to develop the field by pointing out conceptual tools that can enrich and deepen its analyses.

What seems to distinguish critical traditions is their insistence on grounding practice in ideological clarity that explicitly critiques at least one form of collective oppression. Multicultural education that is critical, then, is not simply practice, but very explicitly politically guided practice. Multicultural education writings, however, with their focus on classroom practice, too often assume that educators bring ideological clarity and a sophisticated understanding of oppression, culture, and difference, and will change practice accordingly with guidance. But subsequent practice too often remains grounded in dominant discourses of individualism, implicit Eurocentrism, and naiveté about embedded power relations. In that context, multicultural education is enacted as strategies for sharing information about lifestyles, learning to get along, and examining the "other." Critical race theory, anti-racist education, and critical pedagogy writings generally spend more time examining the nature of oppression and culture in depth in order to develop ideological clarity, even though they may have less to say about teaching practice. This chapter suggests drawing from these fields, as well as additional fields such as multicultural feminism, to steer the course of transforming education more strongly.

At this point, one might reasonably ask to what extent it is possible and useful to attempt to synthesize multicultural education, critical pedagogy, critical race theory, and anti-racist education. After considering this question, we concluded that it is more useful to expand the dialogue between these fields. All four fields emerged as oppositional discourses to dominant discourses about education. Each came about through specific histories to address social justice from specific vantage points. As such, each illuminates some issues and strategies while occluding others, and each speaks to realities of some communities more than others. Conceptually, theoretical differences among the fields can provide overlapping but still distinct lenses for viewing schooling, each revealing somewhat different issues and possibilities. Politically, the fields themselves represent overlapping but distinct groups of people, embedded within histories of power conflicts. It is helpful to think of the differences as creative tensions that are grounded in the theoretical, practical, and political realities of each field.

At a theoretical level, literature in multicultural education, critical pedagogy, anti-racist education, and critical race theory provide somewhat different insights. Let us consider creative tensions around how each views the concept of culture and how each addresses structure and agency, since these concepts directly involve the nature of oppression, social change, and shared ways of making sense of the world. Critical pedagogy, anti-racist education, and critical race theory situate culture within relations of power more explicitly than does much of the multicultural education literature. Yet, even these three do not necessarily agree entirely on the relationship between culture and structures of power. While multicultural education attends actively to ethnic culture that is transmitted from generation to generation, critical pedagogy focuses mostly on the culture of everyday life, viewing culture as created within historic as well as contemporary power struggles. Anti-racist education, particularly in its inception, and critical race theory give far more attention to race and racism than to culture per se. Similarly, at a theoretical level the fields place different emphases on structure versus agency. Multicultural education tends to emphasize, more than the other fields, individual agency and personal attitudes over power structures and institutional practices by highlighting what teachers can do. On the other hand, critical race theory and anti-racist education focus primarily on oppressive structures and racist practices such as tracking, school funding, school (de)segregation, and the media, often leaving teachers unclear what they can do. Critical pedagogy attempts to link the structure agency dichotomy, but with a focus on class, more than on the intersections of multiple oppressions.

Rather than suggesting a grand theory, we find it more useful to ask what insights each perspective can offer, and how these insights might overlap and complement each other. For example, White Americans can be described as being preoccupied with measuring and organizing time, viewing time as linear, tangible, and scarce. Historically one might trace roots of this practice, in part, to German culture (ethnic cultural transmission perspective with an emphasis on agency); one can also connect this practice to industrialization and the construction of factories (institutional perspective with an emphasis on structure) (Alred, 1997). Current intensification of work due to economic shifts has intensified the scheduling of lives (culture within social class relations structured by capitalism). In addition, one can view the clock as a tool of racism that the mono-chronic dominant society uses to regulate subordinate groups (racism perspective with an emphasis on structure). Mono-chronic White Americans (who tend to see individual agency and not culture or structure) judge poly-chronic uses of time—in which time is conceptualized as circular, overlapping, and flexible—as disorganized. At an institutional level, this matters when organizations such as schools operate in a highly mono-chronic manner, penalizing communities that construct time more flexibly (racism and culture conflict perspective with an emphasis on structure). What conception of culture is most helpful and how to address the relationship of structure to agency depends on one's question.

Thompson (1997) cautioned that attempting to create one grand narrative from the left would end up pushing aside too many very significant issues. Therefore, our discussion of the four bodies of literature attempts to illustrate creative tensions and clarify what each field brings to bear on schooling, so that depending on one's question and focus, educators can benefit from the unique insights of multiple frameworks. Learning to use multiple frameworks can help us avoid the dangers of one grand narrative while examining significant issues related to schools, students, and their community contexts.

At a practical and political level, tensions surround the historic and contemporary discourse communities represented by each of the four fields. Each was created by and speaks to a group of people, and these groups do not necessarily blend easily or readily. For example, since critical pedagogy has its conceptual basis in a social-class analysis, and its theorists speak to class issues, it appeals more than the other three fields to a White leftist constituency. Critical race theory, on the other hand, developed as an oppositional discourse to critical theory, as scholars of color sought to place race rather than class at the center of analysis. As such, its discourse community is largely scholars of color. Multicultural education speaks largely to practicing teachers, a community that is not at the center of critical race theory. Each field has historic roots; connecting fields means addressing tensions based on historic as well as contemporary power struggles among the people who have created them. If historically the White working class participated in the subjugation of African Americans, to what extent does the historical baggage of racism accompany critical theory? If K-12 teachers tend to be marginalized in the process of constructing academic theory, to what extent would attempts to merge the fields reproduce this marginalization?

At the same time, there is a need to continue to try to connect various forms of oppression and various communities struggling for social justice. Over the past several years, significant attempts have been made to connect an analysis of racism with an analysis of sexism and class oppression; our chapter is only one additional such effort. Struggles to define the nature of oppression are often couched in terms of binaries: White versus people of color, men versus women, gay/lesbian versus heterosexual, working class and impoverished versus wealthy, and so forth. Binaries help to define power relations and demarcate conflict and struggle, but historically binaries have also been used as a means of control. Okihiro (2001) provided an excellent example by using the vantage point of Asian American history to challenge the binaries of East/West, Black/White, male/female, and heterosexual/homosexual. He showed how each of these was socially constructed within specific historic circumstances, and how each breaks apart when viewed from an angle within Asian American history. For example, eighteenth- and nineteenth-century White Americans constructed images of Chinese men as asexual but Chinese women as prostitutes as a way of controlling the sexuality of White women and making both White women and women of color available to White men. Attempts to connect multiple forms of oppression and multiple diversities end up challenging binaries. Okihiro pointed out, "Binaries resist change, perhaps, because they offer coherence" (p. 125). Binaries may work as conceptual tools, but they also impose simplistic solutions and serve as means of controlling some "Other." Practice uninformed by a critical reanalysis of how one understands social relations may end up reproducing the status quo.

As critical traditions attempt to connect analyses of various forms of oppression, they work to dislodge existing binaries while retaining a critical analysis of power, struggle, oppression, and social change. This is complicated work both theoretically and practically. Since practice is often uninformed by a complex understanding of oppression, culture, and power, one might ask if it is truly possible to use oppositional discourses in mainstream schools. Is it likely that critical theories, as they interact with practice, will be altered or diluted to meet the everyday practical needs of educators? It seems that although multicultural education, critical pedagogy, critical race theory, and anti-racist education emerged as oppositional discourses, there remains a strong possibility for their transmutation in practice, especially if dialogue among the different discourse communities is limited or restrained.

Note

1. Dolores Delgado Bernal is professor at the University of Utah.

PART III

Equipping the Next Generation of Multicultural Social Justice Teachers

9

Teacher Education, Neoliberalism, and Social Justice

Social justice in teacher education can be conceptualized as being comprised of three strands: (1) supporting access for all students to high-quality, intellectually rich teaching that builds on their cultural and linguistic backgrounds; (2) preparing teachers to foster democratic engagement among young people; and (3) preparing teachers to advocate for children and youth by situating inequities within a systemic sociopolitical analysis. These strands resonate with dilemmas that Delpit (1995) discussed regarding teaching other people's children. For communities that have been historically subordinated, gaining access to the dominant culture of power is of paramount importance. Reflected in the first strand above, teachers must be able to teach such children effectively so they can master that culture. At the same time, as the third strand suggests, the culture of power must also be critiqued, particularly for processes by which oppressive relationships are perpetuated. All of this must involve dialogue—the second strand—in which those who occupy positions of privilege, including teachers and teacher educators, learn to listen to, hear, and work with those who do not.

Although possibilities for building teacher education around social justice are rich, it is becoming increasingly difficult to enact them because the culture of power, embedded in global capitalism, is pressing away from social justice. Ironically, a history of weak relationships between teacher education and historically marginalized communities means that many communities do not see teacher educators as allies, even though teacher educators purport to serve them. After discussing neoliberal assaults on teacher education, I will suggest some lines of work that are urgently needed for teacher education to build alliances for social justice through collaborative relationships with historically under-served communities.

Assaults on Teacher Education and Social Justice

As a field, teacher education has never been a bastion of social justice, although many teacher educators have worked tirelessly and creatively to create strong social justice-oriented teacher education programs, and some states and accrediting agencies have had social justice requirements. But the field as a whole has always tended to be fairly traditional, mainly oriented toward preparing young White women for established missions and practices of schools. Teacher education faculty are overwhelmingly White, most having little experience teaching diverse populations (Zeichner, 2003).

Currently, under neoliberalism, teacher education and social justice are under active assault from "the parallel universe from which the business reform agenda springs" (Gelberg, 2007, p. 52). As discussed in the Introduction to this book, this reform agenda, which has taken an exaggerated form by Tea Party advocates, seeks to shrink or completely dismantle government support of public welfare in favor of expanding individualism, privatization, and competition for profit (Hursh, 2005). Neoliberalism has framed schools like businesses designed to turn out workers for the new global economy, and as venues for profiteering (for an insightful analysis of neoliberalism's impact on education globally, see Compton & Weiner, 2008). In this chapter, I argue that neoliberalism is pressing teacher education in the following ways: (1) away from social justice teacher preparation and toward preparing teachers as technicians to raise student test scores; (2) away from being linked with teacher professional knowledge and teacher quality; and (3) toward becoming shorter or by-passed altogether.

Teacher education as preparation of technicians

Teacher education should be directly linked to K-12 schooling. At their best, teacher education programs and schools collaborate to develop high-quality teaching and strengthen democratic participation (Darling-Hammond, 2006). But pressures originating in global capitalism are pushing schools away from democratic participation and even away from rich conceptions of teaching. In the process, they are pushing teacher education away as well. In response to high-stakes testing, school districts across the United States, especially those serving low-income or culturally diverse students, have adopted increasingly prescribed curricula that are aligned with state standards and tests. Much prescribed curriculum emphasizes memorization much more than critical thinking. Increasingly, in schools that serve historically underserved communities, teaching means implementing prescribed curriculum packages "with fidelity" rather than responding to students, let alone developing teacher-made curricula (Achinstein, Ogawa, & Speiglman, 2004; Valli, et al., 2008). In this context, teacher education programs are being compelled to reduce or eliminate not only explicit social justice teacher preparation, but also learner-centered teaching in general.

Standards for teacher preparation are under pressure to reduce or eliminate reference to social justice, multicultural education, or bilingual education. For example, in 2002, Iowa replaced the requirement of a multicultural education course with more reading methods coursework. In 2006, National Council for the Accreditation of Teacher Education (NCATE), following a complaint by the National Association of Scholars and other conservative organizations, withdrew the term social justice as a possible desirable teacher disposition. While NCATE does not explicitly discourage member institutions from incorporating social justice into teacher education programs, this move undercut a source of support that many teacher educators had used on their own campuses. In California, the earlier emphasis in Culture, Language and Academic Development (CLAD) was folded into standards for all teacher education candidates, but in a way that de-emphasized bilingualism and biculturalism in favor of English-language acquisition. California's revised standards made "clear repeatedly that the role of teacher education is to prepare teachers to teach the state-adopted content standards using state adopted materials" (Sleeter, 2003, p. 20). The phrase "state-adopted academic content standards" appears throughout the standards documents, but the term *culture* appears only occasionally in reference to learning about culture, and the terms *bilingual, culturally relevant* and *culturally responsive* do not appear. To investigate the impact of this change, Montaño and colleagues (2005) surveyed faculty members in 16 California teacher education programs, finding that content addressing culture and language, formerly taught in designated courses, had now been "infused" or reduced.

School districts are also pressuring teacher education programs. For example, Selwyn (2005–2006), a teacher educator at Antioch College, commented that it is increasingly difficult to find classroom field placements serving low-income students that model anything except scripted teaching. Recently a colleague who has long been active in social justice teacher education told me that school principals now insist that they need teachers trained to use the highly scripted elementary reading package *Open Court* rather than multicultural social justice education. New teachers who resist routinized, scripted teaching in order to teach in student-centered ways are subject to being pushed out, even when their students score very well on tests (Achinstein & Ogawa, 2006).

Growing national discussions about linking assessment of teacher candidates with student test scores when those candidates begin to teach, then evaluating teacher preparation programs based partially on the test scores of their graduates' students, further harnesses what it means to teach to test preparation (see Nelson, 2012). The shift away from support for critical, multicultural, and social justice perspectives and toward technical training reinforces an ideological shift away from education as preparation for democratic participation, toward education as work preparation only. It also reflects a narrowing of how equity is to be understood, away from addressing high-poverty communities' chronic lack of basic resources, including education resources (e.g., Anyon, 2005; Berliner, 2005; Gándara, Rumberger, Maxwell-Jolly, & Callahan, 2003), and toward focusing on test scores only. Programs that build awareness of a larger view of equity disrupt attempts to directly address a much narrower, test-score driven conception of it.

Disconnecting teacher education from teacher quality assessment

Teacher quality has been redefined in a way that allows teacher education to be regarded as unnecessary. Zeichner's (2003) three conceptions of teacher quality help to clarify what has happened. A professional conception, reflected in the work of professional groups such as the National Commission on Teaching and America's Future and the National Board for Professional Teaching Standards, emphasizes teachers' professional pedagogical knowledge base and ability to use that knowledge in the classroom. A social justice conception, reflected in the work of organizations such as the National Association for Multicultural Education, emphasizes teachers' knowledge of and ability to use culturally responsive instructional strategies. Both conceptions link teachers' professional pedagogical knowledge with subject-matter competence.

A deregulation conception, reflected in reports by conservative think tanks such as the Fordham and Abel Foundations, emphasizes subject-matter preparation only, seeing little or no professional pedagogical knowledge of value that can be learned other than through experience. This conception is supported by statistical research that correlates increases in students' test scores with teachers' verbal ability and the proportion of teachers in a school who hold subject matter rather than education degrees (Johnson, 2000; Monk, 1994). *No Child Left Behind* made the deregulation conception law by defining a highly qualified teacher as: "one who has full state certification as a teacher (including certification through alternative routes); or passed state teacher licensing exam and holds a license in that state" (Norfolk Public Schools, n.d.). The law places a premium on teachers' demonstrated subject matter knowledge aligned to the state's content standards, and on teacher testing. The Bush family has long-standing ties to McGraw-Hill, one of the main corporations selling curriculum packages and tests, and thus had a vested interest in pressing toward test-based systems for judging quality (Trelease, 2006).

Shifting conceptions of teacher quality away from professional knowledge and toward traditional measures of academic content knowledge and pedagogy serves as a control on university-based teacher education by pressing toward alignment of curriculum with assessment. State-mandated performance-based teacher assessment systems also have the potential to codify what teaching should look like, emphasizing some teaching processes and approaches over others (such as learner-centered teaching). State and national systems, such as PACT (Performance Assessment for California Teachers) also remove decision-making about teaching from the local level (Berlak, 2010), as well as enabling national corporations to turn performance-based teacher assessment into a profitable enterprise, as is currently happening as Pearson takes over PACT.

Disconnecting systems for teacher evaluation from formal teacher education also enables any agency to certify teachers as long as it tests them according to state standards. This shift elevates testing as a way of determining teacher quality over other means, reducing the significance of that which is not testable, such as racial dispositions, expectations for student learning, or ability to connect academics with culturally diverse students. Defining teacher quality through testing also ignores social justice problems connected with testing. A long history of disproportionate failure rates among teachers of color is due to a variety of factors, including biases in whose knowledge is valued on tests and whose is not (Alberts, 2002; Epstein, 2005), the arbitrariness of cutoff scores and their relationship to the racial composition of who passes and who does not (Memory, Coleman, & Watkins, 2003), and connections between testing and perception of stereotype threat (Bennett, McWhorter, & Kuykendall, 2006; Steele & Aronson, 1995). Increased testing undercuts attempts to diversify the teacher population, tacitly dismissing the value of teacher diversity (Epstein, 2005; Flippo, 2003).

In addition, testing shifts power to determine what it means to learn and teach away from educators, and toward legislatures and the corporations that produce and sell tests. Harrell and Jackson (2006), based on an analysis of science teacher testing in Texas, for example, noted that although higher education was still expected to provide content knowledge, it was "the state legislature partnered with test companies" that defined what teachers should know; the greatest beneficiary appeared to be test companies.

Shortening professional teacher education

Assaults on teacher education have juxtaposed teachers' content knowledge against pedagogical knowledge, arguing teachers need the former but not the latter. This, coupled with cuts in state spending on higher education, has led to a shortening of professional teacher education, reducing and in some cases squeezing out preparation for social justice.

Preservice teacher education programs had gradually lengthened from the 1970s through the early the 1990s. For example, between 1973 and 1983, required semester hours for elementary teachers in general studies increased from an average of 41 to 62, and in clinical experiences from 10 to 17 (Feistritzer, 1999). During that time, programs developed more intentional series of field experiences and added coursework that reflected changes in schools, such as mainstreaming exceptional children, working with technology, and teaching diverse learners. By 1999, required semester hours in general studies for elementary teachers had dropped to 51, in clinical experiences to 15, and in professional studies from a high of 38 down to 31 (Feistritzer, 1999). Keep in mind that while teacher education was shrinking, student diversity was growing rapidly; for example, it was becoming increasingly likely that teachers would have English learners in their classrooms that they would be expected to know how to teach.

Teacher education has been shortened through several venues. One venue has been the emergence of test-based programs with minimal professional preparation and no contact with a college of education. The American Board for Certification of Teacher Excellence (ABCTE) program Passport to Teaching, for example, is a test-based system in which holders of a bachelor's degree can complete certification exams online, to teach in states that accept this form of teacher certification. Teachers certified through test-based systems receive no training in any form of social justice education. Fast-track programs, such as Teach For America, briefly prepare teachers before placing them in the classroom. Although surveys of teachers prepared through fast-track programs find them to feel unprepared and many leave teaching after a year or two (National Academy of Education, 2009), school districts around the country have established relationships with fast-track providers, particularly Teach for America, often reserving slots for them. Competition with fast-track providers creates pressure to shorten university-based teacher education.

Most teachers are still certified through university-based programs, but many such programs have shrunk or reduced enrollment as colleges of education have been pressured to reduce time to degree in the wave of financial pressures on university budgets. Reduction in taxes coupled with rising costs of public services in most states has resulted in reductions of public expenditures on higher education. Cuts in teacher education programs, along with the other pressures described above, have squeezed curricular space for social justice work in teacher education. Rather than complementing methods coursework, increasingly coursework in multicultural and social justice education now competes with it. Shortened teacher preparation fits with a "trickle down" theory of teaching and learning in which what children should know is codified into standards and tests, to be delivered using materials that detail each concept and step for teaching it, and teachers need minimal preparation to deliver that content. Darling-Hammond (2006) explains, historically, "Limited training for teachers was seen as an advantage for the faithful implementation of newly designed 'scientific' curricula" (p. 78).

Managing Dissent through Science

It is in the interest of the corporatocracy to manage dissent while building consensus for its expansion. Science has emerged as a useful tool for this purpose. Martin (1999) pointed out that, "Because scientific knowledge is widely believed to have an authority derived from nature, undisputed scientific knowledge claims can play a powerful legitimating role" (p. 105). In several fields, the Bush administration was charged with using science as a political tool, promoting findings that supported its agenda while suppressing those that did not. Based on an examination of the Bush administration's political interference with science, the Government Reform Minority Office (2003) noted that misleading statements, suppressed reports, and the like benefit mainly "important supporters of the President, including social conservatives and powerful industry groups"—the corporatocracy.

In education, a drastically narrowed conception of what counts as science is being used to support education reforms and suppress dissent. Renaming what had been the Office of Educational Research and Improvement as the Institute for Education Sciences, signaled this shift. The Institute defines "scientifically based research" as involving "a randomized controlled trial or a quasi-experiment (including quasi-experiments with equating, regression discontinuity designs, and single-case designs)" (What Works Clearinghouse, 2006). Other ways of framing and conducting research, such as phenomenological research, do not count. This conception of science affirms testing as a primary measure of success, while removing from consideration a huge amount of knowledge derived through research processes other than experimental research, such as that reviewed in Chapters Four and Six of this volume.

This redefinition casts most social justice work as irrelevant, since the only "legitimate" question left on the table is: What teaching strategies have been found to raise student test scores, using experimental or quasi-experimental research? Using that question and research so defined, the government is then able to identify schools in which test scores have risen, highlighting those to show that neoliberal reform is working, and which "scientifically based" teaching strategies to promote. Teacher educators who question this framing of knowledge, or who value teaching strategies that have not been validated as "scientifically based," are then cast as impediments to school improvement. Newspaper articles that appear periodically, for example, affirm the suspicion that "those who can, do; those who can't, teach; and those who can't teach, train teachers."[1]

Teacher education has for too long, in general, failed to serve historically underserved communities well. Currently, many historically underserved communities see neoliberal reforms that focus on the achievement gap as doing more to improve education for their children than teacher educators have been doing. In a letter to Congress, over 100 African-American and Latino superintendents emphasized their support for accountability reforms that focus directly on the achievement gap, writing that underachievement of students of color and students who live in poverty "has been swept underneath overall averages for too long" ("Don't Turn Back the Clock," 2003). The broader sociopolitical restructuring that is occurring under neoliberalism is probably detrimental to historically underserved communities in the long run, by rapidly widening gulfs between rich and poor and dismantling public services (Harvey, 2005). If we take social justice seriously in teacher education, what can we be doing, recognizing that the landscape has become much more difficult?

Teacher Education for Social Justice

A wide repertoire of existing practices and programs illustrate ways in which teacher education can help to ensure diverse communities equitable access to quality teaching, prepare teachers to advocate for diverse children, and prepare all students for democratic participation in a diverse society. From recruiting diverse candidates who demonstrate commitment to equity, to constructing fieldwork and professional coursework to build capacity for social justice education, there are many intervention points and strategies that are supported in the research.

Below I suggest a few of these. Possibilities in teacher education for social justice work are summarized in Table 9.1. Across the top are the three social justice strands I am using in this chapter. Down the left-hand side are three areas of teacher education that will be discussed: recruitment and admission, professional coursework, and guided fieldwork.

Table 9.1 Teacher Education and Social Justice Themes

	Build equitable access to high-quality, intellectually rich, culturally affirming teaching	Prepare teachers to foster democratic engagement among children and youth	Prepare teachers as equity advocates for children and youth
Recruit, admit:	More diverse teacher candidates	Candidates committed to multicultural democracy	Candidates who believe in equity advocacy
Professional coursework that includes:	Self analysis, Sociocultural framework for teaching and learning, Teaching strategies linking what students bring to academics	Strategies for building multicultural democracy in classroom	Nature of institutional discrimination in society and schools
Guided fieldwork:	In culturally diverse and/or low-income settings, Inquiry-based to disrupt deficit theorizing, In communities to learn culture of students	In classrooms that support democratic decision-making	Inquiry into school and community patterns of inequity

Recruitment and admission

Teacher education can help to ensure that all students, and particularly those in historically underserved communities, have equitable access to high-quality teachers who believe in them, are committed to working with them, are convinced they have cultural and linguistic resources on which academic learning and democratic participation can be built, and know how to facilitate that learning. Although in part this is a teacher preparation challenge, it is also a recruitment and admission challenge. It is widely recognized that the demographic gap between students and teachers is large and growing. In 2010, enrollment in U.S. public schools was only slightly more than half White (54%), and only slightly under half students of color; 14% of students spoke a language other than English at home (National Center for Education Statistics, 2012). Yet, as explored in more detail in Chapter Eleven, the teaching force remains about 82% White.

Although many studies have found most White teacher candidates bring deficit-oriented stereotypes and very little cross-cultural background, knowledge, and experience (Sleeter, 2008), admission to teacher education is rarely denied on the basis of unwillingness to learn to teach diverse students well. Preservice teachers of color tend to bring a richer multicultural knowledge base than their White counterparts, and are more likely to bring a commitment and sense of urgency to multicultural teaching, social justice, and providing children of color with an academically challenging curriculum (Dee & Henkin, 2002; Knight, 2004; Rios & Montecinos, 1999; Su, 1997). Teachers who are willing to stay in challenging urban schools are more likely to be older adults who are from the community in which they are teaching, rather than young White teachers (Haberman, 1996).

It is possible for teacher education to recruit, admit, and prepare a significantly more diverse mix of prospective teachers than is currently the case; Chapter Eleven of this volume reviews various program models in some detail. Such efforts are not intended to replace White teachers with teachers of color, but rather to build a teaching force that not only looks more like today's students, but also brings more knowledge from their communities into the profession. If teacher education seems irrelevant to many historically underserved communities, working actively with them to bring more members of such communities into teaching, via well-conceived teacher preparation programs, would be a start in making change.

Professional coursework

Although social justice coursework should be woven through the entire professional preparation program, commonly it is added on without addressing the rest of the program as a whole. Quite often such additions are made by a small number of faculty members who have a commitment to teaching for social justice. Holistic, coherently planned programs that thoughtfully weave multicultural and social justice coursework throughout, have much more impact on teacher candidates than single courses (Darling-Hammond, 2006; Villegas & Lucas, 2002).

Professional coursework that develops social justice begins by having teacher candidates examine their own backgrounds and experiences to identify assumptions, beliefs, and values they hold, as well as cultural contexts in which they have grown up that impact their understandings of schooling, children, and families (Feiman-Nemser, 2001). Gaining awareness of these powerful filters through which teacher candidates interpret students and teaching opens candidates to learning. Many teacher educators have teacher candidates write autobiographies or personal cultural histories (Lea, 1994) that discuss who was present and absent in communities where they grew up, core values they learned in their families, beliefs they hold about people who differ from themselves, and their conceptions of what "good teaching" looks like. For example, Kumashiro (2004b) begins teaching about sexual orientation by having candidates write anonymously about how they honestly feel about issues involving sexual orientation, so that teaching can begin with their questions and concerns. As coursework then moves outward from candidates' lives, experienced teacher educators systematically use interactive, reflective processes that continue to engage candidates in examining their beliefs and experiences in relationship to analytical frameworks and key concepts.

In professional coursework, teacher candidates can learn a sociocultural framework of learning and teaching strategies that offers equitable access to quality education for diverse learners, such as scaffolding, using instructional conversations, and differentiating instruction. As Gutiérrez and Rogoff (2003) explain, learning occurs through intellectual participation in cultural practices. The classroom is one site of cultural practice; so also are communities and homes in which children live. As teacher candidates gain understanding of language use and cultural practices that are familiar to the students, coursework can help them learn by building on the language, frames of reference, and patterns of relationships with which students are familiar.

Professional coursework focusing on multicultural democracy lays the foundation for building community in the context of diversity and developing children's awareness of complexities of culture, difference, and equity. Teacher candidates can learn to guide students in open and constructive conversations about differences they see and experience, and help them learn to make collective decisions that balance competing interests and demands. Reading the work of theorists such as Freire (1998), Banks (2003), Kincheloe and Steinberg (2006) and Knoester (2012) can prompt candidates to distinguish between democracy and the marketplace, in which the concept of "freedom" has migrated from meaning political and cultural freedom to meaning freedom to buy and make money. *Rethinking Schools* regularly features articles that help teacher candidates envision what it looks like to build democracy in diverse contexts. Professional coursework is most powerful when teacher candidates are diverse, and not only read about, but also experience building democratic communities in the context of diversity.

Learning to address barriers encountered by students from historically oppressed communities in schools requires teacher candidates to understand the nature of institutional discrimination. Without this understanding, teachers too often attribute students' difficulties to home or community "cultural deficiencies," rather than to institutionalized sociopolitical factors that can be addressed. Andrzejewski's (1995) comprehensive framework links macrolevel systems of oppression with local, everyday inequalities, and connects diverse forms of oppression, including racism, sexism, heterosexism, and classism. In the context of studying systems of oppression, she also has teacher candidates examine how media shape belief systems, juxtaposing social analyses embedded in alternative media with those in mainstream media. She emphasizes identifying and acting on local issues, while situating those within larger issues that require organizing in order to change.

As teacher candidates identify school and classroom barriers to equitable student learning, they can learn to construct alternative inclusive practices. For example, curricula, including state standards and textbooks, still reflect mainly the experiences and perspectives of White, middle-class, heterosexual Americans, although diverse peoples are usually sprinkled throughout. In professional coursework, teacher candidates can explore the relationship between who is in curriculum and how students respond, then create multicultural curricula that teach core academic concepts through diverse groups' experiences (Sleeter, 2005).

Promising practices in guided fieldwork

Various forms of fieldwork throughout teacher education is essential. An extensive, carefully designed mix of field experiences can have several purposes, including: helping candidates to decide whether they actually want to teach diverse students; helping them examine their assumptions about children and teaching; exposing them to varied models of teaching; teaching them to identify the intellectual resources students bring to school; helping them gather and use data to guide instruction and to examine schools as institutions; and providing guided teaching practice. Most fieldwork in teacher education, however, encourages replication of the status quo rather than critically questioning and transforming it (Feiman-Nemser, 2001). And simply requiring an experience in a low-income or minority school is just as likely to reinforce negative stereotypes (e.g., Marx, 2000; Tiezzi & Cross, 1997; Wiggins & Follo, 1999) as to challenge them (e.g., Chance, Morris, & Rakes, 1996; Fry & McKinney, 1997; Lazar, 1998).

One promising practice that is used far too little is guided inquiry in cross-cultural community-based learning. Such fieldwork has tremendous potential for building familiarity with diverse students and adults in their lives, investigating institutional discrimination, and learning to view schooling from another point of view. In cross-cultural community-based field experiences, candidates learn how to learn in a community that is culturally different from their own, using strategies such as active listening and nonjudgmental observation. In classrooms, teacher candidates see students reacting to school, but often attribute their reactions to students' lives outside school. By learning from their community contexts, teacher candidates can gain a much better understanding of students' capabilities, strengths, and interests.

Field experiences can vary widely in intensity and duration. Immersion experiences involve living in another cultural context for a period of time, ranging from days or weeks (e.g., Aguilar & Pohan, 1998) to a semester (e.g., Mahan & Stachowski, 1993–1994). In less-intensive experiences (which often take the form of service learning), teacher candidates visit neighborhoods or communities where they have a role to play (such as tutoring) or a specific guided-learning activity (such as interviewing senior citizens or constructing a community portrait) (Boyle-Baise, 2002). For example, teacher candidates can work in an agency such as a community center, ethnic club, church, or homeless shelter, in connection with coursework addressing culture and community. Guided-inquiry activities might explore why people come to the agency, what kinds of needs people have, what the local community is proud of, what its residents do well, what its children do when not in school, and so forth. In well-structured experiences, candidates see functioning communities and everyday cultural patterns first-hand, form relationships with people, confront stereotypes, and hear stories of lives that reflect abstractions they may have read about in textbooks.

Ultimately, this provides a basis for learning to construct culturally relevant teaching in the classroom. For example, Noordhoff and Kleinfeld's (1993) case study of the impact of a semester-long immersion experience in a small indigenous Alaskan community demonstrated this potential. The teacher candidates lived in the community and became involved in activities such as sewing or beading groups, or local church activities. The researchers videotaped them student teaching three times over the semester, documenting their shift from teaching as telling, to teaching as engaging the children with culturally relevant knowledge connected with academic knowledge.

Guided-inquiry projects can investigate patterns of discrimination in the community context that impacts on families. For instance, teacher candidates can compare the prices of gasoline and groceries in low-income and upper-income neighborhoods, then the type of transportation available to a low-income resident who might want to shop outside his or her neighborhood. Or, they might investigate availability and accessibility of medical care to immigrants who are not yet fluent in English and who live in low-income neighborhoods. The notion of institutional discrimination begins to take on substance during such investigations. Numerous case studies have found teacher candidates to question prior stereotypes and become familiar with cultural strengths and community resources they had not seen before as a result of community-based learning (e.g., Bondy & Davis, 2000; James & Haig-Brown, 2002; Melnick & Zeichner, 1996; Moule, 2004; Seidl & Friend, 2002).

In classrooms, teacher candidates need cooperating teachers who can support inquiry-based, democratic, social justice-oriented practice. Programs that are able to provide this support generally involve close collaboration between schools, universities, and communities. The Bilingual/Multicultural Department at Sacramento State University, for example, produced enough graduates to create a deep network of cooperating teachers who understand, model, and support social justice teaching. In addition, the department has forged Professional Development School relationships with several local schools. Faculty members engage in professional development there, which improves "coherence between practices in the student teaching placements and the theory and practices highlighted in coursework" (Wong et al., 2007).

Conclusion

Quality teacher education is a valuable public resource. However, to be a quality resource to communities that have historically had least access to excellent teaching, teacher education must be relevant. Relevance requires that teacher educators collaborate directly with such communities, and social justice demands it. In the process of collaborating with communities, teacher educators can forge strategies to recruit and prepare a more culturally and linguistically diverse cadre of teacher candidates who reflect local communities more than is currently the case. Through collaboration built on dialogue across communities of difference, teachers can be prepared to advocate for children and youth and to foster democratic engagement, taking into account how local inequities are embedded within systems of oppression as well as movements for action.

Neoliberalism is actively dismantling public services, including teacher education. Based on a comprehensive analysis of its track record globally, Harvey (2005) finds that "the universal tendency [is] to increase inequality and to expose the least fortunate elements in any society...to the chill winds of austerity and the dull fate of increased marginalization" (p. 118). The fate of teacher education is directly linked with fates of broad segments of the public, particularly those who can least afford the impact of massive privatization. For that reason, teacher educators must take social justice seriously.

Note

1. The original source of this phrase is unknown. The phrase appears on several websites, attributed to an unknown original source.

10

Teaching Whites about Racism

As student populations become increasingly diverse in racial and cultural composition and as the teaching force remains overwhelmingly White, interest in training teachers in multicultural education has grown. Many educators conceptualize this task as helping White teachers and preservice students replace negative attitudes about communities of color with positive attitudes, and as helping them acquire a knowledge base about race, culture and various racial groups. I see the task as more complex than that: White women teachers, many of whom have worked themselves up from working-class origins, already have considerable knowledge about social stratification in America, but that knowledge tends to be fairly conservative.

Part of the task for teacher educators is to help teachers examine and reconstruct what they know. Otherwise, they simply integrate information about race into the knowledge they already have and in the process distort it. This chapter describes a process I have used with White preservice students to help them recognize the limits of what they know about social stratification so that they can begin to reconstruct what they know.

How White Teachers Think about Social Stratification and Race

Anthony Giddens (1979) advanced his analysis of social theory on the premise that "every social actor knows a great deal about the conditions of reproduction of the society of which he or she is a member" (5). Regardless of how little experience with racial or cultural diversity White teachers have had, they enter the classroom with a considerably rich body of knowledge about social stratification, social mobility, and human differences based on their life experiences. The analogies they draw between racism and what they know about sexism, class mobility, and White ethnic experiences tend to minimize the importance of racism as they see it.

Race is one axis of oppression in America; social class and gender are equally important axes. About 82% of the teaching population is White (National Center for Education Statistics, 2010), making most teachers, as Whites, members of the dominant racial group. As such, most never have been victims of racism in America nor have experienced racial minority communities in the same way Americans of color do. Whites draw on their own experience to understand inequality, and their interpretation of that experience usually upholds their belief that the rules of society apply roughly the same to everyone. Haves and have-nots rise or fall by their own merit or effort, for the most part.

White Americans and Americans of color grow up in different locations in the racial structure, although Whites usually deny that there is a significant racial structure. Based on his study of White perceptions of race, David Wellman (1977) argued that a contradiction Whites face is how to interpret racial inequality in a way that defends White interests in publicly acceptable terms. Generally, sociobiological explanations for inequality are not acceptable today, so Whites construct alternative explanations, resolving "the contradiction by minimizing racism. They neutralize it" (219), viewing racism as individual prejudice and inequality as due mainly to cultural so-called deficiencies" (see also Bonilla-Silva 2010; Hunt, 2007)

While denying structural racism, Whites usually spend their lives in White-dominated spheres, constructing an understanding of race and social equality from that vantage point. According to Wellman (1977), "Given the racial and class organization of American society, there is only so much people can 'see.' The positions they occupy in these structures limit the range of their thinking. The situation places barriers on their imaginations and restricts the possibilities of their vision" (235). Consequently, they assume the opportunity structure works the same for all Americans.

A large proportion of teachers are women, and a large proportion have also worked their way up from lower- or working-class origins. In that regard, they are members of oppressed groups, and their experiences with social class and gender provide teachers with a perspective about how they believe social stratification works. Historically, teaching has provided members of the lower- and working-class entrée into middle-class status; many teachers have experienced working their way up by attaining education (Lortie 1975). Ashton and Webb (1986) noted that, "The life experiences of most teachers demonstrate their allegiance to the ethic of vertical mobility, self-improvement, hard work, deferred gratification, self-discipline, and personal achievement. These individualistic values rest on the assumption that the social system…works well, is essentially fair, and moves society slowly but inevitably toward progress" (29–30).

For example, I interviewed twenty-three teachers about their parents' occupations (Sleeter 1992). Four of their fathers had held jobs that normally require college education, two had owned small businesses, and the fathers of the other seventeen had worked as laborers of various sorts. Some of the teachers had experienced the stigma of being poor. But they had raised their own social-class standing by earning college degrees and becoming teachers. Education had served them as an effective vehicle of upward mobility and personal betterment. Several teachers also talked about their European ethnic backgrounds (or those of their spouses). Their parents or grandparents had come to America very poor and had worked hard; gradually the family had moved up the social ladder. These life experiences taught teachers that the social system is open to those who are willing to work, regardless of ethnicity (a view that equates White ethnicity with race). As a result, researchers consistently find White teachers and White preservice teachers to minimize attention to racism, locating racism in the past and embracing colorblindness as a way of understanding race (e.g., Lensmire, 2010; Picower, 2009; Trainor, 2005).

Many Americans regard their own social standing as higher than that of their parents. While most social mobility has been due to an expansion of middle-class jobs and widespread improvement of the living standard of Americans in general, people tend to attribute their own improved status to their own individual efforts (Kluegel & Smith 1986). Teachers' experience with sexism also provides them with an experiential basis for thinking about social stratification. As women, many teachers have experienced prejudice and stereotyping, which offers a perspective about how discrimination works that very often locates sexism (and classism) mainly in biased attitudes of individuals who limit the opportunities of others by treating them stereotypically. The main solution to discrimination from this perspective is to try to eliminate stereotyping so that all may strive as individuals.

Most teachers' understanding of sexism and social class is cast within a conservative framework that emphasizes individual choice and mobility within a relatively open system. One's progress may be hindered by prejudices and stereotypes, as well as by meager economic and cultural resources from home. However, these blocks can be compensated for by hard work. Structural bases for gender and social class oppression are rarely studied in school in any depth, so most teachers' understanding of their personal experience stays rooted within a naïve individualistic framework. But it is important to recognize the power of personal experience in reinforcing this framework.

When concerned White teachers define classism, sexism, and by extension racism as a matter of individual prejudice, they then strive to keep racial prejudices and stereotypes from coloring their interactions with individuals. I interviewed twenty-six teachers over a period of time as they participated in a two-year staff development project in multicultural education. How to think about race, color, and culture was a major issue they grappled with and often discussed in interviews and in the staff development sessions. Many of them upheld the "colorblind" perspective, believing that one is not participating in racism if one learns to ignore color and feel comfortable around children of color. Yet most White teachers had an unresolved dilemma: how to accept all children regardless of race while explaining their difficulties in school without seeming racist. Some blamed the "culture of poverty," asserting that race was not the issue. Several tried to ignore explanations that "blamed the victim." But they unconsciously used such explanations anyway for lack of means to explain children's classroom behavior and achievement. First, they mentioned the racial and socioeconomic composition of their students; then they immediately described those students (Sleeter 1992).

Those who attempt to teach White teachers about racism commonly encounter defenses that are difficult to penetrate. Convinced that individual attitudes and stereotypes form the basis of racism, Whites try very hard not to see color and therefore not to hear race-related information; Whites also experience guilt when confronted with information about racism. Reducing social organization to individual relationships, many Whites define "getting along" in face-to-face interactions as the solution to racism, then maintain that they already do this well. Many Whites equate race with what they know about White ethnicity, drawing on what they know about their own ancestors' experiences pulling themselves up "by the bootstraps." The European ethnicity analogy assumes that every group faced difficulties but that most overcame those difficulties through hard work; it ignores the importance of skin color in perpetuating racial discrimination. However, drawing parallels between racism, sexism, and classism, many Whites resentfully interpret civil rights laws and social interventions as people of color wanting "special attention and privileges."

The European ethnic immigrant experience provides a template for thinking about diversity that White teachers commonly use to try to construct race in what they construe as a positive rather than negative manner. According to the ethnicity paradigm, members of diverse groups voluntarily came to America to partake in its freedom and opportunity; while systems were not always fair in the past, opportunity has gradually been extended to everyone. In his study of how Euro Americans think about ethnicity, Alba (1990) found them to view it as voluntary participation in a group, in which the meaning of ethnicity is tied mainly to family history and expressions of so-called old-world culture, especially cuisine, holidays, and ethnic festivals. Among Euro Americans, ethnic differences no longer define opportunities or social participation: marriage, housing, employment, education, and so forth are almost unrelated to European ethnic background. So, it makes sense for Euro Americans to view their own ethnicity as voluntary and to define it as they do. However, colonized groups as well as immigrant groups who are visibly identifiable have not had the same history; the European ethnic experience does not provide an appropriate framework for understanding non-European groups (Jacobson, 2006; Omi & Winant, 1986). Trying to apply it to everyone, in fact, is another defense Whites use.

One approach to penetrating these defenses is to affirm to Whites that their beliefs are valid but also limited—valid for Whites, but not necessarily for people of color. Since Whites tend to deny that a racial structure locates them differently from people of color, one can begin by helping them recognize structural racism and the importance of visible differences among people when defining access. This shifts attention away from feelings of guilt, reliance on the White ethnic experience, or the possibility of being colorblind.

In what follows, I describe a process I have used to help White preservice students articulate some of what they know about the social system, recognize that what they know may be true for White people but does not necessarily generalize to Americans of color, and develop some sensitivity to how the rules of American society work differently for people of color than they do for Whites. It is significant to my teaching that I am White. I deliberately use my race and my background to try to relate to the White students, for example, by telling them that I used to think X until I experienced Y, that "we as Whites" experience advantages we are often aware of, or that I have made some big mistakes that Whites commonly make. Professors of color can draw on different advantages than White professors to teach about race. A lifetime of personal experience with a group and with racial discrimination arms a professor of color with a rich repertoire of experiences and examples (as an African American friend put it to me once, "I've been Black all my life and taking notes"). Students may attempt to dismiss professors of color as advocating a cause (as well as women professors who teach about gender); this avoidance technique should be pointed out directly, and students should be redirected to the information the professor is attempting to teach.

Analytic Framework

Before describing some specific teaching strategies, I will present a framework that structures how I teach about race and other axes of oppression.[1] I share this framework with students, referring back to it repeatedly. The framework directs them to analyze social institutions rather than characteristics of individuals and groups and to examine how institutions work differently for different groups; it is based on conflict theory.

In a fair social system individuals generally get what they strive for according to predictable rules that apply equally to everyone. This is a tenet of U.S. society that most citizens, regardless of race or any other ascribed characteristic, believe ought to be the case. Figure 10.1 represents this visually, in which "Reward" refers to whatever an individual is striving for (such as a job, or a decent place to live, or education), and the arrow indicates the social rules governing distribution of that resource.

However, in reality the rules do not work the same way for everyone. Conflict theorists postulate that dominant groups make the rules in order to retain control over the resources of society. Different groups actually experience society's rules differently, and as a consequence, view society and have not groups differently. Figure 10.2 illustrates differences in perspective between dominant and oppressed or marginalized groups with respect to the nature of society and why some groups fare better than others. The figure helps orient students visually to a major idea of the course: that society operates differently for different groups, and consequently different groups construct opposing explanations for inequality, based on people's lived experiences.

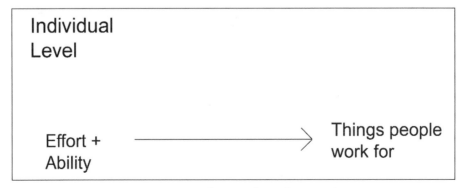

Figure 10.1. How do we explain who gets what?

	Dominant Groups	Oppressed Groups
Nature of society	Fair, open	Unfair, rigged
Nature of have not groups	Lack ambition, effort, culture, language, skills, education	Strong, resourceful, work to advance

Figure 10.2. Different perspectives.

Most Americans analyze who gets what in terms of individual effort and ability only. Figure 10.3 illustrates two additional levels of analysis that explain group differences in status: the institutional level and the cultural level. At the institutional level, one examines both formal and informal or unwritten rules and processes that are used to regulate human behavior. For instance, one can also examine the degree to which any given reward (such as housing or higher education) is actually available to everyone who works for it. At the cultural level, one examines beliefs people have about society and diverse groups, how and by whom those beliefs are encoded, and how and to whom they are transmitted. The relationship between cultural beliefs and individuals, and between cultural beliefs and institutions is reciprocal; both levels influence one another.

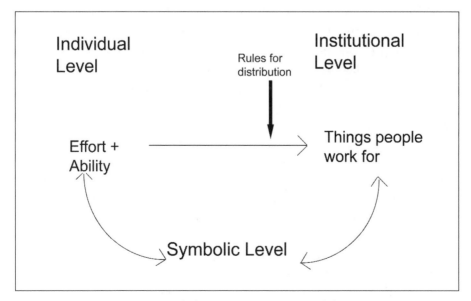

Figure 10.3. Framework for examining institutional discrimination.

When teaching Whites about racism, my main goal is to help them ask and begin to answer questions about racism at the institutional and cultural levels, those levels that people of color generally direct their attention toward to explain and challenge racial disparities. Such analyses are foreign to the way most White people think about racial disparities, and it takes a good deal of practice to be able to think in institutional and cultural terms. As Whites gain practice in doing so, however, they begin to understand (sometimes for the first time) what people of color are saying about racism. Below, I will describe some specific strategies I have used to help students learn to ask and answer questions at the institutional and cultural levels.[2]

Helping White Preservice Teachers Rethink Race

I began the semester by having students describe and discuss some of their beliefs about teaching and about how society works, first in writing, then in small group discussions, addressing questions such as the following. What is proper student behavior in the classroom? What does it mean to be late, and how do you interpret someone who is late? Why do most people live in racially homogeneous neighborhoods? What do you consider to be the greatest works of literature? I also had students fill out a questionnaire examining how much contact they have had with members of other racial groups and social class backgrounds in various areas of their lives, including school, college, work, neighborhood, and church (see Grant & Sleeter, 2011, Chapter One for sample questionnaires).

Students generally approached these tasks puzzled by their obviousness. On the one hand, their beliefs have a transparently "obvious" character, such as the belief that proper classroom behavior consists of students showing respect and interest by attending to the teacher, asking questions politely, obeying, sitting quietly, raising one's hand before speaking, and so forth; or the believe that people live in relatively homogeneous neighborhoods because they prefer to do so. In small group discussions about their beliefs, there was usually so much agreement (especially when groups are all White) that they were unclear why they were asked to do this. On the other hand, the questionnaire about their backgrounds showed the extent to which the great majority had fairly little contact with people of a different background; this, too, had a certain obviousness about it. Some students at this point maintained that they are not prejudiced; others admitted that their beliefs are limited by their backgrounds, though they were not clear to what extent.

I would then tell the class that all of their answers are correct, but also that multiple correct answers, varying by race, culture and other factors, for every question they had been discussing. At this point, I introduced two related but somewhat different ideas that subsequent class sessions developed.

First, all social behavior is culturally constituted, often differently across cultural groups. One example of how something that seems obvious can be viewed differently across cultures is interpretation of time. I would ask students what time they would arrive someplace if told to come at 9:00. Even within an all-White class, students suggest different appropriate arrival times. Someone would inevitably ask whether the event is an appointment or a social gathering, which led to consideration of time as culturally interpreted. I provided examples of correct arrival times in contexts that do not surface in the discussion, such as on an Indian reservation, in Switzerland, or for a Black as opposed to White party. I then discussed the concept of code-switching, emphasizing that they (and every one else) have learned a set of correct cultural codes in their own environment, that the codes they know are not the only correct ones, and that anyone can learn another set of codes if taught.

Second, I suggested that a color line exists, in addition to gender and social class lines, differentiating those who make the rules of society and for whom the rules operate fairly consistently from those who do not make the rules and for whom they do not operate consistently. I would point out that we all see color and that visible differences become important social marks of who belongs on which side of the line. (On some occasions, I have asked White students or other White audiences for a show of hand for who lives in a racially integrated neighborhood. When few hands go up, I ask why White people tend to choose to live in White neighborhoods, since true colorblindness would lead to different results. This question usually catches Whites by surprise.)

The line is socially constructed, although we may associate it with biological features. Over time (and in different cultures), the line may be positioned differently. For example, southeastern Wisconsin (where I taught for over a decade) was a popular destination for eastern and southern European immigrants historically, and some of their descendants were usually students in my class. Sometimes we would discuss whether Italians are White or not; students varied in their responses. Those who were familiar with the history of discrimination against Italians locally would point out that they were not considered White for a long time but generally (although not universally) are now. When Latinos were class members, we discussed whether Latinos are White, which opened up consideration of the importance of visible characteristics, especially to White people, in making this determination, and how visible characteristics feed into racial profiling. These kinds of discussions helped to blur students' assumptions about race as tied to biology, leading them to understand racial lines as socially drawn.

We then would move to consider the idea that education is supposed to pay off equally for everyone. To explore this idea, I would show statistical information illustrating that it actually pays off (in terms of income and employment) differently based on race and sex; data are easily accessible from the U.S. Census Bureau website. Students' main reaction at this point has been that this is not fair, and they began asking why.

I then assigned students to read the book *The Education of a WASP* (Stalvey, 1988), which traces the experience of a White middle-class woman as she relearns how race in America works for African Americans.[3] The book, which is autobiographical, opens with Stalvey's description of her growing up in Milwaukee during the 1940s and 1950s and of her naïve beliefs about the essential fairness and justice of American society. At this point, most of my students could identify with her. The book then chronicles her life and the change in her perspective over a four-year period as she became increasingly involved with struggles within the Black community. She describes how she learned about institutional racism in a variety of areas: housing, schooling, media coverage, job opportunities, and so forth. Over the four years, Stalvey crossed a color line that most White Americans never cross, and she learned first-hand how African Americans experience America, from the other side of a color line that Stalvey earlier had believed did not exist.

When I first assigned the book, I was afraid my White students would find it too offensive, too angry, or even too dated to take seriously. Generally, this was not their reaction, and many of them could not put it down once they start reading it. Overwhelmingly, they would tell me that it is very interesting and eye-opening. Some said it made them cry, some said it was the first textbook they had read cover-to-cover, a few confessed they were not reading assignments for other classes because they want to finish it. Some loaned it to friends and neighbors; one class commented that there will probably be few used copies in the bookstore because this is one book no one would want to sell. One student who had studied about racism in high school, wrote later:

"I must admit now that I have received this education with my eyes and heart closed. For example, I know how Blacks were historically forced into slavery and about the Black inventors who made many contributions for American society....I am sure that I can go on with more historical knowledge, but the point is that even though I have been taught these accounts, I have never experienced any of them. This is because I am White and have never really had any contacts with people outside of my race until after I entered college."

The Education of a WASP provokes a strong reaction from most White readers, as students found themselves emotionally engaged in a struggle against racism for the first time in their lives. The engagement is vicarious but strongly felt. Students of color also found the book worth reading, commenting that it made them think about issues they had not thought deeply about for a while and that it gave them a better idea of how White people think. As one African American student put it, "I knew White people were naïve, but I didn't know they were that naïve."

The book focuses on institutional racism as well as media production of imagery that rationalizes racist actions. It provides a very different template for thinking about race than the European ethnic immigrant experience does. But it also describes one woman's experience, decades ago. Subsequent activities engaged students in examining the same factors the book describes, here and now, focusing on institutional processes and on cultural beliefs and images.

I found two simulations very helpful. The one I used first, because it was the less threatening of the two, was *BaFa BaFa* (Shirts, 1977). In this simulation, the class is divided into two groups in two different rooms where each learns and practices a different culture. After each group has mastered its culture, observers and visitors are exchanged for a few minutes at a time and are encouraged to share with members of their own culture what they saw. The simulation is followed by a discussion. During the simulation itself, which lasts about one hour, contact experiences with the other culture invariably produce a set of stereotypes, antagonisms, and feelings of confusion. Members of each culture rather quickly learn to view theirs as best and most sensible, and they use it as a benchmark against which to judge others negatively. After discussing their reactions to each other, we draw parallels between the simulation and real-life denigration of members of other groups. The example I provided earlier about cultural differences in time orientation is helpful again here. Often, White students commented that this was the first time they experienced feeling left out and confused by encountering a different set of cultural rules, and that now they have a sense of what code-switching means.

The other simulation I used, usually two or three weeks later, was *Star Power* (Shirts, 1969). In this simulation, participants are divided into three groups to play a trading game, the purpose of which (they are told) is to compete in the accumulation of points. The trading game in the simulation is rigged so that one group continues to accumulate more than the rest, but they are led to believe their success is due to their skill. Part way through the simulation, the top group (Squares) is given power to make rules for the rest of the simulation. The Squares invariably use this power to further their own advantages (e.g., they restrict membership, impose taxes, make rules for themselves that differ from rules for everyone else, and sometimes establish a welfare system to keep everyone else playing). The other two groups react in a variety of ways to their powerless position: sometimes they stop playing, usually they find ways to subvert the rules, sometimes they revolt. The discussion that follows the simulation helps participants move from their own particular experiences with the simulation to broader issues of power and social structure. In the discussion, I try to draw from the group as many real-life examples that parallel the simulation as possible. I have also found the simulation helpful in providing the class with a common vocabulary and set of experiences I can use throughout the semester to make points (such as, Why might this set of parents be behaving like Triangles? What power relations might they be reacting to?) Typically students need help connecting both simulations to racial issues around them; some draw parallels easily, but others have needed to walk them through specific examples (such as race relations in the university) before they start to make connections.

Invariably, a few students dismissed the book as outdated and the simulations as unreal. Therefore, we also investigated some aspects of racism ourselves, locally. We used the framework in Figure 10.3 to generate questions, brainstorming questions one could ask at each of the three levels of analysis (I instructed students to focus on the institutional or cultural levels). For example, they could interview a realtor to find out if color is taken into account when selling a house, investigate whether there is a relationship between racial composition of neighborhoods and accessibility of voting places, ask university students of color why students at the university are disproportionately White, and so forth.

For example, in one class a White student interviewed a family friend who is a realtor. This individual explained to her that he does not care who he sells a house to, but the neighbors often do, believing that Blacks do not keep up their houses and contribute to neighborhood crime. Therefore, like the respondents to Bonilla-Silva's (2010) questions, although he personally does not agree with this view, he honors it. Another student telephoned several local industries and banks to find out how many people of color they had hired in management positions. Most of the individuals he tried to talk to refused to answer his questions or gave him a runaround; he interpreted their refusal to discuss this with him as indication that few if any people of color occupied management positions. Still another student asked a Black university student about obstacles he encountered getting into college and was told that a major one was money. The part-time jobs that paid most were located in the suburbs (near where this White student lived), too far away from him and most other Blacks to be accessible. The White student then realized that he held a part-time job that the Black student did not have access to. Yet another student counted the racial representation of people on cereal boxes, then shared his findings with an African American friend. She found his figures interesting, but suggested things that were more important, from her perspective, such as the preponderance of White women used to portray beauty.

I encouraged students to share what they find out. I also supplemented their sharing with a barrage of statistical information on distribution of income across racial lines, unemployment, housing discrimination, life expectancy, access to health insurance, and so forth. By then, students are usually willing to listen to me, especially if their own personal investigations validated the idea that society's rules operate differently for people of color than they do for Whites, just as Stalvey found out.

I also showed a video of Dr. Charles King talking about racism on the Phil Donahue show several years ago. This particular video is no longer available, but one can locate other excellent films and videos that expand on the workings of racism (for a list of excellent resources, see nameorg.org/resources/teaching-resources/videos/name-film-festival). In the videotape, Dr. King (who was Black) deliberately showed his anger and impatience toward White racism and White denials of racism, attempting to direct viewers away from blaming Blacks for their condition toward examining the racist structures that are responsible for the condition in which Blacks find themselves. Since Dr. King did not mince words with the audience and shows his emotion, most Whites found the video offensive unless they had been prepared for it. Having prepared students with the above activities, most are able to listen to him fairly non-defensively. In a follow-up discussion, one of the main points I stressed was the difficulty we as Whites experience listening to people of color talking honestly about racism, but we have a need to listen nonetheless in order to learn, just as Stalvey did.

In May of 1992, I showed a class Dr. King's videotape shortly after the riots in Los Angeles following the acquittal of White police officers accused of police brutality and after we had completed the rest of the activities above. Many class members told me that the idea of racism finally made sense: they were for the first time able to see what people of color were angry about. The combination of the book, the class activities, and the videotape—so very directly connected to a current issue—finally came together.

In Wisconsin, I taught a two-course sequence in Multicultural Education; this chapter describes only the beginning of that sequence. In subsequent sessions we examined how schools institutionalize racism, as well as the institutionalization of classism and sexism, and then explore things they can do differently. I also direct students to find out more about children and youth whose background differs from their own, from people of the children's own background, including community members, teachers, and scholars. (White preservice students are often very resistant to seeking information from anyone other than teachers they encounter, the great majority of whom are White.)

I also tried to help students move beyond their understanding of sexism, heterosexism, and classism as matters of individual stereotyping. Discussion of these areas is beyond the scope of this chapter, but I will note that most students have been quite resistant to examining institutional sexism or the social-class structure outside the school itself. To many of them, questioning the class structure sounds like what they call "socialism" or "communism," which they have been trained to regard as anti-American. Questioning sexism leads to an analysis of family roles and structures; young women who are preoccupied with establishing their own families resist this tenaciously. These forms of resistance need to be addressed seriously in ways that acknowledge and build on what students know and value, while at the same time opening up alternative analytical frameworks and points of view.

Teaching Whites about Racism

I have found the processes described above to be fairly effective, although they do antagonize a few students to a point where some drop out. I judge its effectiveness based on connections students make in papers and class discussions, and on their receptivity to ideas that build upon this foundation over the two-course sequence. I believe the approach has been effective with many students for several reasons.

First, having students articulate some of their own beliefs, and then attempting to validate that what they know is correct for themselves but at the same time not correct for all Americans, defuses some resistance. All of us become angry and defensive when told our experience is wrong; we are much more receptive when one acknowledges what we experienced when we experienced, even if others have had substantially different experiences. While it is difficult for many people to accept that there are multiple perspectives and multiple experiences, it is even more difficult for an individual to accept that she or he is completely wrong. Multicultural education is about multiple realities, not about one "correct" reality. The point is to seek understanding across differences, rather that agreement with one point of view.

Second, directing students' attention toward barriers to access, rather than characteristics of people of color, which is where Whites normally direct their attention, and encouraging them to investigate some barriers for themselves, helps students understand disparities they see, but in a new light. Stereotypes, which arise from the consequences of barriers, become justification to the barriers. The books, the simulations, and their own investigations help to reinforce this point and help keep their attention directed toward barriers to access. A student's response to *The Education of a WASP* illustrates: "We learned that the Black people learn at a very early age just where their place in society is, and the consequences for stepping over that line. Their reactions are a form of self preservation." Later explorations of strengths and resources among oppressed groups (such as community self-help groups, or linguistic resources in one's first language or dialect, upon which a second language or dialect can be built), contrast this view with the cultural deficiency view.

Third, trying to involve students actively in constructing a sense of how discrimination works, drawing ideas out of their experience with the simulations and their investigations, is much more effective as a teaching ad learn process, than imposing my ideas on students. Again, this approach validates their ability to construct for themselves an understanding of how society works, but it introduces a different set of questions and materials on which to draw than most have used previously.

The approach I have described is not a panacea. I strongly suspect that many White students continue to regard it as an academic exercise, giving me what I want but not taking it very seriously. Some who are actively interested and engaged at the time shift their attention to other things later on in their preservice program; Whites have the luxury of being able to forget about racism, and my students are no exception. A variation of the forgetfulness is that many students learn the vocabulary I have used to examine racism without connecting it with much in their own lives; instead they revert to blaming "cultural deficiencies" of students of color when they get into schools and are confronted with behavior they do not really understand. White students also frequently react by wanting to solve racism, taking a "savior" stance, which continually needs to be confronted and problematized with the idea of learning to become an ally in a long-term struggle.

However, I also believe that the emotional impact of the combination of teaching processes described here, interpreted through a provided vocabulary and set of concepts, equip many White preservice students with a foundation on which they can continue to rethink how racism works and their own participation in racist institutions. (Contact I have had with some former students who are now teaching supports this belief.) As a student concluded in a paper: "After having some exposure to the harsher realities of life, I now hope that I will not be as blind to them as I was before, and that my education never stops, for my sake and the sake of others."

Notes

1. In this chapter, I focus on race and racism rather than culture and cultural identity. As a teacher educator, I have also given considerable attention to helping White preservice teachers understand themselves as cultural beings, a process that is highly supported by the professional literature. However, that process is not the focus of this chapter.

2. At the time of the updating of this chapter, I am retired and no longer teaching courses in teacher preparation. As a result, I describe the process in the past rather than present tense.
3. This particular book worked exceptionally well for the time and place in which I was teaching when I taught in Wisconsin. Many books get at the same ideas; instructors need to choose readings that open up the workings of institutional racism in ways that their own students can relate to.

11

Researching Successful Efforts in Teacher Education to Diversify Teachers

With H. Richard Milner, IV[1]

Introduction: A Demographic Urgency

The cultural, gendered, racial, ethnic, socioeconomic, and linguistic background of teachers is an important issue because research suggests that an overwhelmingly White teaching force cannot meet the needs of increasingly diverse P–12 students (Gay & Howard, 2000; Milner, 2006; Sleeter, 2001b). The demographic divide imperative (Banks, 2003)—what we are calling a demographic urgency—is present in an important body of literature that makes a case for the preparation of teachers for the diversity they will face (cf. Gay & Howard, 2000; Sleeter, 2008; Zumwalt & Craig, 2005). Emphases on demographics in teacher education and subsequently P–12 operate on at least two levels: (1) teachers in teacher education programs (who are mainly White and female) need to be (better) prepared to meet the needs of racially and ethnically diverse learners; and (2) teacher education programs need to be more persistent and innovative in selecting, recruiting, and inducting a more diverse teaching force.[2]

While available teacher education demographic data suggest that the teaching force is diversifying slightly, the rate and consistency of its diversification remains a serious problem. Almost a decade ago, analyzing statistics from the U.S. Department of Education, Gay and Howard (2000) found that

> 86% of all elementary and secondary teachers are European Americans. The number of African American teachers has declined from a high of 12% in 1970 to 7% in 1998. The number of Latino and Asian/Pacific Islander American teachers is increasing slightly, but the percentages are still very small (approximately 5% and 1% respectively). Native Americans comprise less than 1% of the national teaching force. (pp. 1–2)

The demographics of teachers between 2003 and 2004 are captured in Table 11.1 below. The data represent the most current statistics available at the time of this review. As it shows, there has been fairly little change in the demographics of the teaching force over the last decade.

Table 11.1. Teaching Demographics in Public Elementary and Secondary Schools (in percent)

	Elementary	Secondary
White	81.6	84.2
Black	8.8	7.5
Hispanic	7.0	5.5
Asian	1.3	1.3
Pacific Islander	0.2	0.2
American Indian/Alaska Native	0.4	0.6
More than One Race	0.7	0.7

Source: U.S. Department of Education (2007)

Value of Teachers of Color [3]

There are at least two lines of thinking regarding the diversification of the teaching force. These lines of thinking are not mutually exclusive—both are important. One line of thinking suggests that the real emphasis should be placed on better preparation of teachers, regardless of their racial and ethnic background, for the students they will face. This line of thinking sometimes builds on the compelling qualitative research of Ladson-Billings (1994) who found that teachers from any racial and ethnic background could learn to be successful pedagogues of African American students. In this sense, what teachers know and have the skills to learn about themselves, their students, the contexts in which they teach, their curriculum development, and their teaching matter more than teachers' racial and ethnic backgrounds. Another line of thinking suggests working to recruit and retain teachers of color for the benefit of the diverse students teachers will encounter. Following the latter line of thinking, cultural and racial congruence and incongruence (Irvine, 2003) are often used as frames to discuss the complexities embedded in the urgency to prepare teachers to meet the needs of *all* students. Because White teachers and students of color often possess different racialized and cultural experiences and repertoires of knowledge and knowing both inside and outside the classroom, racial and cultural incongruence may serve as a roadblock for academic and social success in the classroom (Foster, 1997; Irvine, 2003; Nieto, 2000).

For instance, research suggests that teachers of color can have a positive influence on the achievement among students of color, especially when teachers and students share the same racial background (Irvine, 2003; Nieto, 1999). Irvine (2003) reported on the research of Meier, Stewart, and England (1989) who investigated the impact of African American educators on African American students' success and found that in contexts with high percentages of African American teachers: "fewer African American students were placed in special education classes. Fewer African Americans were suspended or expelled. More African Americans were placed in gifted and talented programs. [And] more African Americans graduated from high school" (p. 54).

Teachers of color can be invaluable for student success in the classroom (Siddle-Walker, 2000) because they can serve as role models for students (Cole, 1986; Milner & Howard, 2004; Villegas & Clewell, 1998) and understand and respect the cultural knowledge students possess, using this knowledge as a foundation for their teaching practices (Irvine, 1988; Siddle-Walker, 2000). In their observations on why teachers of color are needed Villegas and Clewell (1998) wrote:

> If children do not see adults of color in professional roles in schools and instead see them overrepresented in the ranks of non-professional workers, they are taught implicitly that

White people are better suited than racial/ethnic minorities to hold positions of authority in our society. (p. 121)

Pang and Gibson (2001) maintained that "Black educators are far more than physical role models…they bring diverse family histories, value orientations, and experiences to students in the classroom, attributes often not found in textbooks or viewpoints often omitted" (pp. 260–61). Teachers of color are valuable, not only because students of color benefit, but all students can benefit from what the teachers bring into the learning environment. Villegas and Clewell (1998) also stressed how important it is for White students to have teachers of color: "By seeing people of color in professional roles, White youngsters are helped to dispel myths of racial inferiority and incompetence that many have come to internalize about people of color" (pp. 121–22).

Building from her research as well as that of others, Irvine (2003) formulated three central propositions related to the importance of a diversified teacher force. She explained that teachers of color (1) serve as "cultural translators" (p. 55) in the classroom, (2) have high expectations for their students, they are reliable mentors for their students and advocate for them, and (3) provide a culturally based teaching approach in the classroom. Teachers of color are likely to deeply understand students of color and their cultural references because teachers of color experience life outside of the classroom in ways similar to many of their students. Teachers understand some of the problems students face because they grapple with similar issues with their own children. In terms of building and establishing racial and cultural knowledge about their students, teachers of color sometimes attend the same church as their students, frequent the same beauty and barber salons (also see Siddle-Walker, 2000), and understand the structural challenges that their students face such as being followed around in a department store due to their racial and ethnic background. These experiences outside of the classroom allow teachers to build on and from these experiences for opportunities to connect and learn in the classroom. This allows teachers to empathize with, not pity, their students (McAllister & Irvine, 2002). Thus, students do not want to let their teachers down because the teachers are concerned for the students (Foster, 1997), a concern that has been described as *other mothering* (Collins, 1990). The teachers want for their students the best—just as they would want for their own biological children.

We also see teacher race and ethnicity as an indicator of the worldviews available within any school's professional teaching corps. The more homogenous the teachers, the more homogenous the worldviews that are likely to be used to analyze teaching and student needs, which is particularly problematic when those world-views and the experiences underlying them diverge from those of students.

It is important to note that while we believe that diversifying the teaching force is a critical component to student success, we are not asserting that such diversification is a panacea for increasing student achievement and student-learning opportunities. Rather, we understand that teachers operate within and through systems and institutions that shape their work with students. A teacher's racial or ethnic background does not determine a teacher's ideology, shared background with a particular group of students, or ability to teach. Further, the systemic and institutional support or lack thereof that teachers receive can sometimes serve as roadblocks for teachers of color in their work with students.

Buendia, Gitlin, and Doumbia's (2003) research highlights tensions between established discourses in a context and the pedagogical, as well as philosophical, beliefs teachers of color may bring. In their study, the discourse in the school context carried "deficit views of immigrant students" (p. 315). Teachers believed that the immigrant students needed to be "socialized…into things like being responsible…[and] how to handle all of the freedom" (p. 302) in the new context. This ingrained discourse seemed to convey the message that the students did not bring intellectual and social assets and capital to the learning environment. In that context, the teachers of color struggled to develop and implement curricular and pedagogical strategies that, from their experiences, could more appropriately meet the needs of English-language learners—in opposition to the permeating dominant discourse in the school. Although teachers of color may find racial and cultural conditions and experiences appropriate and relevant because of their personal experiences (for instance, with racism and sexism), the pervasive (and White) belief systems, goals, missions, and discourses of the school can circumvent highly capable teachers' desires to transform the curriculum. Buendia, Gitlin, and Doumbia declared that "the present-day contexts of schools may push critically minded teachers of color in ways that undermine their desires" (p. 317).

Still, the research on the value of diversifying the teaching force is too compelling to ignore the potential benefits for students of color and all students. Thus, because of its value, in addition to preparing all teachers for diverse students, it is urgent that attention be given to diversifying the teaching force itself. In what follows, we review programs to recruit and prepare teachers of color. We then critically examine the nature of research reported on such programs, and sketch out what a research agenda might look like to advance the area. We conclude with implications for policy, practice, and research.

Programs to Recruit and Prepare Teachers of Color[4]

Programs that have been designed to recruit and prepare teachers of color usually take into account at least some of the following factors related to the teaching workforce and reasons why there are relatively few teachers of color. (1) Most teachers prefer to teach close to home; "growing your own" teachers of color has been recommended as a promising strategy for that reason (Boyd, Lankford, Loeb & Wyckoff, 2005). (2) At the P–12 levels, students of color are sometimes not well prepared for higher education, nor do they receive much guidance about navigating into higher education. (3) Related, teacher testing disproportionately washes out teachers of color (Alberts, 2002). (4) Research focusing on Black teachers suggests that, while teaching used to be seen as a profession to gain entry into the middle class, with the increase in job prospects, university students of color are often selecting different careers instead (Foster, 1997; Milner & Howard, 2004; Zumwalt & Craig, 2005). (5) Some university students of color are put off by the Whiteness and irrelevance of teacher education programs they see.

We divided programs we review into two categories: those that bring candidates of color into and through existing teacher education programs, and those that tailor teacher education programs specifically for racially and ethnically diverse working adults. We began by seeking published journal articles or book chapters that had substantive descriptions, if not actual empirical studies, about specific programs; we excluded those in which descriptions were very brief (such as one page). We searched several databases (such as ERIC), not limiting our search to any particular years or journals. To keep our review manageable, we limited it in three ways. First, we limited the review to preservice level programs, although we recognize that there are also efforts to retain teachers of color at the professional development level. Second, we limited it to programs in the United States, although we recognize that similar efforts are taking place elsewhere (c.f., Solomon, 1997; Wang, 2001). Third, we limited it to programs that have been intentionally designed to diversify who goes into teaching, rather than including those with relatively diverse student populations achieved by virtue of location.

Bringing candidates of color into and through existing teacher education programs

Many programs attempt to build the pipeline of potential teacher candidates of color either prior to or while they are in the university. Such programs do not attempt to change teacher education programs but rather to build support systems into, around, and through them. Pipeline programs work with youth to demystify higher education and increase the likelihood that youth will be prepared academically for college, while also exposing them to experiences that may attract them into teaching. Programs to support university students of color typically offer financial and academic support, as well as social and cultural support to combat alienation on predominantly White campuses.

Pipeline programs. Pipeline programs involve collaboration between university-based teacher education programs and feeder institutions, mainly secondary schools. Magnet high school programs for potential teachers of color are an intensive kind of pipeline program that have been implemented in a few cities. For example, the Teaching Professions Program at Coolidge High School in Washington, D.C., was designed to interest African American students in teaching (Hunter-Boykin, 1992), and the Socratic Institute at Riverside High School was designed in collaboration with the University of Texas at El Paso to interest Latino students in teaching (Oliva & Staudt, 2003, 2004). Both programs, which serve grades 9–12, recruit academically capable students, add coursework related to teaching (such as Orientation to Teaching) to their academic curriculum, and involve participants in tutoring younger children. As of 1992, the Teaching Professions Program had about 130 students, with a fairly high retention rate; all 15 graduates that year had been accepted into universities (Hunter-Boykin, 1992). The more recent Socratic Institute reported having 82 students in 2004, 98% of whom were Latino; none had yet reached graduation (Oliva & Staudt, 2004).

Less intensive pipeline programs to build interest in teaching typically include activities such as bringing secondary students onto the college campus, strengthening their academic skills, and involving them in tutoring younger children. Project FUTURE at Texas Tech University works with cohorts of students from sixth grade through their first year of college. Between 2005 and 2006, 440 students, over 80% of whom were of color, participated. Activities include a day-long conference on the university campus, other events on campus throughout the school year, and mentoring by a Texas Tech student (Stevens, Agnello, Ramirez, Marbley, & Hamman, 2007). Much smaller projects with high school students included the Teacher Track Project at California State University at Fullerton (Yopp, Yopp, & Taylor, 1992) and "Project: I Teach" at the University of Texas at San Antonio (Zapata, 1988).

Connecting prospective teachers of color with excellent mentors appears to be a critical component to success. Padak, Stadulis, Barton, Meadows, and Padak (1994) described the results of mentoring in the Urban Teachers Project that was designed to recruit future urban teachers. The partnership (which still exists) represented participation of school personnel, Kent State University, and the project staff. Like the programs above, this one supported high school students interested in education and urban teaching with a Saturday program to assist students with building knowledge about education and teaching and also in-school academic support through tutoring. A third component of support was mentoring, which was the main focus of the study. The authors summarized the success of the mentoring component of the project stating:

> The development and maintenance of mentoring relationships may offer a partial solution to the problem of encouraging talented minority students to become teachers in urban settings. Our experience suggests that mentoring focused on professional socialization can be successful while future teachers are still in high school. Becoming a well-prepared and committed teacher involves professional socialization…mentor teachers can effectively support students' [mentees'] transition into college and ultimately into the teaching profession. (p. 351)

Programs to support university students of color. Programs designed to support university students of color who may be interested in completing teacher certification typically offer scholarships (often with the expectation that graduates will teach in local schools) and additional academic and cultural support. The nature of the support differs somewhat depending on whether the program targets mainly traditional-age students or working adults.

The University of Texas at San Antonio, in collaboration with San Antonio College, developed the Academy for Teaching Excellence, a large, comprehensive program to support Latino college students interested in becoming teachers. A central feature is the Teacher Academic Learning Community, which recruits mainly Latino freshmen, then offers them summer bridging and other academic support (particularly for passing academic proficiency exams), personal support (such as cultural seminars and life-planning assistance), and professional support (such as mentoring in field experiences). As of 2006, about 750 students, mostly Latino, had participated, with a very high retention rate (Flores, Clark, Claeys, & Villarreal, 2007). Hopi Teachers for Hopi Schools, which involved collaboration between Northern Arizona University and the Hopi Nation, one of twenty similar projects funded by the Office of Indian Education, served two cohorts of about twenty students each between 2000 and 2006. In addition to financial support, it offered academic advising, tutoring, monthly meetings, and workshops designed to help participants negotiate challenges at the university. As of 2006, it had certified thirty-eight Hopi teachers (White, Bedonie, de Groat, Lockard, & Honani, 2007).

The Freshman/Sophomore Minority Teachers Grant Program involved collaboration among a university and two community colleges in Arkansas to help

African American students navigate the transition from a community college to a four-year institution and an education major. Students were supported through stipends, mentoring, and various community-building activities (Holmes & Couch, 1997). Similarly, the Career Opportunity Program 2000 in Des Moines, Iowa, involved collaboration between a school district, a community college, and a private four-year college; most of its students were non-traditional-age African Americans. Although about 130 students participated, as of 1998 only 12 had completed the program, probably due to the cost of tuition and the traditional nature of the four-year college (Hall Mark, 1998). Project TEAM (Transformative Educational Achievement Model) at Indiana University, which began in 1996, successfully served cohorts of fifteen to twenty students of color per year, beginning with the freshman year. In addition to financial support, a key feature of this program was its honors seminar that addressed concerns of students of color that are often ignored in predominantly White programs, such as how teachers of color can negotiate predominantly White schools (Bennett, 2002; Bennett, Cole, & Thompson, 2000). Many fairly small programs incorporate features of some of the larger programs described above but support fewer than a dozen students at any given time. Project TEACH, which involved collaboration among a four-year college, a community-based organization, and a school district, brought in one or two students of color per year for twelve years, supporting the education and certification of eighteen teachers of color (Irizarry, 2007). A collaborative effort between the Marietta City School District in Georgia and Kennesaw State College brought in two new freshmen per year, assisting a total of seven scholars of color with completing their degrees in education (Fielder, 1996).

The importance of linking identities of students of color with teaching and academic research cannot be underestimated. For example, Dillard (1994) reported on an eight-week summer research institute, Opening Doors: The Worlds of Graduate Study for Minority Students in Education, that occurred summer of 1992. She planned and directed the institute for twenty-one undergraduate students of color interested in careers in education and graduate school. Results pointed to the importance of teacher identity and the maintenance of teachers' ethnic identities in particular. The idea that programs in education and also educational contexts expect teachers to divorce themselves from their racial and ethnic identities was problematized and used as a site of critique and discussion in the institute.

Programs aimed toward working adults take into account not only ethnic identity and cultural support but also pragmatic concerns associated with adults' need to continue to work and barriers adults may experience in higher education institutions.

Two California State University Teacher Diversity Projects that were described in published articles served paraprofessionals, most of whom were Latino and bilingual, and whose education levels ranged from high school through university graduates. At California State University at San Bernardino, the Excellence and Equity in Teaching Project collaborated with community colleges. Participants were selected based partly on their commitment to teaching. Academic counselors monitored their progress through coursework and helped them navigate the transfer from the community college to the CSU campus. Support groups at the community colleges offered academic and cultural support. As of 1996, the project had forty participants (Gutiérrez, 1992; Gutiérrez & Murphy, 1996).

Similarly, the Teacher Track Project at California State University at Fullerton, in collaboration with two community colleges and three school districts, recruited and supported instructional aides, most of whom were Latinos and some of whom were credentialed teachers from other countries. Support included advisement on course taking, monthly meetings, small financial stipends, and occasional special events such as guest speakers. At the time of writing, sixty-six instructional aides were involved (Yopp, Yopp, & Taylor, 1992). Newcomers Entering Teaching involves collaboration between the University of Southern Maine and the Portland, Maine, public schools to help immigrant university-educated adults, most of whom had been teachers in their home countries, to complete the university's certification program. The program helps them navigate university bureaucracies, develop their use of academic English, prepare for the GRE, and meet entry requirements of the certification program. It also offers financial help to those who need it and an internship during the final semester. At the time of writing, six immigrant teachers had completed the program (Ross, 2001).

In summary, programs that are designed to bring candidates of color into and through teacher education tend to share several features. They build an interest among students of color in a teaching career, often taking steps to link students' racial or ethnic identities with teaching, such as by connecting them with mentor teachers from their same background or engaging students in projects that are culturally relevant to them. Such programs also offer academic support as well as support navigating college requirements. Programs aimed toward secondary education students attempt to demystify college by bringing students to the college campus; programs aimed toward college students offer scholarships as well as any other support that will enable them to successfully enter and succeed within the teacher education program.

Redesigning teacher education programs

Ultimately, we believe that teacher education programs themselves should be transformed to attract, welcome, and prepare diverse teachers. Implicitly, most programs are designed mainly with traditional-age White students in mind, a reality that may be invisible to those in such programs but is visible to those who sense not belonging. In Agee's (2004) study, she explained that "the teacher education texts used in the course made recommendations for using diverse texts or teaching diverse students based on the assumption that preservice teachers are White" (p. 749). This assumption could alienate preservice teachers of color. What about the curricular and instructional needs of Asian or Latino teachers, for instance?

The Multilingual/Multicultural Teacher Preparation Center (M/M Center) in the Bilingual/Multicultural Department at Sacramento State University, which is more than twenty years old, is an excellent example of a program designed around student diversity. About 75% of its candidates are of color and most are bilingual, a mix the program attracts because of its focus, its very diverse faculty, and its commitment to working with communities of color and social justice. Outsiders to California may assume that teacher education programs in California are routinely diverse, but such is not the case. Wong and colleagues (2007) explain, "Race-conscious...and language-conscious policy-making and program development characterize the program's history and current operations" (p. 9). The M/M Center actively recruits, advises, and mentors undergraduates of color on its campus, and over time has developed a network of outreach into schools serving students of color. Its curriculum features multicultural content and the application of theory into practice through extensive field experiences in schools serving low-income and culturally and linguistically diverse students and English-language learners.

Unlike the M/M Center, most redesigned university teacher education programs are alternative versions of existing traditional programs, reworked to serve adults who wish to become teachers—paraprofessionals or other noncertified school district employees, emergency certified teachers, and career-changers—but who generally cannot stop working to return to college.[5] In addition, such programs often capitalize on experiences that adults who are already working in classrooms have. While a higher percentage of teachers of color than White teachers are certified through some kind of alternative program (Shen, 1998), the fact that a program is "alternative" does not necessarily mean that it was designed to appeal to prospective teachers of color. For example, about 75% of new teachers certified through Teach for America (TFA) are "Caucasian, middle-class, female, monolingual English speakers" (Veltri, 2008, p. 522); while TFA attracts a somewhat more diverse population than many other teacher education programs, we do not see it as designed specifically to recruit and prepare a diverse population. Similarly, some urban alternative programs (such as one operated by Los Angeles Unified School District) have quite diverse populations due to location. Because non-university alternatives have been reviewed elsewhere (c.f., Zeichner & Conklin, 2005) and because they tend not to present themselves as having been designed explicitly to diversify the teaching population, we do not review them here.

The DeWitt Wallace–Reader's Digest Fund launched Pathways into Teaching Careers, the largest cluster of such programs, in 1989; eventually there were forty-one sites around the United States. Pathways programs shared several features: (1) they involved partnership between a teacher education institution and local school districts; (2) partnering districts actively helped to recruit and select participants; (3) the selection process combined traditional and nontraditional criteria (such as commitment to teaching in urban schools); (4) the teacher education curriculum was modified to meet participants' needs; and (5) the program offered a system of academic support, social support, and financial support (Clewell & Villegas, 1999). Several Pathways programs have been described in published articles.

The Pathways program at Armstrong Atlantic State University (in collaboration with Savannah State University and Savannah-Chatham County Public Schools) was developed to respond to the immense need for teachers of color in Georgia. Designed mainly for paraprofessionals, it successfully certified about ninety African American teachers (Lau, Dandy, & Hoffman, 2007). Dandy (1998) proposed targeting the paraprofessional pool including "teaching assistants, clerks, and other school employees with or without baccalaureate degrees" (p. 89). A central focus, however, was the recruitment of these individuals who actually live and work in the community of students being taught. The success of the program was credited to (1) strong collaboration between local schools and the universities involved; (2) leadership by university representatives committed to the objectives of the program; (3) program standards that "begin with a strategic selection process and provide financial, emotional, and academic support" (p. 101); and (4) curricular modification.

Other Pathways programs made use of similar ideas. The program at Norfolk State University, also designed for paraprofessionals, had certified sixty teachers as of 1997 (Littleton, 1998). The Alternative Pathways to Teaching Program at Wayne State University served mainly noncertified school district employees and career-changers. A track of that program, funded partially by the National Science Foundation, certifies minority math and science teachers who already have a degree. At the time of writing, forty-one candidates (mainly African American) had either completed or were about to complete it (Cavallo, Ferreira, & Roberts, 2005). "Project 29" at the University of Illinois at Chicago was designed to prepare bilingual teachers for Chicago Public Schools. Its name was taken from a provisional teaching certificate (Type 29) that was about to expire. Although it began as a Pathways program, partly because one of its co-directors became dean and the other became a full-time faculty member, it became institutionalized within the college where it has influenced other teacher education programs. As of 2006, Project 29 had produced 145 teachers, three-fourths of whom are Latino (Sakash & Chou, 2007).

Many other colleges and universities have had alternative programs with similar characteristics to Pathways programs. Two that have been in existence since the mid-1990s and have certified hundreds of teachers, the majority of whom are teachers of color, are the Latino Teacher Project (now called the Latino and Language Minority Teacher Projects) in Los Angeles and the Metropolitan Milwaukee Teacher Education Program. The Latino Teacher Project, established through a partnership among four higher education institutions, three school districts, the county office of education, and labor unions representing paraprofessionals, certifies bilingual teachers for southern California schools. The project first selects schools that have bilingual paraprofessionals and a commitment to working with the project; the schools then nominate paraprofessionals who are already bilingual and committed to becoming certified bilingual teachers. The curriculum is much the same as it is for the traditional university program but made more accessible to participants primarily by scheduling and by allowing participants to student teach in their own classrooms. The project offers financial, academic, and social support (e.g., grouping participants into cohorts, assigning on-site faculty mentors, and providing regular seminars) (Genzuk & Baca, 1998).

The Metropolitan Milwaukee Teacher Education Program was established through collaboration between Milwaukee Public Schools, the teachers union, and the University of Wisconsin at Milwaukee. Using a structured interview and observing candidates working with urban children over a summer, program faculty select candidates on the basis of their perceived ability to succeed in urban schools. Unlike most other programs we review, this one expects participants to pay the $10,000 program fee; assistance is available for those in need. Also unlike most other programs, this one is not only classroom based but also designed and staffed mainly by outstanding urban teachers. Participants teach in their own classroom under the guidance of veteran teachers. Supporting classes and workshops focus on expectations for teachers working in the district; the curriculum, which is aligned with state standards, was developed by urban teachers. The only full-time faculty members who teach in the program are outstanding classroom teachers who are on leave. A separate group of assessors assess participants' classroom performance; those who demonstrate that their students are learning are recommended for certification (K–9, with a bilingual endorsement option), and those who do not are dropped from the program. Completers earn licensure but no college credits or degrees (Haberman, 2001).

Many other small and more temporary programs have also existed. Elementary Certification for Ethnic Colleagues for the Elementary School (EC3) in Wisconsin was created through collaboration between two universities and a local school district, mainly for adult career-changers. The curriculum was adapted from that of both universities, with courses meeting during the evenings; stipends supported students during full-time student teaching. The program successfully certified three cohorts of teachers of color, mainly African Americans (Shade, Boe, Garner, & New, 1998). Similarly, the LeMoyne-Owen Teacher Education Program in Tennessee was designed for adult career-changers through collaboration with four school systems, a local Head Start, private day care facilities, and local businesses. Classes were held in evenings and on weekends, and financial support was available during the student-teaching semester. The program also offered tutorial services, and workshops addressing needs such as test preparation and resume preparation. As of 1995, it had certified seventy-five teachers of color (Love & Greer, 1995). The Teacher Opportunity Program in Kentucky was formed through collaboration between a university and a school district. It compressed coursework from the traditional teacher education program, and it included intense fieldwork in which candidates were hired as teaching assistants; additional scholarship funds were located for candidates who needed them. Over a three-year period, the program certified twenty-two teachers of color (Brennan & Bliss, 1998). The Teacher Early Entry Paraprofessional training program in Texas was designed to assist bilingual paraprofessionals who had completed two years of college in finishing their degree and teacher certification. Participants were placed as interns with experienced classroom teachers and then offered university classes in evenings and on weekends (Torres-Karna & Krustchinsky, 1998).

Table 11.2 summarizes key features programs share in relationship to partnerships between universities and school districts that serve students of color, selection criteria into teacher education programs, support students are offered, features of coursework and field experiences, and ways of linking students' racial and ethnic identities with teaching.

An important consideration that captures our attention is that while some programs we reviewed were temporary, others became institutionalized, producing hundreds of teachers. From our perspective, they illustrate that it is possible to redesign university-based teacher education, working in collaboration with school districts, to substantially diversify the teaching population.

Table 11.2. Common Features Programs Share

Dimension of Teacher Ed. Program	Common Features
Partnership between university program and school districts that serve students of color	• Candidates recruited through partnership • Partnership develops school placements, recruits teacher mentors • Districts hire interns if possible • Districts hire graduates of program
Selection into the program	• Traditional academic criteria • Ability, interest, experience working with children or youth of color
Student support	• Academic: preparation for tests, intensive work in other academic skills as needed; navigation through college requirements and transfer requirements • Financial: scholarships, stipends common; programs for adults assume candidates need income while earning teaching credential • Personal: life planning as needed • Cultural: activities, seminars that acknowledge and build on candidates' cultural backgrounds in relationship to teaching
Coursework	• Accessibility: scheduling and location tailored to working adults • Relevance: builds on knowledge and experiences candidates already have
Fieldwork	• Acknowledges candidates' experience • Paraprofessionals student teach in own classroom • Paid internships where possible
Link student identity with teaching	• Mentors who are teachers of color • Culturally relevant projects, curriculum that uses scholarship by educators/researchers of color • Significant proportion of teacher education faculty are of color

Nature of the Research

Programs designed to recruit and prepare teachers of color have been in existence for a long time but are not well researched and consequently not well known. Thus, successful efforts as well as challenges that programs face are not reported very much in journal articles, which makes it difficult to draw definitive conclusions about the nature, structure, and progress of such work. We examined the nature of research that has been done on the programs above. Three categories of research emerged: narrative descriptions written by those who participated in running a program, internal evaluations by those working in a program, and external evaluations.

Program description only

About one-third of the programs we reviewed report only program descriptions, narrated by someone working in the program (Cavallo, Ferreira, & Roberts, 2005; Fielder, 1996; Genzuk & Baca, 1998; Gutierrez, 1992; Holmes & Couch, 1997; Littleton, 1998; Love & Greer, 1995; Ross, 2001; Shade, Boe, Garner & New, 1998; Torres-Karna & Krustchinsky, 1998). One might classify these loosely as narrative research, in that they offer "insider stories" by those involved with specific programs, providing testimonial that such programs are possible. For the most part, these narratives are contextualized within conceptual frameworks that help readers interpret the program. However, they suffer limitations common to insider stories: selective perception by virtue of the writer being immersed in a program one often has had to fight for, and in some cases an absence of data (such as numbers of program completers) that would help readers make their own analysis. Moreover, such narratives usually fail to critique their own programs in ways that can provide insight into the pervasive struggles and mistakes that shape them.

Internal program evaluations

About two-thirds of the programs reported not only descriptions but also internal evaluations. The great majority used data gathered through interviews and/or surveys with program participants, either while they were in the program or shortly after completing it, to find out how well the program worked for them, how it addressed their needs, and any other information that might help to strengthen the program. For example, Lau, Dandy, and Hoffman (2007) surveyed graduates of the Pathways program at Armstrong Atlantic State University to identify factors that led to its high retention rate during the program and after the teachers were hired. Yopp, Yopp, & Taylor (1992) surveyed instructional aides in the Teacher Track Project to find out how it had addressed their needs, looking particularly at needs of reentry women who felt insecure about their academic abilities but took their studies very seriously. Irizarry (2007) interviewed Project TEACH participants to find out why they entered teaching and how the project helped and supported them. Dillard (1994) used interactive journals, videotaping, and interviews to gauge participant growth in the Opening Doors Project.

Such internal evaluations only rarely included data provided by someone external to the program about graduates' performance in the classroom. An example of using some external data is Haberman's (1999) evaluation, which included not only telephone surveys of graduates but also principals' ratings of graduates' performance in the elementary classroom. Although program reports that include internal evaluation data offer more information that helps readers analyze the program, these studies are still limited. Data about graduates' quality of teaching is limited when it takes the form of general ratings of teachers as excellent, satisfactory, or less than satisfactory, as did Haberman's study. External evaluators often ask questions and bring perspectives that may complement, but are not identical to, those of insiders. Longitudinal studies where program participants are interviewed, surveyed, and/or observed in naturalist settings and studies that are ongoing and that take place over larger periods of time may add to the literature through these internal program evaluations, particularly if some data can point to the attrition or academic success of students.

External program evaluations

An external program evaluation offers a perspective by someone who was not involved in the work of a program. External evaluators may bring questions, considerations, or points of view that differ from those of program insiders. This does not necessarily make external evaluations inherently better than internal descriptions or internal evaluations, but they do help to counterbalance internal accounts. If we are to claim that teacher education can and should work more actively to diversify the teaching population, we need external evaluations of programs as well as the important accounts offered by internal evaluations.

We found very few external evaluations. The largest was for the Pathways into Teaching Careers program (Clewell & Villegas, 1999, 2001; Villegas & Clewell, 1998). Clewell and Villegas gathered data over a six-year period by surveying Pathways participants, staff, teacher supervisors, principals, and teacher evaluators. By the year 2000, Pathways had recruited and served 2,593 participants nationally, which was 18% more than its original goal. Sixty-three percent of its participants were teachers of color. According to Clewell and Villegas (2001), Pathways participants completed teacher certification at a higher rate (75%) than that of traditional teacher education students (60%). At the end of their first year of teaching, Pathways graduates were rated more highly by their principals and by an external assessor using Praxis III than were their traditional counterparts. Clewell and Villegas conclude that it is possible to diversify the teaching force while improving its quality and retention rate in urban schools, using programs like those that had been funded under Pathways. For example, targeting the paraprofessional pool through university- and school-district partnerships has been seen as a logical way to tap prospective teachers of color (Dandy, 1998; Milner & Howard, 2004). Based on their evaluation, Villegas and Clewell (1998) identified five strategies to increase the number of teachers of color through the recruitment of paraprofessionals: (1) the establishment of partnerships with school districts; (2) the use of multiple sources of information in the selection of teacher candidates; (3) the providing of academic and social support services; (4) the modification of teacher education programs (such as when courses are offered); and (5) the availability of tuition assistance.

We located a few other smaller external evaluations, in which data consisted of interviews with program participants and others, as well as examination of documents. González (1997), for instance, evaluated six programs in three regions of the United States that had been funded by the Ford Foundation. Through site visits, he sought to find out students' perceptions of program features that best met their needs. Across all six programs, he found that students appreciated the personal care that they received, and the comprehensive services that were designed to address the variety of their needs. González noted that these programs went beyond a remedial approach, viewing the preparation of teachers of color as a developmental process that cultivates what they bring into the learning contexts in addition to addressing needs and deficits. He noted that these services cost money but argued that investing in teachers of color is worth the cost.

In Brennan and Bliss's (1998) evaluation of the Teacher Opportunity Program in Kentucky, an external evaluator collaborating with a faculty member found that the school district appreciated the maturity and experience of the candidates and the quality of their work in schools; candidates appreciated program support, including involvement of minority teacher mentors. They also found some problems: most candidates needed more content coursework for elementary teaching, which lengthened time of completion; and the school district's commitment to hire graduates of this program was resented by some White graduates of the traditional program. Beckett's (1998) evaluation of the Latino Teacher Project in Los Angeles and the Navajo Teacher Preparation Program at Fort Lewis College, Colorado, found that both programs were continuing to succeed due to their dedicated leaders who were able to develop collaborative relationships with other institutions and to involve skilled professionals in the design and work of the program.

Research We Need

We are suggesting that the literature available regarding the diversification of the teaching force has been an important body of work that has contributed to what we know about this topic. Based on our review, there are four interrelated areas of focus that can move the field forward: (1) more and deeper situated internal self-studies; (2) more and deeper contextualized external evaluations; (3) more and deeper long-term and longitudinal studies; (4) studies that investigate linkages between teacher ethnicity and student learning; and (5) studies that investigate factors beyond instructional considerations.

Situated internal self-studies

The internal evaluation studies that we reviewed in this chapter—those where someone was involved in program development and implementation—need to be more solidly situated in the broader self-study literature because, without such grounding, it will be difficult for the broader field of teacher education to build knowledge in the area, hopefully for systemic changes in the field. In The *Report of the AERA Panel on Research and Teacher Education*, Cochran-Smith and Zeichner (2005) emphasized that, "Without locating empirical studies in relation to appropriate theoretical frameworks regarding teacher learning, teacher effectiveness, and pupil learning, it will be difficult to explain findings about the effects of particular teacher education practices" (p. 32). The self-study strand of teacher education is a logical site for the internal evaluation studies on recruitment and retention of teachers of color, particularly because so many of the studies are conducted by someone very close to the program, such as the project director, planner, or facilitator. In addition, these self-studies need to engage in the difficult work of critiquing these programs as well as reporting their testimonies and successes. Without posing the difficult questions about the programs, about those in them, and about those who develop and implement them, it will be difficult for improvement on a broader scale, especially in terms of practices in teacher education.

Contextualized external evaluations

External evaluations, too, should include broader and deeper contextual features. It would be very useful if studies not only provided superficial descriptions of participants in schools after participants have graduated or reports from principals of teachers who have experienced these programs but also deep descriptions about the kinds of places in which these teachers are placed, the milieu, the support or lack thereof of parents and colleagues in the school, and so forth. Such findings, emerging from an external evaluator, would provide a deeper sense of the effectiveness of the programs themselves and their ability to prepare teachers to succeed in a range of contexts. What types of programs seem to best prepare teachers for urban schools, for instance? We are also calling for external evaluators to provide more context-rich evaluations of the programs themselves in teacher education in order to provide insight into the successful and unsuccessful practices of those participating and facilitating the programs.

Long-term and longitudinal studies

Research programs also need to be long-term and longitudinal. For instance, as revealed in this review, the field only benefits intermediately by studies that capture the beginning of a program or programs that are someplace in the middle of implementation. Reports are needed that capture the (long) range of the program, from program development through years when teachers are actually in the classroom with students. We see these longitudinal studies involving at least three related phases—program development, program implementation, and program evaluation. Early questions that may emerge in program development might include: How did the program develop? Who was involved with the program development? What kinds of philosophical and theoretical grounding shaped the program? What challenges did those involved encounter? How did those involved work through the difficulties? Program implementation would allow for continued study of what is working and not during program evaluation. We see this process as one where those involved in facilitation as well as participants are being evaluated and questioned by both internal and external investigators. In addition, documents and policies, such as the curriculum, course offerings, professional development workshops, funding, mentoring opportunities, and so forth would also be consistently evaluated over long periods of time and adapted where needed. Finally, program evaluation is where teachers are evaluated in their actual teaching practices with overt attention placed on program objectives. Germaine to the third phase of teachers' work in P–12 is student learning, an area to which we turn next.

Teacher ethnicity with student learning

Perhaps the most important and pressing question about recruiting and retaining teachers of color is whether student learning increases when they are taught by a teacher of color and the extent to which matching teacher and student ethnic or racial identity matters. This has been studied, but not extensively (cf. Dee, 2004).

As mentioned earlier, researchers have investigated links between student achievement and teachers of color (c.f., Irvine, 2003; Meier, Stewart, & England, 1989). We recognize that there is an uncountable number of other factors that will influence student learning and that it would be very difficult to determine the extent to which a teacher's racial and ethnic background might influence student learning. However, posing such a question has to be incorporated in studies in order to gain perspective around how students of color fare with teachers of color.

From our view, this line of research should not be atheoretical. Theories, used as analytical and conceptual tools to help explain and elucidate the complexities of studying matters related to diversifying the teaching force—matters such as race, ethnicity, contexts, student learning, and achievement—are needed to continue building the field. Useful theoretical tools about how and why diversifying the teaching force is important can shed light on the empirical literature. For instance, sociocognitive theories might address the question of whether teachers of color make better role models and advocates for students of color. Sociocultural theories might assist researchers in unpacking the learning milieu and how it shapes the teaching and learning exchange. Moreover, theories such as culturally relevant pedagogy (Ladson-Billings, 1994) and culturally responsive pedagogy (Gay, 2010) may prove to be useful tools in understanding what teachers of color bring into the classroom and are able to transfer into their practices. These and other innovative theoretical frames are essential to building a more robust literature base related to the importance of diversification in the teaching force.

We also believe that studies should investigate factors other than student test scores, which is why we deliberately focus on "student learning" and not student achievement (although we recognize that these two areas are not mutually exclusive). A body of research is beginning to investigate, for instance, connections between African American teachers and the reading scores of African American students in comparison to those of students who do not have African American teachers (c.f., Easton-Brooks, Lewis, & Yang, 2011). If there are powerful effects, the literature should reflect the features of these successful teachers of students of color such that others in teacher education can learn and benefit (c.f., Ladson-Billings, 1994; Milner, 2006).

Factors beyond instructional considerations

While our preference is for studies to focus specifically on educational outcomes, namely student learning and student achievement, we also recognize that research needs to occur related to diversifying the teaching force apart from instructional considerations. For example, studies are needed that

- investigate matters of equity in district hiring practices, recruitment efforts, and retention policies with an intense eye towards teachers of color;
- study the recruitment and retention patterns and practices of districts and states;
- consider, qualitatively speaking, the ways in which teachers of color are "socialized" into hostile teaching environments on the district, school, and classroom levels; and
- research connections between and among school- and district-level administrators, such as school-level principals and district-level personnel, and their recruitment and retention of teachers of color.

In addition, research should examine the extent to which schoolwide responses to academic needs of students of color are affected by the composition of professionals within the school. Do schools serving a high proportion of students of color analyze and respond to their students more effectively when a high proportion of the teachers are from similar backgrounds as their students? Finally, research teasing out interactions between teacher and student ethnicity should also examine to what extent social-class background of students and teachers might mediate the impact of racial and ethnic background.

Implications and Conclusions

This review suggests implications for both practice and research. We are past the time when teacher education programs can assume that little can be done to diversify the teaching population. This review suggests several models that have been used with success. Although some models may prove more successful and longer lasting than others, it is still safe to say that there are various options teacher education programs can try, and descriptions of what others have done that can guide new trials. External evaluations, although limited, offer useful information. They consistently find a high degree of satisfaction on the part of school-district personnel with teachers of color certified through programs like those in this review. Evaluations have also found that programs with comprehensive services that take into account the lives and needs of candidates of color, particularly older candidates who are already working, are probably more effective than those with more limited services.

In addition, we believe that institutions that serve highly diverse populations of students should continue working to build programs and to attract students into teacher education. Historically black institutions, for instance, may be good sites for more innovation in recruiting undergraduate students into teacher education and also for partnering with local school systems. Historically black institutions and their long-standing commitment to and practices of preparing large numbers of African American students was compromised, according to Clark (1988), when the HOLMES/Carnegie reports pushed for fifth-year programs for teacher education programs. Black colleges and universities have relied on undergraduate teacher education programs (and undergraduate programs more generally) for financial vitality and a good number of these institutions did not have, and still do not have, graduate-level programs for any discipline—consider private institutions such as Fisk University in Nashville, Tennessee.

Despite the large number of programs to recruit and prepare teachers of color that have existed, however, research on them has been sparse. Because of a dearth of follow-up studies on pipeline programs, for example, we do not have a clear picture of their impact and what features are most essential to a program's success. We know very little about how well graduates of redesigned programs teach in the classroom after they are hired, and virtually nothing about the quality of their teaching in relationship to that of teachers certified through traditional programs. It appears that externally funded programs that do not become institutionalized last only as long as the funding and/or the employment of committed individuals. One might ask to what extent programs that become institutionalized not only last but also change how the institution recruits and supports its students and what factors enable and support institutionalization.

Finally, we found very little conceptual work embedded within many of the studies reviewed. The literature takes more of a reporting format than an intellectually situated one. Deeper, more nuanced questions need posing about not only how to increase the number of teachers of color but also about the very essence of their presence in the classroom with students. Dillard (1994) asserted that

> to address the inadequate numbers of teachers of color in our public schools today, we must move the discussion beyond simple numerics [*sic*]. Solely focusing the work of recruitment on increasing the numbers of people of color denies the very essence of being for those who embrace and love their ethnicity…The question should be: what is it that the teacher of color brings to the teaching and learning setting which is qualitatively different and inherently of value in our increasingly diverse schools? (p. 16)

Future studies might continue examining ways to increase the number of teachers of color in public schools and also pose deeper questions about what it means for teachers of color to teach increasingly diverse students, how well these teachers fare with all their students, including White ones, what support structures enable and hinder their success, and what qualities about these teachers ensure meaningful learning opportunities for their students.

Notes

1. H. Richard Milner, IV, is associate professor at Peabody College, Vanderbilt University.
2. We understand that every person represents racial, cultural, and ethnic diversity, although White people usually are classified as the norm and others are considered diverse. We understand that there is a great deal of diversity among people from every racial, cultural, and ethnic background. However, for the purpose of this discussion and due to page restrictions, we are defining racially, culturally, and ethnically diverse groups of people as those groups that are not White or European American.
3. Throughout this chapter, we use people of color to refer to those individuals who are not White. We realize that this use is problematic because there is variance between and among individuals of color. However, the use of people of color seems to be the most appropriate language at this time as minority is also an inappropriate word choice.
4. Our description of programs represents their status at the time this chapter was originally written. In some cases, programs that existed at that time no longer exist, or have changed substantially.
5. The term "alternative" means a wide variety of program configurations. Generally it refers to either university-based programs that are alternative to the regular program(s), or alternative-route programs that are only loosely connected to universities or not connected at all.

12

Developing Teacher Epistemological Sophistication about Multicultural Curriculum

A Case Study

Teachers are significant curriculum decision makers in their classrooms, although curriculum is given far less attention in professional development for novice teachers than are other classroom concerns (Clayton, 2007). How does teachers' thinking about curriculum develop in the context of teacher education coursework? And how might an analysis of a novice teacher's learning to think more complexly inform teacher education pedagogy?

This chapter presents a case study of a second-year teacher who enrolled in my graduate-level Multicultural Curriculum Design course, which was designed to develop the complexity with which teachers understand and plan curriculum. As a teacher educator, I attempt to 1) disrupt common novice assumptions that there is a "right" way to design and teach multicultural curriculum and that there is a body of "correct" knowledge and attitudes to teach, and 2) help teachers develop more sophisticated epistemological perspectives about the nature of knowledge and their work as teachers. This case study teases out factors that appeared to prompt the growth of one teacher.

Teachers' Epistemological Beliefs

Working with multiple perspectives, frames of reference, and funds of knowledge is at the heart of designing and teaching multicultural curriculum (Banks, 2004b). Developing curriculum that is intellectually rich and relevant to diverse students, in contexts already furnished with a fairly prescribed curriculum, requires teachers to judge what is most worth teaching and learning and to identify space in which they can invite students' knowledge and interests. Making such judgments requires evaluating knowledge in terms of its sociopolitical moorings and intellectual basis. These are issues of epistemology—beliefs about how people know what they know, including assumptions about the nature of knowledge and the process of coming to know (Clayton, 2007).

Schommer (1990) describes three epistemological dimensions of knowledge that have relevance to teachers: certainty, source, and structure. Certainty refers to the extent to which one sees knowledge as being based on a fixed reality that is "out there" and unchanging. Source refers to where valid knowledge can come from (established external authorities, personal experience, etc.) and how one evaluates the relative strength of various sources and forms of evidence. Structure refers to the extent to which one sees knowledge as having, on one hand, its own internal structure and hierarchy or, on the other, an organic relationship to context, knowers, and everyday life.

Research on teachers' and college students' epistemological beliefs suggests growth along a continuum (Schommer, 1998; White, 2000). At one end are those who hold absolutist beliefs, seeing knowledge as being fixed and certain, outside the knower, and established by authority figures. At the other end are reflective individuals who see knowledge as being situated within the context in which people create it: Problems have multiple solutions, and truth claims can be evaluated on the basis of the veracity of evidence on which they rest. In the middle are relativists, who reject anchoring knowledge in established authorities but, not knowing how to evaluate it otherwise, assume that all perspectives are equally valid.

Assumptions that teachers make about the certainty, source, and structure of knowledge affect what they do with curriculum in general and multicultural curriculum in particular. Powell (1996) compares how two teachers with different epistemologies approached multicultural curriculum. One teacher held a developmentalist approach, seeing students' needs and interests as the basis on which academic knowledge should be built. The other saw the structure of his discipline (science) as being fundamental, and he judged students' learning abilities in relationship to their mastery of disciplinary content. The first teacher saw multicultural curriculum as being relevant; the second did not.

So, to help teachers plan and teach intellectually sound multicultural curriculum that engages their students, one should prompt them to question their beliefs about the certainty, source, and structure of knowledge. Teaching a course in higher education, I have 15 weeks in which to do this—a relatively short time in which to disrupt assumptions built over many years of experiencing conventional schooling. The purpose of this case study was to examine the relationship between a teacher's learning and my teaching strategies in the university, coupled with visitation to the teacher's classroom.

Methodology for a Case Study

According to Stake (2000), "a case study is expected to catch the complexity of a single case" (p. xi). Stake maintains that case study research is useful to education because, although school settings, teachers, and students share similarities, they are unique and complex. We cannot fully understand shared patterns without seeing the uniqueness of individual cases.

This case study is drawn from a larger study of teachers working with multicultural curriculum (Sleeter, 2005), in the context of the program discussed in Chapter Seven of this volume. Why did I select Ann (pseudonym) for a case study? Stake (2000) recommends selecting cases that "maximize what we can learn" (p. 4). Beginning teachers in racially or ethically diverse classrooms are commonly involved in induction programs and thus of interest to many teacher educators (Achinstein & Athanases, 2005; Chan & East, 1993). Therefore, I wanted to focus my attention on a beginning teacher who was relatively new to multicultural education, open to learning, and teaching in a diverse classroom. Of the teachers in my course (veterans as well as new teachers, in varying classroom settings), Ann best fit these criteria. She was a 2nd-year teacher who had moved to California from the East Coast about two years previously. A young White woman, she taught fifth grade in an elementary school that serves a diverse, largely low-income student population. She expressed interest in multicultural education, even though it was new to her.

Case study research typically uses a variety of methods to collect data, with an objective toward triangulating findings across methods (Creswell, 2008; Stake, 2000). Data for this study included (1) several papers that Ann completed during the course, including a unit that she designed as a course requirement, (2) a journal that I kept after each class session, (3) notes on two observations of Ann teaching the unit that she designed after the course had ended, and (4) a 40-minute tape-recorded interview with Ann following my observations.

As a heuristic tool for reflection and analysis, I developed a rubric that appears in Table 12.1, which describes a rough progression of levels in learning to think complexly about multicultural curriculum at novice, developing, and accomplished levels. In developing the rubric, l drew from research comparing teachers' thinking at novice, developing, and expert levels, which generally finds that expert teachers, compared to novice teachers, make more distinctions among aspects of curriculum and instruction and bring to bear more elaborated thinking about their judgments (e.g., Cushing, Sabers, & Berliner, 1992; Krull, Oras, & Sisack, 2007; Swanson, O'Connor, & Cooney, 1990). I also drew from my experience planning and teaching multicultural curriculum, as well as collaborating with several colleagues who were investigating the development of cognitive complexity among their students.

Table 12.1. Thinking Complexly about Multicultural Curriculum

Task definition

Novice. Assumes a "right" way to design and teach curriculum. Assumes that one already understands multicultural curriculum and that "new learning" involves adding onto that. Ignores, sees as irrelevant, or lacks confidence to examine what puzzles, feels threatening, or seems impractical.

Developing. Recognizes more than one "right" way that good curriculum could be designed and taught. Willing to question things that one thought one understood and to explore dimensions that are puzzling or new.

Accomplished. Assumes that multiple ways of designing and teaching curriculum emanate from diverse ideologies; able to own and work with one's ideology. Continually tries to recognize new dimensions of curriculum and to figure out the most ethical and practical balance among competing demands.

Perspective taking

Novice. Assumes there is a body of "correct" knowledge or attitudes to teach; tends to interpret and dismiss other perspectives or critical questions as opinion, personal criticism, or simply impractical.

Developing. Willing to consider multiple and possibly conflicting definitions of what is most worth knowing; able to acknowledge how one's viewpoint, identity, and social location shapes one's perspective; willing to own one's judgments about what is best.

Accomplished. Actively seeks multiple perspectives; makes explicit effort to learn from perspectives different from one's own, especially those that have been historically subjugated. Able to articulate own perspective as one of many; able to invite dialogue and discussion across divergent perspectives.

Table 12.1., continued

Self-reflexivity

Novice. Strives for certainty, assumes that questioning oneself is the same as questioning one's competence; seeks approval for one's thinking from authority figures.

Developing. Willing to acknowledge uncertainty, at least tentatively; occasionally asks what is most worth teaching and why; recognizes need to attend to practical consequences of one's teaching while maintaining some level of critical questioning.

Accomplished. Views uncertainty as tool for learning. Consistently monitors, questions, and evaluates practical and ethical impacts of one's work on students. Questions how one's own positionality, experiences, and point of view affect one's work but can move forward while doing so.

Locus of decision making

Novice. Either looks to external authorities (such as the state, well-known people in the field, texts) to find out what and how to teach or ignores them entirely; assumes that educational decision making flows top-down.

Developing. Attends to external authorities but also willing to seek input from students, parents, community members, or other teachers; explores how to make decisions in a way that satisfies authorities and invites bottom-up input.

Accomplished. Negotiates decision making in a way that consciously places well-being of students at the center; regularly engages students and their communities in collaborative decision making while attending to external expectations; able to take ownership for the consequences of one's decisions.

The rubric includes four dimensions along which epistemological beliefs can be examined: task definition, perspective taking, self-reflexivity, and locus of decision-making. Assumptions labeled novice correspond to what White (2000) characterizes as absolutist thinking. Those labeled developing correspond to relativist thinking, and those labeled accomplished, to reflective thinking. I used the rubric to guide my analysis of the case study data. I also used it with teachers in the Multicultural Curriculum Design course as a reflective tool. Ann used the rubric in a paper to reflect on her own growth, which I read after I had made my preliminary analysis of her growth. Her self-analysis was quite similar to mine. Ann also read an earlier draft of this article, offering a few comments while confirming its consistency with her analysis of her growth.

Case Study of Ann

Ann had enrolled voluntarily in Multicultural Curriculum Design. When I asked how she came to be interested in it, she replied,

> I [student-taught] in Eastern London; it was all primarily Afghani and Pakistani descent students. And I was just fascinated with the Arabic that they spoke and the writing and it was so different....And when I came home, I taught this fifth grade about the cultures I learned over there, and they had no idea what Arabic was, what Muslim, what Mohammed, nothing. And I think it's really important to teach about the different cultures and religions. I think a lot of times ignorance brings hate. (January 28, 2004)

On the first day of the course, I asked teachers to write their definition of curriculum. Ann wrote, "Curriculum is what the teacher is required to teach to the students" (September 8, 2003). About three weeks later, I had them write about the extent to which their curriculum is determined by authorities such as the state and about any concerns that they might have about what they are expected to teach. Ann wrote,

> I have concerns with teaching the history textbook content. As a public school teacher, though, you really can't go outside of your prescribed literature and academic standards. So, I believe at this moment that it is my job as a teacher to try and guide the students to question and look at the text differently than what they read in the chapter....So, the dilemma is how to tactfully incorporate other multicultural views in a school-adopted textbook and be able to cover all the standards the state and government expects of you at the same time. (September 30, 2003)

These responses suggest that Ann entered the course with an absolutist perspective about curriculum. A novice, she accepted the legitimacy of external authorities to determine curriculum; she believed that she could tweak it a bit to make it multicultural; and she was looking for strategies and ideas to use. My task, however, was not to simply offer her strategies and ideas but to slow down her learning process so that she could reflect more deeply on her beliefs and assumptions.

Throughout the semester, I used various strategies to do this: analyzing epistemological and ideological assumptions in documents, reading works that reflect multiple ideological perspectives, engaging in personal interactions that challenge thinking, engaging in reflective writing, and developing a curriculum unit one can teach. I examine these in relationship to Ann's growth.

Analyzing epistemological and ideological assumptions in documents

Early in the semester (September), I guided teachers in analyzing epistemological assumptions in various documents related to curriculum, such as curriculum standards and school reform proposals available on the Internet. Teachers examined documents in relationship to questions such as the following: Who produced this document (if it is possible to tell)? How is it intended to be used? By whom? What is its purpose? W/hose view of the world does it support? Whose view does it undermine or ignore? Whose knowledge isn't here? In addition, they analyzed textbooks from their classrooms, with guidance from a textbook analysis instrument (see Grant & Sleeter, 2009).

Ann elected to analyze her social studies textbook. As she explained near the end of the semester, this analysis caused her to realize that

> history is told overwhelmingly in the white European male perspective....The history text teaches the story of American history as "We the People" as a succession. All the chapters from 30,000 B.C. to 1600 are never rethought after colonization....The broader ideology that is being supported in the text is that it is natural for Europeans to succeed prior races without accepting or studying their culture. (December 8, 2003)

She coupled this analysis with interviews with some of her students, for another short paper. She asked her students what they knew about indigenous people of the United States and the history of colonization. She was surprised to discover that they thought that there are no Native Americans left. Ann discovered that "they knew very little about the colonization period of the United States. Looking at my student perspectives paper, the pieces of information that they did know were mostly filled [with] myth and false facts" (December 15, 2003).

Coupling document analysis with student interviews helped Ann to see that U.S. History is told from a perspective that excludes indigenous perspectives; as a result, her students were coming to believe that indigenous people no longer exist. By October, Ann began to question her earlier assumption that a teacher's job is simply to teach what the state demands.

Reading from multiple ideological perspectives

Readings that engage teachers with various ideological perspectives can prompt reflection when used in conjunction with discussion and reflective writing. To that end, we read Macedo's *Literacies of Power* (1994), which examines curriculum, ideology, and power from a critical ethnic studies perspective, and we read online selections from *Rethinking Schools* (http://rethinkingschools.org), a newspaper written from critical perspectives, mainly by classroom teachers. The readings offered a language that many of the teachers had not previously encountered.

As Ann read *Literacies of Power*, she made connections between its critique of schooling and her own belief system. She wrote that she is a registered Democrat with leanings "toward liberal, green, and democratic ideals"; she also described her co-teachers as dismissing conspiracy theories and as being attached to "their Republican government and books and standards" (October 13, 2003). She was not put off by Macedo's radical questioning of dominant beliefs about schools, because his questions supported her disagreements with co-workers and her new awareness that history texts reflect dominant points of view. At the same time, she realized that she did not understand some of Macedo's ideas. Halfway through the semester, in a class discussion, Ann commented that after listening to classmates of color, she better understood Macedo's ideas.

Her reactions to Macedo suggest that Ann sought connections between his ideas and life experience—her own and that of people whom she knew. As she became more able to make those connections, she gradually took up questions that he raised about how dominant groups shape what happens in schools. By November, she was interested in connecting his analysis of power and curriculum with global power. Ann participated in a small-group discussion of an article in which a fifth-grade teacher describes how he helped his students develop a sense of solidarity with struggles of workers across the globe (Peterson, 2000/2001). Ann asked me what the term *globalize* means, whether it is positive or negative. I explained that the author was referring to the process of large corporations' incorporating Third World economies into a capitalist global economy. Ann commented that she was not sure what the term meant. Two weeks later, she wanted to discuss this article, along with another (Bigelow, 2002) that examined how school knowledge constructs Third World peoples from highly Westernized points of view rather than from Third World points of view. These seemed to be new ideas that she wanted to explore further because they appeared to resonate with her political beliefs and, possibly, with her student teaching experience.

To acquire background for a curriculum unit that was the course's culminating project, teachers were to identify a concept that they could teach, and they were to research it from points of view found in the intellectual scholarship of one historically marginalized group. In early October, as Ann became aware that her textbook virtually ignores indigenous people and the impact of colonization on them, she decided to pursue the topic of colonization from indigenous perspectives. She initially suggested starting with the question, what are Native American perspectives on colonization? I advised that she narrow her question to a specific period, place, and tribe or nation; she decided to focus on the Iroquois during the 17th century. Over the next two months, she read *Lies My Teacher Told Me* (Loewen, 1995) and *Rethinking Columbus* (Bigelow & Peterson, 1998), as well as work by indigenous authors such as LaDuke (1999) and Churchill (2002). As she read, she focused on the Haudenosaunee (Iroquois), Wampanoag, and Pequot during the late 17th century. She came to see that books by indigenous scholars present an opposing perspective from that in the school's history text; She was initially confused, commenting in class, "Topics just kept spinning off each other and it was hard to stop or to figure out what to actually use" (journal notes, December 8, 2003). She struggled with how to rethink her curriculum because she realized that she could not simply add information to it. Later I show how she resolved this dilemma. But it was clear to me that readings grounded in a different perspective prompted her over the semester to recognize and question the perspective in her curriculum and textbooks.

Engaging in personal interactions

Throughout the semester, I had teachers engage in various structured and semi-structured interactions to simulate their thinking and self-analysis. The fact that they were from diverse backgrounds produced rich discussions all semester. They were mainly women. About one third were White; one third, Latino; and the rest included an African American, a Korean, two Africans, two Greeks, and some biracial students who identified as Asian American.

A powerful interaction involved sharing from each teacher's life. They were asked to bring one or two objects that reflect membership in a sociocultural group (e.g., based on race or ethnicity, gender, sexual orientation, language) and a struggle for rights or identity related to membership in that group. The objects should prompt sharing about how they have claimed identity, space, and rights (Flores, 2003). Ann is of Italian American descent, as were several other teachers in the class. They discussed the centrality of food to family gatherings and the position of women in traditional Italian families (as well as Mexican families). Ann discussed being a vegetarian, which her family saw as a rejection of Italian food and family; she had struggled to help her family see that one can be an Italian vegetarian. Although her struggle was less intense than those of some of the teachers of color, it gave Ann a basis for hearing where others were coming from. After this session, she commented that Macedo's critique of schooling in the U.S. made more sense to her.

Engaging in reflective writing

Throughout the semester, teachers wrote reflections about various teaching dilemmas they had experienced, such as how they handled conflicts between the demands placed on them as teachers and their political or pedagogical beliefs. Ann found that reflective writing enabled her to link insights from readings with some of her core beliefs about schooling that conflicted with what she was told to do.

In one reflection, teachers were to identify and analyze a teaching practice they favored and had tried but that did not work or was rejected by their students. Ann wrote about her experiences using small-group activities:

> The students did not respond to my group activities as well as when practiced in my student teaching. When given manipulatives in math, they were thrown sometimes. In language arts we worked in writing workshop groups, and more times than not there were disagreements and fights. The science experiments resulted in many referrals and suspensions. (November 3, 2003)

Her new teacher mentor told her that she was giving the students too much freedom, "that this kind of population needs seatwork and a definite routine every day....As a result, I backed off on these activities and have a whole class teaching method instead of learning centers." On reflection, Ann realized, "I gave up too easily." She went on to write,

> My theory on this is that students tend to talk out and voice expressions when interested in a certain subject matter....I feel that some cultures need to be heard, literally, more than others. The quote from Macedo "education so as not to educate" makes me think, is this the type of teaching that I've adopted from my mentor, just silencing students that probably need to speak out? My dilemma here is how to have a classroom where students speak out, learn in different ways and in group settings, without having troublesome discipline problems. (November 3, 2003)

For Ann, writing reflectively about the intersection between her experiences, beliefs, readings, and discussions seemed to prompt self-analysis. In the process, she questioned the basis on which experienced teachers recommended teaching practices, seeing limitations in her co-workers' advice and reclaiming her beliefs about teaching and learning.

Developing a curriculum unit

The course was organized around a culminating assignment: developing a multicultural curriculum unit that one can actually teach. I used this assignment to provide teachers with a way of working through the questions, dilemmas, and new insights they grapple with over the semester. As noted earlier, Ann grappled with two major problems: how to address the fact that "indigenous people's history stops after Columbus is introduced" (December 8, 2003) and how to engage students in active learning without losing control over the class.

To resolve the problem of how to teach history from two opposing perspectives, Ann used a teacher's suggestion of organizing the unit around a trial. It focused on the Wampanoag nation's frustrations with colonists who were misusing natural resources—particularly over-killing the deer population. It was based on the Haudenosaunee Great Law of Peace and Good Mind, which uses a trial process as a tool for building consensus about solutions to community problems. The trial structure helped her figure out how to engage students in active learning.

To prepare this unit for teaching, Ann needed to learn a good deal more. For example, it was not enough to know that the Handenosaunee had a well-developed democratic governmental and legal system; she also had to be able to describe some of its features accurately. She commented on the amount of time it took her to research background material:

> Just when I was planning this lesson, I went and spent another few hours finding those words and finding all the Native American names....I spent time on Native American websites. And researching this is something I'm kind of interested in. I mean, I've looked up some different Native American beliefs and traditions just for my own personal knowledge. (interview, January 28, 2004)

As a second-year teacher, Ann was overwhelmed with preparing lessons for state standards in all the content areas. She recognized that preparing such a unit entailed work above and beyond that required by the state curriculum. Because Native Americans disappear from the social studies curriculum as it traces the story of Europeans and Euro-Americans, she could elect not to teach the unit and be in full compliance with state requirements. But she believed that the unit was too important to drop.

Ann's completed unit included three 45-minute lessons. I visited her classroom in January while she was teaching the second and third lessons. During the third lesson, students role-played the trial, which Ann entitled "The Case of the Missing Deer." In a fictitious trial set in Massachusetts during the 17th century, the Wampanoag tribe sued the European colonists for misusing natural resources. Ann had given each student a role card that included a name, a designation as a Wampanoag or colonist, and role in the trial. She showed who would sit where: defendants at one table, plaintiffs at another, jury at an other table, and judges at the circular table at the front (there were five judges: two colonists, two

Wampanoag, and one from another tribe who would act as a tiebreaker, if needed). Ann directed everyone into his or her place, then passed out worksheets appropriate to each role. When students received their worksheets, they started filling them out. Ann stressed the need for quiet in the courtroom; the students looked very engaged, with only a little fidgety off-task behavior.

Then the trial started. The Wampanoag witnesses were followed by colonist witnesses. Most students stuck to the lines on their role cards, but a few knew their lines and extemporized. After witnesses for both sides had testified, additional witnesses contradicted some of the testimony. Then Ann took the jurors out of the room and gave them two minutes to render a verdict. While they were deliberating, she had the rest of the class finish answers on their worksheets. The jury returned and found the colonists guilty. The judges then left the room to deliberate sentencing. While they were out, Ann asked the colonists what they thought about the verdict. When a boy suggested planting vegetables, Ann pointed out that the colonists came from England and probably did not know what would grow in Massachusetts. After a small amount of silliness, the children started constructive brainstorming, such as suggesting that the colonists could learn from the Indians what grows in the local geography. The judges returned, sentencing the colonists to share all the deer with the Wampanoag people for two years. Ann led a whole-class discussion of the trial and verdict, asking students to consider whether the decisions were fair. She also asked students to consider whether the Native Americans would teach the colonists how to hunt deer without killing them off.

When I interviewed Ann after the unit had concluded, I realized that she was not yet connecting students' engaged behavior with her careful planning for their active involvement. While teaching, she usually expended considerable energy keeping students on task, but during the simulation, she did not need to do so. She initially attributed their on-task behavior to external factors such as the weather, but by prompting her to reflect on the structure of the unit, I helped her see how her planning offered students a way to become involved and interested in the academic lesson.

Implications for Teacher Education

Over a five-month period, Ann moved from a novice level to a developing level in planning multicultural curriculum. She no longer defined the task of curriculum design as finding the "right" way; rather, she sorted through multiple possibilities to plan curriculum that embodied more than one perspective. She no longer accepted the authority of the state and the textbook companies to define what to teach; rather, she considered the scholarship of indigenous people, the perspectives of students, the experiences of teachers of color, and her own experiences with culture and gender. She was supported in working with uncertainty and investing time in reading and thinking to make decisions that she could defend. Her growth, with the kind of support that she received, was similar to that documented in other studies of new teachers in urban schools, in which coursework and mentoring challenge beginning teachers' beliefs—particularly, those related to race, ethnicity, and poverty—focus on pedagogy, and examine tensions between perspectives of new teachers and responses of their students (Achinstein & Athanases, 2005; Chan & East, 1998).

By carefully reflecting on Ann's learning in the context of my teaching, I learned that the following can help guide teacher educators: First, reflective discussions and writings, as embedded in teachers' classroom work, prompt thinking that can dislodge novice assumptions (Clayton, 2007; Krull et al., 2007). This was a graduate course for practicing classroom teachers; as such, the document analyses, reflective writings, and personal interactions asked them to reflect on their work. For Ann, continued connection between the course and her everyday teaching was fruitful. Analyzing one of her textbooks and interviewing her students prompted her realization that state-defined knowledge assumes a perspective that needs to be questioned. This realization caused her to question where curriculum decision-making should be located. Furthermore, the reflective writings helped Ann to name some of her questions and struggles, such as how to build active engagement without losing control over the class.

Second, to facilitate development beyond novice thinking, it is essential to provide space and support for uncertainty. Ann brought a capacity to self-reflect and live with uncertainty; I could not give her this capacity, but I could work with it. In addition to encouraging reflection in written work and discussions, I made a reasonable attempt to allow students to wonder, to make statements that could be considered naïve, and to disagree with one another and with me. As I examined the journal that I had kept over the semester, I identified Ann's expressions of uncertainty all semester, as well as evidence of her pursuit of questions that interested her. Sometimes in multicultural education courses, students feel shut down and unable to say what they think for fear of offending other students or the professor. This case study shows how important it is to work on creating a climate in which students can ask questions, express their thoughts, and disagree, as long as they do so respectfully. Without creating space for uncertainty, as well as support for questioning and disagreeing, it is unlikely that an instructor will help teachers develop epistemological sophistication.

Third, teachers value opportunities to learn from peers in contexts of guided inquiry (e.g., Jennings & Smith, 2002). I had structured the course to provide multiple opportunities for peer learning, particularly inviting novice teachers to learn from more-experienced teachers. In addition to having regular small-group discussions that asked teachers to link readings with their teaching experience, I used many readings written by classroom teachers (articles from *Rethinking Schools* in particular), and I invited an experienced multicultural educator as a guest speaker. These opportunities helped Ann to envision viable possibilities for teaching, which broadened her definition of the task of multicultural curriculum design. In a reflection paper, for example, she mentioned that some of the readings from *Rethinking Schools* had been especially helpful to her because they linked political issues with real-world classroom teaching. It appeared to me that opportunities to learn from more-experienced teachers helped novice teachers such as Ann to see possibilities that they might not otherwise see.

Opportunities to learn from perspectives across racial, ethnic, and cultural boundaries stretched teachers' beliefs, sometimes painfully. As mentioned earlier, the teachers in the course were highly diverse; there was no racial or ethnic majority. Furthermore, I chose readings to reflect points of view usually absent or silenced in predominantly White, mainstream contexts. Many class sessions provided various kinds of opportunities for teachers to dialogue about their diverse life experiences and to reflect on their experiences in relationship to people of backgrounds different from their own. Some of these discussions became heated and painful; as instructor, my role was to organize such discussions, then to mediate as needed. For Ann, the process of learning across cultural boundaries enabled her to reject her co-workers' beliefs that "this kind of population needs seatwork" and to hear Macedo's (1994) assertion that students such as those in her classroom need an education that enables them to think and speak out. As she read viewpoints of indigenous writers, she briefly experienced a crisis: She recognized that there is no one "correct" body of knowledge to teach; she then gradually took responsibility for trying to make multiple perspectives visible in her curriculum. The process of hearing perspectives across cultural boundaries also helped her to see the limitations in her textbook's point of view and summon the time and energy to construct an alternative.

Deepening teachers' epistemological thinking in one course is a challenging task. Teacher education courses generally last 10 to 15 weeks, and they are usually located on the college campus rather than in the classrooms where teachers work. Both conditions limit the potential potency of coursework. Because of her participation in this study, I maintained a relationship with Ann after the course had ended in order to visit her classroom. There, I was able to offer guidance and coaching—particularly, reflection about the unit's structure and how it increased students' engagement and decreased discipline problems. This study emphasizes the extent to which teachers weigh the viability of new insights in relationship to their feasibility and their impact on students in the classroom. Rather than plan discrete courses for the development of teachers' epistemological complexity, we should plan entire teacher education programs to that end.

Conclusion

In today's standards-based context, schools tend to reinforce novice assumptions about knowledge by defining what to teach and expecting teachers to accept the state as the main authority over knowledge. When I teach, I intentionally disrupt that expectation, tapping into historically marginalized points of view about what is worth knowing and into teachers' beliefs about what schooling could be. As Clayton (2007) argues in her case studies of beginning teachers, teachers ultimately need to figure out how to resolve tensions between (1) an institutionalized press toward standardizing knowledge and treating students as passive knowledge consumers and (2) alternative visions of what is worth knowing and what constitutes teaching and learning.

This case study showed how one novice teacher began to question institutionalized assumptions in the context of a graduate course and how she began to think more complexly. The case study reinforced for me the importance of creating contexts in which teachers can examine their own backgrounds and beliefs, interact with one another, and interact with ideas that stretch them intellectually. Of course, no two teachers bring the same prior experiences, beliefs, and commitments. The challenge for an instructor lies in planning a course that activates a variety of experiences and enables uncomfortable questions and disagreements to take place so that teachers can grow. This inquiry into learning has helped me make sense of that challenge.

13

Te Kotahitanga

A Case Study of a Repositioning Approach to Teacher Professional Development for Culturally Responsive Pedagogies

With Anne Hynds,[1] Rawiri Hindle,[2] Catherine Savage,[3] Wally Penetito,[4] & Luanna Meyer[5]

Preface

The study reported in this chapter comes from research on culturally responsive pedagogy that I did with a team in New Zealand. Why New Zealand, and what implications would this work have for a U.S. audience? Although New Zealand, like most other countries around the world, is being impacted by neoliberalism, the impact there is distinctly less than in the U.S. At the same time, Indigenous Māori educators have been working in sustained and interesting ways on decolonizing the education process. Because programs such as the one discussed in this chapter, rooted in student voice and Māori epistemology, have had a chance to grow (although not, of course, without constant struggle for resources and legitimacy), I realized that I would be able to see the impact of culturally responsive education on students in New Zealand better than in the U.S. What are the implications of this work for the U.S.? I will return to this question at the conclusion of this chapter.

Educational disparities in New Zealand between Indigenous Māori students and their Pākehā/New Zealand European[6] peers are most evident in mainstream schools. National studies undertaken in New Zealand secondary schools, such as the Youth2000 surveys, reveal that "45.8% of Māori students live in neighborhoods of high deprivation (compared to 12.6% of Pākehā/NZ European students)"

(Grant, Milfont, Herd & Denny, 2010, p. 190). The Ministry of Education has reported that in mainstream schools Māori students are overrepresented in special education programs, leave school early with fewer qualifications, and are over-represented in school expulsion and suspension figures compared with the dominant Pākehā/New Zealand cultural groups (Ministry of Education, 2006). These patterns mirror those of minoritized students in other countries such as the United States, Canada, Australia, and Great Britain.

Commonly, teachers take such disparities for granted, seeing altering them as beyond the power of teachers. But Shields, Bishop and Mazawi (2005) contend that teachers who place the blame for underachievement and failure on their students are engaging in deficit theorising. Deficit theorising and low expectations for student learning leads to pathologising classroom practices; such teaching is associated with negative outcomes for Indigenous and other minoritized students (Castagno & Brayboy, 2008). Yet, despite widespread acknowledgement that teachers need to learn to teach students whose culture and language differ from their own (e.g., Alton-Lee, 2003; Cochran-Smith, 2004; Gay & Howard, 2000; Shields et al., 2005), research on effective professional development programs is disappointingly thin. In this chapter, we present data based on a case study of such a professional development program (see Sleeter, 2011, for the larger study).

Approaches to Teacher Professional Development

How one conceptualizes the nature and basis of disparities is important in the design of professional development for culturally responsive pedagogy. One can distinguish between two quite different designs: technical-rational designs in which experts teach pedagogical practices to teachers, and designs that attempt to reposition teachers as learners in relationship to their students and students' communities.

Technical-rational approaches to professional development

Technical-rational approaches have long dominated education (Mehan, Hubbard & Datnow, 2010). Sleeter and Montecinos (1999) explain that under a technical-rational model:

> teaching entails a series of technical decisions made by experts who have a claim to authority. This claim rests on two premises: ownership of a domain of a morally neutral set of facts and the belief that those facts represent law-like generalizations that can be applied to particular cases. (p. 116)

It follows then that professional development based on a technical-rational approach assumes that the underachievement of minoritized students can be addressed by experts teaching teachers specific skills and understandings to use in the classroom. Two examples illustrate.

For example, Haviland and Rodriguez-Kiino (2008) reported the results of a program designed to shift White professors' deficit thinking about Latino students in a small college in the Western part of the U.S. They explain that the course was based on the assumption that professors would shift their practices if they were more aware of the problem and knew more about culturally responsive pedagogy. The program entailed a six-week on-line course teaching about Latino culture and culturally responsive teaching, and a three-day summer institute where professors could share ideas and work together. Pre- and post-interviews, structured classroom observations, and student surveys revealed mixed results across the faculty. While some professors reported large gains in awareness, others found the program irrelevant to their practice.

As another example, Zozakiewicz and Rodriguez (2007) studied the impact of professional development for elementary and middle school teachers in California on making science gender inclusive, inquiry based, and multicultural. This program included a summer institute, classroom visits, a workshop focused on teacher-identified needs, and meetings to discuss progress. The summer institute taught theoretical underpinnings for sociocultural transformative teaching, and classroom practices that connect science with learning. Interview, focus group, and survey data revealed high satisfaction with the program and self-reported improvements in teaching for most teachers. However, Zozakiewicz and Rodriguez found that some of the teachers focused more on science aspects of the professional development rather than issues of culture and equity.

While improving teaching of minoritized students may well require teachers to learn new knowledge and skills, unlearning deficit theorising also requires that teachers reframe their construction of students. Timperley, Wilson, Barrar and Fung (2007) reviewed eight empirical studies of professional development programs designed to reframe teachers' constructions of students. The focus of the various professional development programs differed, ranging from gender positioning, to disability positioning, to expectations for achievement of low-income students. The authors identified characteristics common to the programs, such as infrastructural supports, teacher engagement in the learning process, and use of external expertise. What strikes us, however, is that most of the programs used a technical-rational approach to teacher learning in the sense that "experts" taught knowledge and skills to teachers they could use with minoritized students. Implicitly, the programs replicate power imbalances in the wider society in which minoritized students themselves have little or no voice. Teachers occupy the position of "expert" viz a viz the students, just as professional developers occupy the position of "expert" vis-à-vis the teachers.

Professional development that repositions teacher-student relationships

A co-construction model of teacher professional development that repositions teachers as learners, and minoritized students as teachers, would seek to reconstruct this power imbalance, placing students as the "experts" who know best what works for them. Cook-Sather (2006) argues that repositioning students as active agents in the reform of schooling is both profoundly democratic and profoundly difficult. She points out that, "Because schools are set up on premises of prediction, control, and management, anything that challenges those premises is hard to accomplish within formal educational contexts" (p. 381). She argues that convincing educators not only to listen to students, but also to develop an ongoing process of engaging with what students say, even when what students say destabilizes core assumptions teachers hold, contradicts deeply held norms about teaching. Yet, one might truly regard students as the "experts" about teaching and learning since they are the beneficiaries of what happens in school every day.

Several published studies focus on what students have to say about school, with the intention that student voice should inform school reform and teacher learning. In the U.S., these include Poplin and Weeres' (1992) student voice study in southern California, Wilson and Corbett's (2001) extensive body of interviews with students in Philadelphia, and Storz's (2008) study of over 200 students in four Midwestern urban schools. There has been a small amount of research on teachers' learning through listening to their students. Martin and Hand (2009) reported a case study of a science teacher in the U.S. learning to shift from teacher-centred to student-centred teaching; as student voice increased in the teacher's classroom, the researchers found that students' ownership over their learning and the quality of students' argumentation also increased. In New Zealand, Baskerville (2011) reported a process of using storytelling in the classroom to activate student voice and build cross-cultural understandings and relationships—two teachers took part in the storytelling alongside the students, and everyone in the classroom was positioned as both teacher and learner.

There has been some investigation into engaging preservice teachers with student voice as a way of prompting them to rethink their assumptions about students.

Cook-Sather (2007) in the U.S. developed a well-conceptualised process in which high school students act as consultants to preservice teachers about teaching and learning. Her process intentionally disrupts the traditional positioning of the teacher as the source of knowledge and students as passive receivers of knowledge, and works to build a reciprocal relationship in which teachers and students can talk with each other about classroom teaching and learning.

At the professional development level, however, no study has been reported investigating the impact on teachers of a professional development program that is rooted in student voice. The study reported in this chapter was designed to address the following question: How does a professional development program that aims to reposition teachers as learners from their minoritized students change teachers' understandings of teaching?

Method

Context: Te Kotahitanga

While immersion schools designed to empower and enhance Māori student identity, culture, and accomplishments are available across New Zealand, the majority of Māori students attend 'mainstream' schools reflecting New Zealand's British colonialist history. Bishop, Berryman, Tiakiwai, and Richardson's (2003) Te Kotahitanga provides a model for culturally responsive, relationship-based pedagogy that is grounded in the philosophy of Paulo Freire. That is, the answers to the conditions that oppressed peoples find themselves in are not to be found in the language or epistemologies of the oppressors, but rather in those of the oppressed (Freire, 2003). Te Kotahitanga has been implemented widely to challenge low expectations for indigenous Māori students held by mainstream teachers and to shift classroom instruction from transmission to more discursive, interactive models (Bishop, Berryman, Cavanaugh & Teddy, 2009). At its core the Te Kotahitanga approach, rather than emphasising giving teachers the skills to use with Māori students, attempts to help teachers learn to build a reciprocal relationship with their students through Māori concepts such as *ako* (reciprocal teaching and learning) whereby knowledge is co-constructed within the classroom.

The Te Kotahitanga approach to teacher professional development is grounded in Māori student narratives about what does and does not work for them as learners in school, as the basis for the "Effective Teaching Profile" (ETP) regarding teacher-student instructional relationships in the classroom (Bishop, Berryman, Powell, & Teddy, 2007). Te Kotahitanga links culturally relevant/relationship-based classroom pedagogy with on-site embedded processes for working with teachers in classrooms, the primary aim of which is to help teachers respond directly to the Māori students in their own classrooms by repositioning their relationship with those students. At participating schools, facilitators selected for the quality of their own teaching, indigenous knowledge, and other leadership characteristics work directly with teachers to improve their practice through classroom observation and feedback plus regular co-construction teacher team reviews and planning meetings. Specific program components include:

- The initial induction *hui* (workshop) introducing Te Kotahitanga as a culturally responsive pedagogy of relations, initiated by having teachers read Māori students' narratives about relationships with teachers.
- Structured classroom observations by facilitators, which focus on both teachers' physical and discursive positioning within classrooms based on the ETP, followed by individual feedback sessions with teachers.
- Co-construction meetings where teacher teams problem-solve collaboratively, informed by observational and student outcomes data.
- Specific shadow-coaching sessions for individualised teacher professional development.

Throughout the process, the focus is on pedagogical relationships in classrooms, relationships among teachers, and collaborative work with the facilitation team.

Evaluation research approach

This paper presents a case study of professional development drawn from the findings of a large-scale, independent evaluation of Te Kotahitanga (Meyer et al., 2010; Sleeter, 2011). At the time of the evaluation, 33 secondary schools were participating in two phases reflecting different starting points. Data were gathered from all 12 schools that had participated for four years and a representative sample of 10 of the 21 schools that had participated for two years. While the overall evaluation was mixed methods, the interview data reported in this case study emphasise dimensions of relationship-based pedagogies that were the focus of the professional development activities.

Ethics

As this research involved direct contact with, and gathering data from and about school personnel, *whānau* (family), and school-aged students, appropriate and rigorous procedures for participant consent, data collection, and protection of privacy and confidentiality were followed. Participation in observations and interviews was voluntary, according to the evaluation research requirements.

The proposed data collection approach, data collection measures and questions, and processes for obtaining consent and protecting the privacy of persons (and the identities of the individual schools) were comprehensively reviewed and fully approved by the Victoria University Human Ethics Committee. Ethics protocols guaranteed confidentiality to individual participants from the schools, so that their identity would neither be revealed in our publications, nor would their schools be able to associate data with particular persons. All data were kept according to strict ethical guidelines in locked and password-protected files at the Jessie Hetherington Centre for Educational Research at Victoria University.

Research participants

One hundred and fifty teachers were interviewed across 22 secondary schools that participated in the Te Kotahitanga professional development program. In addition, many other school personnel—facilitators, principals, and other school leaders—were also interviewed. While these additional interviews are not the primary source of data for this chapter, selected comments illustrating themes identified in teacher interviews are included where relevant.

Interview procedures

Teachers were interviewed first, guided by three overarching evaluation questions:

(1) To what extent do teachers believe Te Kotahitanga helps them to develop their vision for education outcomes for Māori students and their sense of agency for improving Māori student achievement?

(2) To what extent do teachers believe Te Kotahitanga is helping them improve their teaching of Māori students and of students more generally? What has been its impact?

(3) How do teachers evaluate the various elements of the Te Kotahitanga professional development process and program?

Across interviews, teachers were encouraged to consider the impact of the Te Kotahitanga professional development program on their approaches to Māori students. Teachers also were asked to comment about using Te Kotahitanga approaches, strategies to enhance Māori achievement, caring for Māori students as learners, and other issues.

Interview transcription, coding and analyses

Interviews were recorded, transcribed, and checked for accuracy. Word documents were coded using NVivo after a preliminary review of a large sub-sample of transcriptions by two researchers to identify an initial set of possible nodes and words for coding. The final set of codes was discussed with additional research team members prior to coding all data. Themes were identified, and salient quotes selected to illustrate themes. The main purpose of the interview analyses was to identify patterns in teacher responses regarding how they viewed effective teaching of Māori students towards meeting more effectively the educational aspirations of Māori.

Limitations

As this was not a pre- and post-study, a particular limitation of this research was the lack of teachers' pre-participation perspectives prior to engaging in the Te Kotahitanga professional development program. During interviews, teachers were asked to describe the impact of the Te Kotahitanga professional development on their own understandings of effective teaching for Māori students. It was clear from analysis that teachers were starting in different places with regard to their own knowledge of culturally responsive pedagogies.

Another limitation is related to characteristics of teacher identity. The quotes provided in the following section represent themes from data analysis. Quotes came from both individual and focus group interviews in which Māori and non-Māori teachers participated. No information was collected on teacher characteristics, such as ethnicity, gender, age or years of teaching. Hence, in the following results section we have used generic terms for teachers.

Results

The analysis of interview data provided strong support for teachers valuing relationship-based pedagogies. With rare exception, virtually all teachers referred to a positive impact on their own learning and how they had operationalized the ETP in classrooms. Teachers highlighted the importance of positive relationships and interactions in the classroom/school environment to enhance Māori student achievement. The analysis aligns with other evidence emerging from the overall evaluation reporting that the majority of teachers (approximately 75%) were observed to demonstrate either moderate or high implementation of the ETP. Across subjects and schools, more than one in five teachers demonstrated a high level of implementation of the ETP in year 9–10 classrooms (Savage et al., 2011). The following section details changes in teachers' understandings of their teaching as a consequence of their engagement in the Te Kotahitanga professional development program.

Change in teacher understandings: Effective learning relationships and interactions in the classroom

Teachers emphasised strategies with a relational/interaction focus as being most helpful in improving practices and outcomes for Māori students. They reported significant shifts in their understandings of the importance of relationship-based pedagogies and policies for supporting Māori student achievement:

> At the start I wasn't aware that the learning method, the social method would be widely advantageous to them; the style of learning would be culturally bound. But once you're made aware of that, and you think about it, you practise it a bit, and you look at it—you know what I mean? And yes, I can see the change, and I can understand it. I found it inspirational, because when you get to my age, we've been through so many educational changes. (Teacher)

Teachers frequently reported that the professional development had raised their 'consciousness' of Māori students, their learning needs in the classroom, and the importance of dialogue with the students as a way of learning what their needs are. As the quotation below illustrates, many teachers came to see themselves as better teachers because they had learned to share power with students:

> It was a paradigm shift between what you (as a teacher) perceive as power or control or authority in the classroom, you don't lose that by sharing it, and I think that was a major paradigm shift. You don't actually become weaker, you become a stronger teacher by sharing it [power with students]. (Head of Department)

Teachers commented on shifts in their biases and assumptions, particularly in relation to expectations for Māori students:

> Expectation, definitely. Because before Te Kotahitanga, I did drop into that trap of thinking, "Oh, these difficult Māori students, I'll just never get through to them. Whatever am I going to do with them?" I didn't give up on them, but I did develop this view just not to expect as much from them as I would from other students, and that has changed. I do now have the same expectations of them as of the other ones. (Teacher)

Descriptions of changes to teaching practice reflected changes in teachers' expectations for Māori students along with an enhanced sense of agency and commitment to work harder towards positive results. Teachers reported increased efforts to improve teacher-student and student-student relationships and interactions in classrooms, and they regarded the focus on positive learning relationships in Te Kotahitanga as essential to establishing classroom climates conducive to learning.

Teachers also emphasised the importance of getting to know their Māori students as well as relating lessons to students' prior knowledge, experiences, and interests. They emphasised the importance of valuing, respecting, including, and caring about Māori culture, demonstrated by correct Māori pronunciation and through learning about cultural protocols and activities. Teachers emphasised high expectations for Māori students, and they talked about shifting from deficit thinking. They acknowledged the importance of setting appropriate challenges in the classroom, expecting students to be responsible for their own learning as well as supporting others' learning and behaviour, and used strategies such as cooperative learning so that students could learn to work with and from one another.

Some teachers believed a significant change in their own practice had been their repositioning, co-construction, and power-sharing with students that enabled them to 'care for students as culturally located individuals.' This was how they demonstrated they valued, respected and included Māori student perspectives, knowledge and voice; it also demonstrated respect for student contributions to knowledge-building in the classroom (reciprocal learning). For example:

> I think it's important that students have that input into their own learning and we've done a project based on a Māori sculptor. And part of that project, I integrated the Māori students into helping me to come up with that project and asking them, what would be really a good project for you to do that would be interesting for you? And I think it was one of the most successful projects that we've done this year, and that came from the students. (Teacher)

Teachers talked about experimenting with negotiation and co-construction of learning and behaviour strategies, whereby student voice was welcomed and acknowledged. Such approaches were considered important in developing more discursive teaching approaches to enhance student motivation, engagement, and achievement. Others emphasised shifting to more 'student focused' classrooms, with students taking responsibility for their own and others' learning and behaviour. Teachers spoke about experimentation with paired, group and cooperative learning activities. They frequently reported learning through such experiences that students were often 'the best teachers' for their peers, and school personnel described this as a profound change:

> I was a traditional classroom teacher, forever, from way back. My job was to provide knowledge for the students. Their job was to use that knowledge in a wise way, but the whole exposure to Te Kotahitanga makes you question what you're doing in the classroom. That shift to the discursive rather than traditional has actually opened a whole lot of doors, in terms of what you can do in the classroom, started to question the whole foundation on which you built your concept of teaching. (Deputy Principal)

Teachers talked about personal learning in relation to Māori concepts like *whānau* (family), *mana* (status), and *manākitanga* (demonstrating care) and their relevance to engaging in learning conversations within the classroom:

> Just to take on board the big Māori concepts, I think looking after the *mana* of the student in particular....I also think one of the things that I'm certainly learning over the process is…that attitude as a teacher....to learn how to engage in conversations with your students is really important. It's probably one of the most valuable things that I've been getting out of the process. How am I going to take the students forward while maintaining the *mana* of that student....I've found it really important to personally take on some of the Māori terminology and the *mana* framework....things like *manākitanga*, how am I actually [doing that]? So….you are going right back to the treaty in the sense that you've got both the European and the Māori framework operating side by side....And just [that] awareness…it's kind of got a focus and a clarity to it that I wouldn't have necessarily had before. (Teacher)

Reciprocity, with teachers sharing their own lives and interests, was also considered important in establishing trusting relationships in the classroom. This was seen as teacher repositioning—as moving away from 'the traditional teacher who did not smile until Easter.' This repositioning enabled students to reciprocate by letting teachers know more about their lives and interests outside the classroom, which was seen as useful knowledge in creating learning activities relevant to Māori students:

> It's also about sharing a bit of me as the teacher…so that they feel comfortable sharing some of their own knowledge and experiences from outside of the classroom with me…and that's important knowledge to have because I can use that in my teaching to link into things that they are familiar with, and their prior knowledge. So it's also creating learning contexts that they are familiar with. (Teacher)

Many participants explained the difference that the professional development program had made to teachers' practice towards creating more student-focused classrooms, particularly through paired activities and cooperative group learning. Developing cooperative classrooms required students to take responsibility for their own and others' learning and behaviour. In describing changes to classroom practice, teachers emphasised they had learned about the value of structuring learning activities whereby students learned from one another and pushed one another to learn. At times, this process was challenging for some teachers:

> I used to be very put off by doing group work, because I was much more goal-orientated, and holding individuals accountable for what I wanted done now, and I push my thing

from the front. Working in groups didn't gel for me in terms of the kinds of things I was stressing about. And as soon as I found out about it I thought, oh, this is going to be a huge waste of my time, having to sit back, and structure groups, and then allow them to work in groups, and provide them with some resource material, maybe assistance, just facilitate for them, but leave them to it, to a much greater extent than I normally would. I would want to be intervening there, much more. And I found the fact that I could actually leave, that—well, for me personally—that I could change my methodology. But then, to see them respond, and then later when I look at the results and the work, you know, even when we do pieces of individual work further down the line and I then I go back and I say well, this is great, where did you get this from, and they said oh, it came out in the discussion, during that day when we were working in groups. (Teacher)

I think Te Kotahitanga is making the classroom less teacher focused and more student focused…In the past I was very business focused…come on in and do this and this…whereas now I trying different techniques, like the group work or think-pair-share so that the kids can talk about their own ideas or share their own experiences…and those discussions are valuable…and I think I've grown as a teacher through the Te Kotahitanga program…because it's made me aware much more of the students' own perspectives, and what they are interested in and their skills and abilities which I can use in the classroom. (Teacher)

Many participants reported increased monitoring of Māori students' on-task behaviour and use of new assessment activities, such as explicit use of learning intentions, feedback and feed-forward.[7] Teachers also said they were more able to identify those students who were Māori, whereas before Te Kotahitanga they did not know which students were Māori or what Māori students were doing in classrooms. Teachers said that having this awareness was a key expectation for their engagement in the professional development program and was linked to broader monitoring and related assessment responsibilities. For example, teachers were seen to be circulating more around the classroom in order to monitor better Māori students' work and engagement. They made more of an effort to clarify the learning and achievement focus for students:

Being aware of making the students more aware of what they're learning, so, hence the learning intentions. But my success criteria don't come from myself, I'm more about the kids so I try to get "well, how are we going to learn this?" and they usually come up with it. (Teacher)

Ongoing challenges

Although the majority of teachers supported and were enthusiastic for relationship-based pedagogies, interview data also emphasised ongoing challenges. Facilitators acknowledged that the development of relationship-based approaches had challenged many teachers' thinking:

> And there are some people…who still can't get their head around, you know, this…*whakawhanaungatanga* (relationship building)…you know. There's teachers here that still can't get their head around that. (Facilitator)

For Pākehā/New Zealand European teachers who have learned through processes of colonisation to devalue the perspectives and worldviews of Māori, it can be very difficult not only to value what Māori adults say, but also to take Māori students' views and opinions seriously. Learning to confront assumptions about Māori students and their learning was a serious and necessary challenge if change is to occur. One facilitator explained:

> The fact that it focuses on Māori students [is] challenging for a lot of our staff, to focus on Māori students. Someone might feel like the others are missing out, so, I think it's challenging to actually sell that to the staff really. The data's showing that [focussing on Māori] is important. National data's saying that this is where the need is. (Facilitator)

The Te Kotahitanga approach required teachers to reflect on their own position and relationship with Māori students within their classrooms, and this meant learning an entirely new approach to teaching that challenges views of authority and expertise that many teachers previously held:

> The biggest challenge is challenging someone's positioning…especially if I'm dealing with a teacher that is a lot more experienced that I am as a teacher. So that's um, quite scary, we've got someone who's been teaching for 25 years, to say 'well…have you thought about doing something differently?' And so that's challenging. (Facilitator)

Some teachers struggled with negotiating co-construction approaches in class whilst also holding high expectations for learning and behaviour. If co-construction means sharing authority with students, they felt that this suggested that teachers abdicate their own authority in the classroom:

> I really lost control of the classroom and I had to work hard with the lead facilitator to get it back…I just went overboard with it. (Teacher)

> We found a teacher who was avoiding confronting Māori students in her class. She didn't realise things had got out of control, she wasn't telling them off, and they were being naughty. (Facilitator)

While considering that it was important to get to know their Māori students, several teachers emphasised that this could not be at the expense of high expectations. Teachers were challenged to develop high expectations alongside positive relationships, rather than one being at the expense of the other. For students to be responsible for their own and others' learning and behaviour, teachers were required to co-construct 'non-negotiables' in the classroom:

> Sure if you have a positive working relationship it helps…but you need to, as the teacher.…you…need to have clear and high expectations for the kids…don't threaten things that you're not going to follow up on…you need to have clear consequences for things…and that's not just for Māori kids that's for all kids…you need to recognise and celebrate their achievements…and you need to challenge them to 'step up' and if you set that challenge for them and help them they will do it…they can achieve…I'm quite tough on my kids…I set up my classroom so that they have to take responsibility for themselves but also the others in the group…We have rules and guidelines for working in this class…and there are also clear consequences if those rules are broken…if kids are off-task and distracting their mates then that affects the learning for all…so it's not all lovey-dovey…(Teacher)

We found a relationships between these challenges and the approaches to teaching we observed. Participant interview data were compared with in-class observation data. In classes where teachers evidenced low implementation of the ETP, discursive teaching approaches were not evident, and student experiences were not utilised within either the lesson content or format (Savage et al., 2011).

Discussion

We began by distinguishing between technical-rational versus teacher repositioning approaches to teacher professional development for culturally responsive pedagogies. Te Kotahitanga exemplifies the latter approach. Our interview data illustrate potentials of a repositioning approach, as well as some limitations.

The teachers we interviewed expressed enthusiasm for improving teaching by building relationships with their students, and by listening to them and valuing their perspectives. We would suggest that, since teachers generally go into the teaching profession because they enjoy young people, focusing their attention on the quality of their relationships with their students capitalizes on this motivation to enter teaching. Te Kotahitanga, however, prods teachers to develop relationships that go beyond being friendly and personable with students.

Using relationships as a fulcrum for communication with students about teaching and learning, and for co-constructing classroom processes with them, is a bit more challenging. The interviews show that most of the teachers understood that Te Kotahitanga aims to develop their ability to work with such relationships, and facilitator support in their classrooms appears to be crucial. As one of the facilitator interview quotes above illustrates, as teachers struggle with what it means to share authority with students while also using their authority as teachers, having someone there in the classroom to guide them is very important. Perhaps more challenging is getting teachers to recognise that Māori students in particular have historically not enjoyed strong pedagogical relationships with most teachers, and that these are the students with whom teachers should focus their efforts. The majority of teachers we interviewed did not see a focus on Māori students as problematic, and many described their learning about Māori culture and Māori language as occurring through positive relationships. As teachers conveyed their interest in getting to know students better, students shared more in return. Not all conversations were specifically about cultural issues, yet over time teachers increased opportunities for students to co-construct curricular elements. Yet many teachers did express concerns about focusing their efforts on building pedagogical relationships with Māori students, viewing this focus as a form of reverse discrimination.

However, there may be a limit to the cultural knowledge that teachers can learn solely through teaching and learning relationships with their students, which suggests a role for technical-rational learning alongside learning through repositioning. First, sharing authority with students will not replace teachers' pedagogical skills. For example, teachers who are unclear how to construct an academically rich, coherent lesson in their content area probably will not become better at doing so without assistance that goes beyond learning relationship-based learning.

More importantly, teacher repositioning needs to encompass knowledge of *te ao Māori* (the Māori world), historical experiences of *whānau* (family), *hapū* (sub-tribe) and *iwi* (tribe) with schools (see Chapter Six of this volume regarding the impact of ethnic studies). Mainstream schooling systems in New Zealand have been designed to assimilate Māori into the dominant group of Pākehā/European New Zealanders and eliminate cultural and language differences (Penetito, 2010). Māori worldviews, language, and so forth, can be learned better through more traditional approaches to professional development than through relationships with students. At the same time, teachers should also develop reciprocal relationships with Māori communities where they teach. Castagno and Brayboy (2008) warn that teachers require authentic learning connections with, and knowledge of, Indigenous communities and worldviews to develop culturally responsive pedagogies. Relationship-based learning, we would argue, provides a foundation on which to build, but closer linkages between schools and their local

Indigenous Māori communities are also needed if teachers are to extend their cultural knowledge and understandings.

Postscript

What do we learn about teacher professional development and culturally responsive pedagogy that has implications beyond New Zealand? Essentially, we found that ongoing professional development, based on a relationship-based approach to teacher professional learning and grounded in a powerful theory about culture and disparities, can improve the quality of minoritized students' education and achievement. Most teachers who participated in the professional development did shift their observable classroom pedagogy, and students responded positively and enthusiastically to that shift (Savage et al., 2011). Schools in which most of the teachers had participated in the professional development retain Māori students at a higher rate than comparison schools, prepared all of their students for university entrance at a much higher rate, and yielded higher achievement results in some academic areas. Culturally responsive pedagogy can be taught to teachers and it does make a difference for minoritized students—a greater positive difference, I would argue, than the standards and test-driven, market-based, privatized reforms that are being pushed in the U.S.

This particular project did not emphasize bringing more Māori teachers into the profession, nor on changing the curriculum substantively from the point of view of Māori intellectual knowledge. The reason it did not do these things is that most Māori students are in mainstream schools now, being taught by non-Māori teachers. How much more impactful would changes be if the curriculum were decolonized (along the lines of the research in Chapter Six), and if the teaching force reflected the student population (as discussed in Chapter 11)? I hope that nations around the world—including the U.S.—are able to address these questions. Indeed, doing so is essential to constructing schools for democracy and social justice, in diverse societies that have a legacy of racism, and in the context of a non-democratic movement to restore elite power.

Notes

1. Anne Hynds is Senior Lecturer, School of Educational Psychology and Pedagogy, Victoria University of Wellington, New Zealand.
2. Rawiri Hindle is Lecturer, Te Kura Māori, Victoria University of Wellington, New Zealand.
3. Catherine Savage is Executive Director, Tahu's Te Tapuae o Rehua, New Zealand.
4. Wally Penetito is Professor, Te Kura Māori, Victoria University of Wellington, New Zealand.

5. Luanna Meyer is Professor, School of Educational Psychology and Pedagogy, Victoria University of Wellington, New Zealand.

6. Pākehā/New Zealand Europeans, largely of British and Scotch descent, occupy much the same social position as Whites in the U.S.

7. While feedback focuses on work that the student has already completed, feed forward directs the student on work that hasn't been completed yet. When giving feed forward, the teacher offers explicit guidance or coaching on what the student is about to do, or should do next.

References

Aboud, F. E., & Fenwick, V. (1999). Exploring and evaluating school-based interventions to reduce prejudice. *Journal of Social Issues 55* (4), 767–786.

Achinstein, B., & Athanases, S. Z. (2005). Focusing new teachers on diversity and equity. *Teaching and Teacher Education*, 21 (7), 843–862.

Achinstein, B., & Ogawa, R. T. (2006). (In)Fidelity: What the resistance of new teachers reveals about professional principles and prescriptive educational policies. *Harvard Educational Review, 76*(1), 30–63.

Achinstein, B., Ogawa, R. T., & Speiglman, A. (2004). Are we creating separate and unequal tracks of teachers? The effects of state policy, local conditions, and teacher characteristics on new teacher socialization. *American Educational Research Journal, 41*(3), 557–603.

Ada, A. F. (1988). The Pajaro Valley experience. In T. Skutnabb-Kangas & J. Cummins (Eds.), *Minority education: From shame to struggle* (pp. 223–238). Philadelphia: Multilingual Matters.

Agee, J. (2004). Negotiating a teaching identity: An African American teacher's struggle to teach in test-driven contexts. *Teachers College Record, 106* (4), 747–774.

Aguilar, T. E., & Pohan, C. A. (1998). A cultural immersion experience to enhance cross-cultural competence. *Sociotam, 8*(1), 29–49.

Aguirre, A. (2000). Academic storytelling: A Critical Race Theory story of affirmative action. *Sociological Perspectives,* 43, 319–339.

Alba, R. D. (1990). *Ethnic identity.* New Haven, CT: Yale University Press.

Alberts, P. (2002). Praxis II and African American teacher candidates (or, "Is everything Black bad"?). *English Education, 34*(2), 105–125.

Allegretto, S. A. (2011). The state of working America's wealth, 2011. Economic Policy Institute briefing paper #292. Retrieved from www.epi.org/publication/the_state_of_working_americas_wealth_2011/

Allen, W. R. (1992). The color of success: African-American college student outcomes at predominantly White and historically Black public colleges and universities. *Harvard Educational Review, 62*(1), 26–44.

Alred, G. J. (1997). Teaching in Germany and the rhetoric of culture. *Journal of Business & Technical Communication* 11 (3), 353–378.

Alridge, D. P. (2006). The limits of master narratives in history textbooks. *Teachers College Record 108* (4), 662–686.

Alton-Lee, A. (2003). *Quality teaching for diverse students in schooling: Best evidence synthesis*. Wellington: Ministry of Education.

Altschul, I., Oyserman, D., & Bybee, D. (2006). Racial-ethnic identity in mid-adolescence: content and change as predictors of academic achievement. *Child Development, 77* (5), 1155–1169.

Altschul, I., Oyserman, D., & Bybee, D. (2008). Racial-ethnic self-schemas and segmented assimilation: Identity and the academic achievement of Hispanic youth. *Social Psychology Quarterly 71* (3), 302–320.

Andrzejewski, J. (1995). Teaching controversial issues in higher education: Pedagogical techniques and analytical framework. In R. J. Martin (Ed.), *Practicing what we teach* (pp. 3–26). Albany, NY: SUNY Press.

Antonio, A. L., Chang, M. J., Hakuta, K., Kenny, D. A., Levin, S., & Milem, J. E. (2004). Effects of racial diversity on complex thinking in college students. *Psychological Science 15* (8), 507–510.

Anyon, J. (2005). *Radical possibilities*. New York: Routledge.

Apple, M. W. (2000). *Official knowledge: Democratic education in a conservative age*. New York: Routledge.

Apple, M. W. (2001). *Educating the "right" way*. New York: RoutledgeFalmer.

Apple, M. W. (2004). *Ideology and curriculum*, 3rd ed. New York: RoutledgeFalmer.

Arkansas Department of Education (1992). *Multicultural Reading and Thinking (McRAT): Proposal submitted to the effectiveness panel of the National Diffusion Network*. Washington, DC: US Department of Education.

Aronowitz, S. (2000). *The knowledge factory: Dismantling the corporate university and creating true higher learning*. Boston: Beacon Press.

Ashton, P. T. & Webb, R. B. (1986). *Making a difference: Teachers' sense of efficacy and student achievement*. New York: Longman.

Astin, A. W. (1993). Diversity and multiculturalism on campus: How are students affected? *Change 25* (2), 44–50.

Au, K. H. (2003). *Literacy instruction in multicultural settings*. New York: Harcourt Brace.

Bakhtin, M. M., Holquist, M., & Emerson, C. (1986). *Speech genres and other late essays*. (V. W. McGee, Tran.). Austin: University of Texas Press.

Bales, B. L., & Saffold, F. (2011). A new era in the preparation of teachers for urban schools. *Urban Education, 46*, 953–974.

Ball, A. F. (2009). Toward a theory of generative change in culturally and linguistically complex classrooms. *American Educational Research Journal, 46*, 45–72.

Banks, J. A. (1984). Multicultural education and its critics: Britain and the United States, *The New Era* 65 (3): 58–65.

Banks, J. A. (1993). The canon debate, knowledge construction, and multicultural education. *Educational Researcher, 22*(5), 4–14.

Banks, J. A., Ed. (2003). *Diversity and citizenship education: Global perspectives*. San Francisco: Jossey-Bass.

Banks, J. A. (2004a). Introduction: Democratic citizenship in multicultural societies. In J. A. Banks (Ed.), *Diversity and citizenship education* (pp. 1–16). San Francisco: Jossey-Bass.

Banks, J. A. (2004b). Race, knowledge construction, and education in the United States. In J. A. Banks & C. A. M. Banks (Eds.), *Handbook of research on multicultural education* (2nd ed., pp. 228–239). San Francisco: Jossey-Bass.

Banks, J. A. (2007). *An introduction to multicultural education*, 4th ed. Needham Heights, MA: Allyn & Bacon.

Barnes, R. (1990). Race consciousness: The thematic content of racial distinctiveness in critical race scholarship. *Harvard Law Review*, 103, 1864–1871.

Barton, P. E. (2006). The dropout problem: Losing ground. *Educational Leadership, 63*(5), 14–18.

Baskerville, D. (2011). Developing cohesion and building positive relationships through storytelling in a culturally diverse New Zealand classroom. *Teaching and Teacher Education, 27*, 107–115.

Bean, T. W., Valerio, P. C., Senior, H. M., & White, F. (1999). Engagement in reading and writing about a multicultural novel. *Journal of Educational Research 93* (1), 32–37.

Beane, J. A., & Apple, M. W. (1999). The case for democratic schools. In M. W. Apple & J. A. Beane (Eds.), *Democratic schools* (pp. 1–12). Buckingham, England: Open University Press.

Beauboeuf-LaFontant, T. (1999). A movement against and beyond boundaries: Politically relevant teaching among African-American teachers. *Teachers College Record, 100*, 702–723.

Begay, S., Dick, G. S., Estell, D. W., Estell, J., McCarty, T. L. & Sells, A. (1995). Change from the inside out: A story of transformation in a Navajo community school. *Bilingual Research Journal 19* (1), 121-139.

Bell, D. (1985). The civil rights chronicles. *Harvard Law Review*, 99, 4–83.

Bell, D. (1987). *And we are not saved: The elusive quest for racial justice*. New York: Basic Books.

Beckett, D. R. (1998). Increasing the number of Latino and Navajo teachers in hard-to-staff schools. *Journal of Teacher Education, 49*(3), 196–205.

Bennett, C. I. (1998). *Comprehensive multicultural education*, 4th ed. Needham Heights, MA: Allyn & Bacon.

Bennett, C. I. (2002). Enhancing ethnic diversity at a Big Ten university through Project TEAM: A case study in teacher education. *Educational Researcher, 31*(2), 21–29.

Bennett, C., Cole, D., & Thompson, J. (2000). Preparing teachers of color at a predominantly White university. *Teaching and Teacher Education, 16*(4), 445–464.

Bennett, C. I., McWhorter, L. M., & Kuykendall, J. A. (2006). Will I ever teach? Latino and African American students' perspectives on PRAXIS I. *American Educational Research Journal, 43*(3), 531–575.

Berger, R. (2003). *An ethnic of excellence*. Portsmouth, NH: Heinemann.

Bergeron, B. S. (2008). Enacting a culturally responsive curriculum in a novice teacher's classroom. *Urban Education, 43*(1), 4–28.

Berlak, A. (2010). Coming soon to your favorite credential program: National exit exams. *Rethinking Schools 24*(4), 41–45.

Berlak, A., & Moyenda, S. (2001). *Taking it personally*. Philadelphia: Temple University Press.

Berliner, D. C. (2005). Our impoverished view of educational review. *Teachers College Record*, August 2, 2005. Retrieved from http://www.tcrecord.org

Berliner, D. C., & Biddle, B. J. (1995). *The manufactured crisis.* Cambridge, MA: Perseus Books.

Bernstein, B. (1975). *Class, codes and control,* revised edition. London: Routledge & Kegan Paul.

Bernstein, B., & Solomon, J. (1999). Pedagogy, identity, and the construction of a theory of symbolic control: Basil Bernstein questioned by Joseph Solomon. *British Journal of Sociology of Education* 20(2), pp. 265–279.

Beyer, L., & Liston, D. (1996). *Curriculum in conflict.* New York: Teachers College Press.

Bigelow, B. (2002). Rethinking primitive cultures: Ancient futures and learning from Ladakh. In B. Bigelow & B. Peterson (Eds.), *Rethinking globalization* (pp. 308–315). Milwaukee, WI: Rethinking Schools.

Bigelow, W. (1990). Inside the classroom: Social vision and critical pedagogy. *Teachers College Record* 91 (3): 437–448.

Bigelow, B., & Peterson, B. (1998). *Rethinking Columbus.* Milwaukee, WI: Rethinking Schools.

Bigler, R. S. (1999). The use of multicultural curricula and materials to counter racism in children. *Journal of Social Issues* 55 (4), 687–705.

Bigler, R. S., Brown, C. S., & Markell, M. (2001). When groups are not created equal: Effects of group status on the formation of intergroup attitudes in children. *Child Development, 72,* 1151–1162.

Bishop, R., Berryman, M., Powell, A., & Teddy, L. (2007). *Te Kotahitanga: Improving the educational achievement of Māori students in mainstream education Phase 2: Towards a whole school approach* (Report to the Ministry of Education). Wellington, NZ: Ministry of Education.

Bishop, R., Berryman, M., Cavanagh, T., & Teddy, L. (2009). Te Kotahitanga: Addressing educational disparities facing Maori students in New Zealand. *Teaching and Teacher Education, 25,* 734–742.

Bishop, R., Berryman, M., Tiakiwai, S., & Richardson, C. (2003). *Te Kotahitanga: The experiences of year 9 and 10 Māori students in mainstream classrooms.* Report to the Ministry of Education. Wellington, NZ: Ministry of Education.

Blackwell, D. M. (2010). Sidelines and separate spaces: Making education anti-racist for students of color. *Race Ethnicity & Education 13* (4), 473–494.

Bloom, A. C. (1989). *The closing of the American mind.* New York: Simon & Schuster.

Blumer, I., & Tatum, B. D. (1999). Creating a community of allies: How one school system attempted to create an anti-racist environment. *International Journal of Leadership in Education* 2 (3), 255–267.

Bondy, E., & Davis, S. (2000). The caring of strangers: Insights from a field experience in a culturally unfamiliar community. *Action in Teacher Education, 22*(2), 54–66.

Bondy, E., Ross, D. D., Gallingane, C., & Hambacher, E. (2007). Creating environments of success and resilience. *Urban Education, 42,* 326–348.

Bonilla-Silva, E. (2010). *Racism without racists,* 3rd ed. Lanham, MD: Rowman & Littlefield.

Bonnett, A. (1990). Anti-racism as a radical educational ideology in London and Tyneside. *Oxford Review of Education,* 16 (2), 255–267.

Bonnett, A., & Carrington, B. (1996). Constructions of anti-racist education in Britain and Canada. *Comparative Education* 32 (3), 271–288.

Bowman, N. A. (2010a). Disequilibrium and resolution: The non-linear effects of diversity courses on well-being and orientations towards diversity. *The Review of Higher Education 33* (4), 543–568.

Bowman, N. A. (2010b). College diversity experiences and cognitive development: A meta-analysis. *Review of Educational Research 80* (1), 4–33.

Boyd, D., Lankford, H., Loeb, S., & Wyckoff, J. (2005). The draw of home: How teachers' preferences for proximity disadvantage urban schools. *Journal of Policy Analysis and Management, 24*(1), 113–132.

Boyle-Baise, M. (2002). *Multicultural service learning*. New York: Teachers College Press.

Boyte, H. C. (2003). Civic education and the new American patriotism, post-9/11. *Cambridge Journal of Education, 33*(1), 85–100.

Bracey, G. W. (2005). *No Child Left Behind: Where does the money go?* Arizona State University: Educational Policy Studies Unit. Retrieved from www.asu.edu/educ/epsl/EPRU/documents/EPSL-0506–114-EPRU.pdf

Brandt, G. L. (1986). *The realization of anti-racist teaching*. Lewes, England: The Falmer Press.

Brayboy, B. McK. J. (2005). Toward a tribal critical race theory of education. *Urban Review 37*(5), 425–446.

Brayboy, B. M. J., & Castagno, A. E. (2009). Self-determination through self-education: Culturally responsive schooling for Indigenous students in the U.S.A. *Teaching Education, 20*(1), 31–53.

Brennan, S., & Bliss, T. (1998). Increasing minority representation in the teaching profession through alternative certification: A case study. *Teacher Educator, 34*(1), 1–11.

Bromley, H. (1989). Identity politics and critical pedagogy. *Educational Theory* 39 (3), 207–223.

Brophy, J., & VanSledright, B. 1997. *Teaching and learning history in elementary schools*. New York: Teachers College Press.

Brown, D. F. (2004). Urban teachers' professed classroom management strategies. *Urban Education, 39*, 266–289.

Brown, K. D., & Brown, A. L. (2010). Silenced memories: An examination of the sociocultural knowledge on race and racial violence in official school curriculum. *Equity & Excellence in Education 43* (2), 139–154

Brozo, W. G., & Valerio, P. C. (1996). A walk through Gracie's garden: Literacy and cultural explorations in a Mexican American junior high school. *Journal of Adolescent and Adult Literacy 40* (3), 164–170.

Buendia, E., Gitlin, A., & Doumbia, F. (2003).Working the pedagogical borderlands: An African critical pedagogue teaching within an ESL context. *Curriculum Inquiry, 33*(3), 291–320.

Bunch, W. (2010). *The backlash*. New York: Harper.

Buras, K. L. (2010). *Pedagogy, policy, and the privatized city*. New York: Teachers College Press.

Business Roundtable (1997). A business leader's guide to setting academic standards. Retrieved from http://www.brtable.org/TaskForces/TaskForce/

Business Roundtable (1999). *Transforming education policy: Assessing ten years of progress in the states*. Washington, D. C: The Business Roundtable.

Business Roundtable (2005, July 27). Citing "critical situation" in science and math, business groups urge approval of new national agenda for innovation. Retrieved from www.businessroundtable.org/newsroom/document.aspx?qs=5876BF807822B0F1AD1448722FB5171 1FCF50C8

California Department of Education. (1996). *Recommended literature: Kindergarten through grade twelve* [online]. Sacramento, CA: Author. Retrieved from www.cde.ca.gov/ci/literature.

California Department of Education. (1997). *English-language arts content standards for California public schools*. Sacramento, CA: Author.

California Department of Education. (1999a). *English language development standards* Sacramento, CA: Author.

California Department of Education. (1999b). *Reading/language arts framework for California pub-*

lic schools. Sacramento, CA: Author.

California Department of Education. (2001). *History-Social Science Framework and Standards for California Public Schools.* Sacramento, CA: Author.

California Department of Education. (2012). *Student and school data reports.* Retrieved from www.cde.ca.gov/ds/sd/cb/.

California State University Monterey Bay. (2002). *Strategic plan.* Retrieved from http://csumb.edu/strategicplan.

Camangian, P. (2010). Starting with self: Teaching autoethnography to foster critically caring literacies. *Research in the Teaching of English, 45,* 179–204.

Cambium Learning and National Academic Educational Partners. (2011). *Curriculum audit of the Mexican American Studies Department, Tucson Unified School District.* Retrieved from http://saveethnicstudies.org/state_audit.shtml.

Cammarota, J. (2007). A social justice approach to achievement: Guiding Latina/o students toward educational attainment with a challenging, socially relevant curriculum. *Equity & Excellence in Education, 40,* 87–96.

Cammarota, J., & Romero, A. (2006). A critically compassionate intellectualism for Latina/o students. *Multicultural Education, 14*(2), 16–23.

Cammarota, J., & Romero, A. (2009). The Social Justice Education Project: A critically compassionate intellectualism for Chicana/o students. In W. Ayers, T. Quinn & D. Stovall (Eds.), *Handbook for social justice education* (pp. 465–476). Mahwah, NJ: Lawrence Erlbaum.

Carter, D. (2008). Achievement as resistance: Development of a critical race achievement ideology among Black achievers. *Harvard Educational Review 78*(3), 466–497.

Castagno, A., & Brayboy, B. (2008). Culturally responsive schooling for indigenous youth: A review of the literature. *Review of Educational Research, 78,* 941–993.

Cavallo, A. M. L., Ferreira, M. M., & Roberts, S. K. (2005). Increasing student access to qualified science and mathematics teachers through an urban school-university partnership. *School Science and Mathematics, 105*(7), 363–372.

Center for Research on Education, Diversity and Excellence. (2002). *Research evidence: Five standards for effective pedagogy and student outcomes.* Technical Report No. G1, March 2002. Santa Cruz, CA: University of California, Santa Cruz. Retrieved from http://crede.ucsc.edu/pdf/evidence_g1.pdf

Chan, S. M., & East, P. (1998). Teacher education and race equality: A focus on an induction course. *Multicultural Teaching, 16*(2), 43–46.

Chance, L., Morris, V. G., & Rakes, S. (1996). Fostering sensitivity to diverse cultures through an early field experience collaborative. *Journal of Teacher Education, 47*(5), 386–389.

Chang, M. J. (2002). The impact of an undergraduate diversity course requirement on students' racial views and attitudes. *The Journal of General Education 51* (1), 21–42.

Chavarin, J. L. (2002). *Culturally congruent critical pedagogy for preschool children.* Unpublished master's thesis, California State University Monterey Bay.

Chavous, T., Hilkene, D., Schmeelk,Cone, K., Caldwell, C. H., Kohn-Wood, L., & Zimmerman, M. A. (2003). Racial identity and academic attainment among African American adolescents. *Child Development 74* (4), 1076–1090.

Churchill, W. (2002). *Struggle for the land.* San Francisco: City Lights.

Cixous, H. (1988). Conversations. In K. M. Newton (Ed.), *Twentieth century literary theory.* New York:

St. Martin's Press.

Clark, V. L. (1988). Teacher education at historically Black institutions in the aftermath of the HOLMES/CARNEGIE reports. *Teacher Education Quarterly, 15*(2), 32–49.

Clayton, C. D. (2007). Curriculum making as novice professional development: Practical risk taking as learning in high-stakes times. *Journal of Teacher Education, 58*(3), 216–230.

Clewell, B. C., & Villegas, A. M. (1999). Creating a nontraditional pipeline for urban teachers: The Pathways to Teaching Careers Model. *Journal of Negro Education, 68*(3), 306–317.

Clewell, B. C., & Villegas, A. M. (2001). *Absence unexcused: Ending teacher shortages in high-need areas: Evaluating the Pathways to Teaching Careers Program.* Washington, DC: Urban Institute. ERIC Document ED460235.

Cochran-Smith, M. (2004). *Walking the road: Race, diversity and social justice in teacher education.* New York: Teachers College Press.

Cochran-Smith, M., & Zeichner K. M. (2005). Executive summary. In Smith, M. C. & Zeichner, K.M. (Eds). *Studying teacher education* (pp. 1–36). Mahwah, NJ: Lawrence Erlbaum Associates.

Cole, B.P. (1986). The black educator: An endangered species. *Journal of Negro Education, 55*(3), 326–334.

Coles, G. (2000). *Misreading reading: The bad science that hurts children.* Portsmouth, NH: Heinemann.

Collins, P. H. (1990). *Black feminist thought.* New York: Routledge.

Comber, B., & Nixon, H. (2009). Teachers' work and pedagogy in an era of accountability. *Discourse: Studies in the Cultural Politics of Education, 30*, 333–345.

Compton, M., & Weiner, L. (2008). The global assault on teaching, teachers, and their unions. Basingstoke, UK: Palgrave Macmillan.

Cook-Sather, A. (2002). Re(in)forming the conversations: Student position, power and voice in teacher education. *The Radical Teacher, 64*, 21–48.

Cook-Sather, A. (2006). Sound, presence, and power: "Student voice" in educational research and reform. *Curriculum Inquiry, 36*(4), 361–390.

Cook-Sather, A. (2007). What would happen if we treated students as those with opinions that matter? The benefits to principals and teachers of supporting youth engagement in school. *NASSP Bulletin, 91*(4), 343–362.

Copenhaver, J. (2001). Listening to their voices connect literary and cultural understandings: Responses to small group read-alouds of *Malcolm X: A Fire. New Advocate, 14*, 343–359.

Cornbleth, C., & Waugh, D. (1995). *The great speckled bird: Multicultural politics and education decision-making.* New York: St. Martins Press.

Crenshaw, K. (1993). Beyond racism and misogyny: Black feminism and 2 Live Crew. In M.J. Matsuda, C. R. Lawrence, R. Delgado, & K. W. Crenshaw, (Eds.), *Words that wound: Critical race theory, assaultive speech, and the first amendment* (pp. 111–132). Boulder, CO: Westview Press.

Crenshaw, K., Gotanda, N., Peller, G., & Thomas, K., (Eds.) (1995). *Critical race theory: The key writings that formed the movement.* New York: The New Press.

Creswell, J. W. (2008). *Research design: Qualitative, quantitative, and mixed methods approaches.* Thousand Oaks, CA: Sage.

Crocco, M. S., & Costigan, A. T. (2007). The narrowing of curriculum and pedagogy in the age of accountability. *Urban Education, 42*, 512–535.

Cummins, J. (1996). *Negotiating identities: Education for empowerment in a diverse society.* Ontario,

CA: California Association for Bilingual Education.

Cushing, K. S., Sabers, D. S., & Berliner, D. C. (1992). Olympic gold: Investigations of expertise in teaching. *Educational Horizons, 70*, 108–114.

Dakari, A. (2009). Rolling up their sleeves: Venture philanthropists pitch in for Chicago's schools. *Education Week, 28*, 23–25.

Dandy, E. B. (1998). Increasing the number of minority teachers: Tapping the paraprofessional pool. *Education and Urban Society, 31*(1), 89–103.

Darder, A. (1995). Buscando America: The contributions of critical Latino educators to the academic development and empowerment of Latino students in the U.S. In C. E. Sleeter & P. McLaren (Eds.), *Multicultural education, critical pedagogy, and the politics of difference* (pp. 319–348). Albany, NY: SUNY Press.

Darder, A. (1991). *Culture and power in the classroom: A critical foundation for bicultural education.* Westport, CT: Bergin & Garvey.

Darling-Hammond, L. (2006). *Powerful teacher education.* San Francisco: Jossey-Bass.

Deakin, C. R., Coates, M., Taylor, M., & Ritchie, S. (2004). *A systematic review of the impact of citizenship education on the provision of schooling.* London: EPPI-Centre, Social Science Research Unit, Institute of Education.

Dee, J. R., & Henkin, A. B. (2002). Assessing dispositions toward cultural diversity among preservice teachers. *Urban Education, 37*(1), 22–40.

Dee, T. S. (2004). Teachers, race and student achievement in a randomized experiment. *Review of Economics and Statistics, 86*(1), 195–210.

Dei, G. J. S. (1993). The challenges of anti-racist education in Canada. *Canadian Ethnic Studies* 25 (2), pp. 36–52.

Dei, G. J. S. (1996). *Anti-racism education.* Halifax, Nova Scotia: Fernwood Publishing.

Dei, G. J. S. (1999). Knowledge and politics of social change: The implication of anti-racism. *British Journal of Sociology of Education*, 20 (3), pp. 395–410.

Delgado, R. (1989). Storytelling for oppositionists and others: A plea for narrative. *Michigan Law Review,* 87, 2411–2441.

Delgado, R. (1993). On telling stories in school: A reply to Farber and Sherry. *Vanderbilt Law Review,* 46, 665–676.

Delgado, R. (1995). *The Rodrigo chronicles: Conversations about America and race.* New York: New York University Press.

Delgado, R. (1999). *When equality ends: Stories about race and resistance.* Boulder, CO: Westview Press.

Delgado, R., & Stefancic, J. (Eds.). (2000). *Critical race theory: The cutting edge*(2nd ed.). Philadelphia: Temple University Press.

Delgado, R., & Stefancic, J. (2001). *Critical race theory: An introduction.* New York: New York University Press.

Delgado Bernal, D. (1999). Chicana/o education from the civil rights era to the present. In J.F. Moreno, (Ed.), *The elusive quest for equality: 150 Years of Chicano/Chicana education,* (pp. 77–108). Cambridge, MA: Harvard Educational Review.

Delgado Bernal, D. (2002). Critical race theory, Latino critical theory, and critical raced-gendered epistemologies: Recognizing students of color as holders and creators of knowledge. *Qualitative Inquiry,* 8(1): 105–126.

Delpit, L. (1995). *Other people's children.* New York: The New Press.

Denson, N. (2009). Do curricular and co-curricular activities influence racial bias? A meta-analysis.

Review of Educational Research 79 (2), 805–838.

Derman-Sparks, L., & Phillips, C. B. (1997). *Teaching/learning anti-racism.* New York: Teachers College Press.

Dewey, J. (1938). *Experience and education.* New York: Touchstone.

Diamond, B. J., & Moore, M. A. (1995). *Multicultural literacy: Mirroring the reality of the classroom.* New York: Longman.

Díaz, M. I. (2002). *Edifying and strengthening English literacy for Latino second-language learners through the use of their native language: A language arts curriculum.* Unpublished master's thesis, California State University Monterey Bay.

Dicker, S. 1996. *Languages in America: A pluralist view.* Clevedon, U.K.: Multilingual Matters Ltd.

Dickson, S. V., Chard, D. J., & Simmons, D. C. (1993). An integrated reading/writing curriculum: A focus on scaffolding. *LD Forum, 18*(4), 12–16.

Dillard, C.B. (1994). Beyond supply and demand: Critical pedagogy, ethnicity, and empowerment in recruiting teachers of color. *Journal of Teacher Education, 45*(1), 9–17.

"Don't turn back the clock!" (2003). *The Education Trust.* Retrieved from www2.edtrust.org.

Du Bois, W. E. B. (1903). *The souls of Black folk.* Chicago: A.C. McClurg & Co.

Duncan-Andrade, J. (2007). Gangstas, wankstas, and ridas: Defining, developing, and supporting effective teachers in urban schools. *International Journal of Qualitative Studies in Education, 20,* 617–638.

Duncan-Andrade, J. M. R., & Morrell, E. (2008). *The art of critical pedagogy.* New York: Peter Lang.

Durdin, T. R. (2007). African centered schooling: Facilitating holistic excellence for Black children. *The Negro Educational Review, 58* (1–2), 23–34.

Dutro, E., Kazemi, E., Balf, R., & Lin, Y. S. (2008). "What are you and where are you from?" Race, identity, and the vicissitudes of cultural relevance. *Urban Education, 43,* 269–300.

Easton-Brooks, D., Lewis, C., & Zhang, Y. (2011). Ethnic-matching: The influence of African American teachers on the reading scores of African American students. *Urban Education, 46*(6), 1280–1289.

Edelman, M. W. (1996, April). Needed: A massive moral movement to leave no child behind. *Intercultural Research Development Newsletter.* Retrieved from www.idra.org/Newslttr/1996/Apr/Marian.htm#Needed_A_Massive_Moral

Educational Demographics Office. (2004). *Enrollment in California Public Schools by Ethnic Designation, 1981–82 through 2002–03.* Sacramento: California Department of Education. Retrieved from http://goldmine.cde.ca.gov/demographics/reports/index.html

Elenes, C. A. (1997). Reclaiming the borderlands: Chicana/o identity, difference, and critical pedagogy. *Educational Theory* 47 (3): 359–375.

El-Haj, T. R. (2003). Practicing for equity from the standpoint of the particular: Exploring the work of one urban teacher network. *Teachers College Record, 105,* 817–845.

El-Haj, T. R. A. (2006). *Elusive justice: Wrestling with difference and educational equity in everyday practice.* New York: Routledge.

Ellsworth, E. (1989). Why doesn't this feel empowering? Working through the repressive myths of critical pedagogy. *Harvard Educational Review* 59 (3): 297–324.

Emery, K., & Ohanian, S. (2004). *Why is corporate America bashing our public schools?* Portsmouth, NH: Heinemann.

Emig, J. (1982). Inquiry paradigms and writing. *College Composition and Communication, 33,* 64–75.

Engberg, M. E. (2004). Improving intergroup relations in higher education: A critical examination of the influence of educational interventions on racial bias. *Review of Educational Research 74* (4), 473–524.

Epstein, K. K. (2005). The whitening of the American teaching force: A problem of recruitment or racism? *Social Justice, 32*(3), 89–102.

Epstein, T. (2000). Adolescents perspectives on racial diversity in U.S. history: Case studies from an urban classroom. *American Educational Research Journal 37* (1), 185–214.

Epstein, T. (2001). Racial identity and young people's perspectives on social education. *Theory into Practice 40* (1), 42–47.

Epstein, T. (2009). *Interpreting national history*. New York: Routledge.

Farber, D., & Sherry, S. (1993) Telling stories out of school: An essay on legal narratives. *Stanford Law Review*, 45, 807–855.

Farber, D., & Sherry, S. (1997) *Beyond all reason: The radical assault on truth in American law*. New York: Oxford University Press.

Fashola, O. S., & Slavin, R. E. (1997). Promising programs for elementary and middle schools: Evidence of effectiveness and replicability. *Journal of Education for Students Placed at Risk 2* (3), 251–307.

Feeney, T. (2004). Principles count (Heritage Lecture #854). *The Heritage Foundation*. Retrieved from http://www.heritage.org

Feiman-Nemser, S. (2001). From preparation to practice: Designing a continuum to strengthen and sustain teaching. *Teachers College Record, 198*(6), 1013–1055.

Feistrizter, E. (1999). *The making of a teacher: A report on teacher preparation in the U.S.* National Center for Education Information. Retrieved from www.ncei.com/MakingTeacher-rpt.htm

Fickel, E. H. (2005). Teachers, tundra, and talking circles: Learning history and culture in an Alaskan native village. *Theory and Research in Social Education, 33*, 476–507.

Fielder, D. J. (1996). Diversifying from within: the minority teacher scholarship program. *Phi Delta Kappan, 77*(6), 445–446.

Flecha, R. (1999). Modern and postmodern racism in Europe: Dialogic approach and anti-racist pedagogies. *Harvard Educational Review* 69 (2), 150–171.

Flippo, R. F. (2003). Canceling diversity: High-stakes teacher testing and the real crisis. *Multicultural Perspectives, 5*(4), 42–45.

Flores, B. B., Clark, E. R., Claeys, L., & Villarreal, A. (2007). Academy for teacher excellence: Recruiting, preparing, and retaining Latino teachers through learning communities. *Teacher Education Quarterly, 34*(4), 53–70.

Flores, J. (2003). *Dismantling the master's house: Using whose tools?* Unpublished master's thesis. Seaside, CA: California State University, Monterey Bay.

Flores, M. T. (2007). Navigating contradictory communities of practice in learning to teach for social justice. *Anthropology & Education Quarterly, 38*, 380–402.

Flores, W. V., & Benmayor, R., Eds. (1997). *Latino cultural citizenship*. Boston: Beacon Press.

Foorman, B. R., Francis, D. J., Fletcher, J. M., & Scatschneider, C. (1998). The role of instruction in learning to read: Preventing reading failure in at-risk children. *Journal of Educational Psychology* 90, 37–55.

Ford, D. Y., & Harris III, J. J. (2000). A framework for infusing multicultural curriculum into gifted education. *Roeper Review*, 23 (1), 4–10.

Foster, M. (1997). *Black teachers on teaching*. New York: New Press.

Foster, S. J. (1999). The struggle for American identity: Treatment of ethnic groups in United States history textbooks. *History of Education 28* (3): 251–278

Freire, P. (1970). *Pedagogy of the oppressed*. New York: Continuum.

Freire, P. (1973). *Education for critical consciousness*. New York: Seabury Press.

Freire, P. (1976). *Education and the practice of freedom*. London: Writers and Readers Publishing Cooperative.

Freire, P. (1998). *Pedagogy of freedom*. Lanham, MD: Rowman & Littlefield.

Freire, P. (2003). From *Pedagogy of the oppressed*. In A. Darder, M. Baltodano & R. Torres (Eds.), *The critical pedagogy reader* (pp. 57–68). London: Routledge Falmer.

Fry, P. G., & McKinney, L. J. (1997). A qualitative study of preservice teachers' early field experiences in an urban, culturally different school. *Urban Education, 32*(2), 184–201.

Fuller, E. J., & Johnson, J. F., Jr. (2001). Can state accountability systems drive improvements in school performance for children of color and children from low-income homes? *Education and Urban Society, 33*(3), 260–283.

Gallegos, B. (1998). Remembering the Alamo: Imperialism, memory, and postcolonial educational studies. *Educational Studies, 29*(3), 232–247.

Gándara, P., Rumberger, R., Maxwell-Jolly, J., & Callahan, R., (2003). English learners in California schools: Unequal resources, unequal outcomes. *Education Policy Analysis Archives, 11*(36). Retrieved from http://epaa.asu.edu/epaa/v11n36/.

Gandhi, L. (1998). *Postcolonial theory: A critical introduction*. New York: Columbia University Press.

Garcia, R. (1995). Critical race theory and Proposition 187: The racial politics of immigration law. *Chicano-Latino Law Review*, 17, 118–148.

Garza, R. (2009). Latino and white high school students' perception of caring behaviors. *Urban Education, 44*, 297–321.

Gay, G. (1983). Multiethnic education: Historical developments and future prospects. *Phi Delta Kappan, 64*, 560–563.

Gay, G. (1995a). Curriculum theory and multicultural education. In J. A. Banks & C. A. M. Banks (Eds.). *Handbook of Research on Multicultural Education* (pp. 25–43) New York: Macmillan.

Gay, G. (1995b). Mirror images on common issues: Parallels between multicultural education and critical pedagogy. In C. E. Sleeter & P. McLaren (Eds.), *Multicultural education, critical pedagogy, and the politics of difference* (pp. 155–190). Albany, NY: SUNY Press.

Gay, G. (2010). *Culturally responsive teaching* (2nd ed.). New York: Teachers College Press.

Gay, G. & Howard, T. (2000). Multicultural teacher education for the 21st century. *The Teacher Educator 36*, 1–16.

Gelberg, D. (2007). The business agenda for school reform. *Teacher Education Quarterly, 34*(2), 45–58.

Genzuk, M., & Baca, R. (1998). The paraeducator-to-teacher pipeline. *Education & Urban Society, 31*(1), 73–88.

Gibbons, P. (2002). *Scaffolding language, scaffolding learning: Teaching second language learners in the mainstream classroom*. Portsmouth, NH: Heinemann.

Giddens, A. (1979). *Central problems in social theory*. Berkeley: University of California Press.

Gillborn, D. (1995). *Racism and anti-racism in real schools*. Buckingham: Open University Press.

Gillborn, D., & Youdell, D. (2000). *Rationing education*. Philadelphia: Open University Press.

Ginwright, S. (2004). *Black in school: Afrocentric reform, urban youth, and the promise of hip-hop culture*. New York: Teachers College Press.

Giroux, H. A. (1983). *Theory and resistance in education*. South Hadley, MA: Bergin & Garvey.

Giroux, H. A. (1985). Critical pedagogy, cultural politics, and the discourse of experience. *Journal of Education* 167 (2), 22–41.

Giroux, H. A. (1988). *Teachers as intellectuals*. South Hadley, MA: Bergin & Garvey.

Giroux, H. A. (1992). *Border crossings*. New York: Routledge.

Giroux, H. A., & McLaren, P. (1992). Writing from the margins: Geographics of identity, pedagogy and power. *Journal of Education* 174 (1): 7–30.

Giroux, H. A., & Simon, R. I., Eds. (1989). *Popular culture, schooling and everyday life*. Granby, MA: Bergin & Garvey.

Goldstein, B. S. C. (1995). Critical pedagogy in a bilingual special education classroom. *Journal of Learning Disabilities* 28 (8), 463–475.

González, F. (1998). The formations of Mexicananess: Trenzas de identidades multiples. Growing Up Mexicana: Braids of multiple identities. *International Journal of Qualitative Studies in Education*, 11(1), 81–102.

González, J. M. (1997). Recruiting and training minority teachers: Student views of the pre-service program. *Equity & Excellence in Education, 30* (1), 56–64.

Goodman, K., & Goodman, Y. (1979). Learning to read is natural. In L. Resnick & P. Weaver (Eds.) *Theory and practice of early reading* (Vol. 1). Hillsdale, NJ: Erlbaum.

Gordon, E. (1990). On the other side of the war. In Watanabe, S, & Bruchac, C., Eds. *Home to stay: Asian American women's fiction* (1st ed.) (48–51). Greenfield Center, New York: The Greenfield Review Press.

Graman, T. (1988) Education for humanization: Applying Paulo Freire's pedagogy to learning a second language. *Harvard Educational Review* 58 (4): 433–448.

Grande, S. M. A. (2000). American Indian geographies of identity and power. *Harvard Educational Review* 70 (4): 467–498.

Grant, C. A., & Sleeter. C. E. (2009). *Turning on learning* (4th ed.). New York: Wiley.

Grant, C. A., & Sleeter. C. E. (2011). *Doing multicultural education for achievement and equity*. New York: Routledge.

Grant, S., Milfont, T., Herd, R., & Denny, S. (2010). Health and well-being of a diverse student population: The Youth2000 surveys of New Zealand secondary school students and their implications for educations. In V. Green & S. Cherrington (Eds.), *Delving into diversity: An international exploration of issues of diversity in education* (pp. 185–193). New York: Nova Science.

Graves, D. (1982). How do writers develop? *Language Arts, 59* (2), 173–179.

Green, A. (1982). In defence of anti-racist teaching: A reply to recent critiques of multicultural education. *Multicultural Education* 10 (2): 19–35.

Grice, M. O., & Vaughn, C. (1992). Third graders respond to literature for and about Afro-Americans. *Urban Review 24* (2), 149–164.

Government Reform Minority Office. (2003, August). About politics & science: The state of science under the Bush administration. Retrieved from http://democrats.reform.house.gov/features/politics_and_science/index.htm.

Gurin, P. Y., Dey, E. L., Gurin, G., & Hurtado, S. (2003). How does racial/ethnic diversity promote education? *Western Journal of Black Studies 27* (1), 20–29.

Gurin, P. Y., Dey, E. L., Hurtado, S., & Gurin, G. (2002). Diversity and higher education: Theory and impact on educational outcomes. *Harvard Educational Review 72*(3), 330–367.

Gurin, P., & Nagda, B. R. A. (2006). Getting to the what, how, and why of diversity on campus. *Educational Researcher 35* (1). 20–24.

Gutiérrez, G. (2000). Deconstructing Disney: Chicano/a children and critical race theory. *Aztlán* 25(1), 7–46.

Gutiérrez, J. (1992). Expanding the teacher pool. *School Community Journal, 2*(2), 23–30.

Gutiérrez, J. M., & Murphy, J. A. (1996). Persistence and impediments in minority students becoming teachers. *School Community Journal, 6*(1), 113–125.

Gutiérrez, K. 2001. So what's new in the English language arts: Challenging policies andpractices, ¿y qué?, *Language Arts Journal, 78* (6), 564–569.

Gutiérrez, K., Asato, J., Santos, M., & Gotanda, N. (2002). Backlash pedagogy: Language and culture and the politics of reform. *Review of Education, Pedagogy, and Cultural Studies, 24,* 335–351.

Gutiérrez, K. D., & Rogoff, B. (2003). Cultural ways of learning: Individual traits or repertoires of practice. *Educational Researcher, 32*(5), 19–25.

Gutiérrez, R. (2002). Beyond essentialism: The complexity of language in teaching mathematics to Latina/o students. *American Educational Research Journal, 39,* 1047–1088.

Haberman, M. (1996). Selecting and preparing culturally competent teachers for urban schools. In J. Sikula, T. J. Buttery, & E. Guyton (Eds.), *Handbook of research on teacher education* (2nd ed., pp. 747–760). New York: Macmillan.

Haberman, M. (1999). Increasing the number of high-quality African American teachers in urban schools. *Journal of Instructional Psychology, 26*(4), 208–212.

Haberman, M. (2001). The creation of an urban normal school: What constitutes quality alternative certification? *Educational Studies, 32*(3), 278–288.

Hacker, J. S. & Pierson, P. (2010). *Winner-take-all politics.* New York: Simon & Schuster Paperbacks.

Hakuta, K. (1986). *Mirror of language: The debate on bilingualism.* New York: Basic Books.

Halagao, P. E. (2004). Holding up the mirror: The complexity of seeing your ethnic self in history. *Theory and Research in Social Education 32* (4), 459–483.

Halagao P. E. (2010). Liberating Filipino Americans through decolonizing curriculum. *Race Ethnicity & Education 13* (4), 495–512.

Hall, S. (1993). What is this "black" in black popular culture? *Social Justice* 20(1–2): 104–115.

Hall Mark, D. L. (1998). Growing our own: A three-way partnership. *Urban Education, 32*(5), 591–615.

Harrell, P. E., & Jackson, J. K. (2006, May). Teacher knowledge myths: An examination of the relationship between the Texas examinations of educator standards and formal content area coursework, grade point average and age of coursework. Paper presented at the Science, Technology, Engineering and Mathematics Education Institute, University of Massachusetts, Amherst. Retrieved from http://www.stemtec.org/act.

Harris, A. (2000). Race and essentialism in feminist legal theory. In R. Delgado, & J. Stefancic, (Eds.). *Critical race theory: The cutting edge,* 2nd ed. Philadelphia: Temple University Press.

Harris, C. I. (1993). Whiteness as property. *Harvard Law Review,* 106, 1707–1791.

Harvey, D. (2005). *A brief history of neoliberalism.* New York: Oxford University Press.

Hauser-Cram, P., Sirin, S. R., & Stipek, D. (2003). When teachers' and parents' values differ: Teachers' ratings of academic competence in children from low-income families. *Journal of Educational Psychology, 95*(4), 813–20.

Haviland, D., & Rodriguez-Kiino, D. (2008). Closing the gap: The impact of professional development on faculty attitudes toward culturally responsive pedagogy. *Journal of Hispanic Higher Education, 8,* 197–212.

Haycock, K. (2001). Closing the achievement gap. *Educational Leadership, 58*(6), 6–11.

Heath, S. B. (1983). *Ways with words*. New York: Cambridge University Press.

Henderson-King, D., & Kaleta, A. (2000). Learning about social diversity: The undergraduate experience and social tolerance. *The Journal of Higher Education 71* (2), 142–164.

Hess, F. M. (2001). The work ahead. *Education Next, 1*(4), 8–13.

Hickman, H., & Porfolio, B. J., Eds. (2012a). *The new politics of the textbook: Critical analysis in the core content area*s. Boston: Sense Publishers.

Hickman, H., & Porfolio, B. J., Eds. (2012b). *The new politics of the textbook: Problematizing the portrayal of marginalized groups in textbooks*. Boston: Sense Publishers.

Hill, M. L. (2009). Wounded healing: Forming a storytelling community in hip-hop lit. *Teachers College Record, 111*, 248–293.

Hillocks, G. (2002). *The testing trap: How state writing assessments control learning*. New York: Teachers College Press.

Hogan, D. E., & Mallott, M. (2005). Changing racial prejudice through diversity education. *Journal of College Student Development 46* (2), 115–125.

Holmes, B. D., & Couch, R. (1997). Seamless collaboration for student success: Effective strategies for retaining minority students. *Michigan Community College Journal, 3*(2), 43–51.

hooks, b. (1994). *Teaching to transgress: Education as the practice of freedom*. London: Routledge.

Howard, T. C. (2001). Telling their side of the story: African American students' perceptions of culturally relevant teaching. *Urban Review, 33*(2), 131–149.

Hu-DeHart, E. (2004). Ethnic studies in U.S. higher education: History, development, and goals. In J. A. Banks & C. A. M. Banks (Eds.). *Handbook of research on multicultural education,* 2nd ed. (pp. 869–881). San Francisco: Jossey-Bass.

Hughes, R. L. (2007). A hint of whiteness: History textbooks and social construction of race in the wake of the sixties. *The Social Studies*. Sept/Oct., 201–207.

Hughes, J. M., & Bigler, R. S. (2007). Addressing race and racism in the classroom. In G. Orfield & E. Frankenburg (Eds.), *Lessons in integration: Realizing the promise of racial diversity in America's schools* (pp. 190–206). Charlottesville: University of Virginia Press.

Hughes, J. M., Bigler, R. S., & Levy, S. R. (2007). Consequences of learning about historical racism among European American and African American children. *Child Development, 78*, 1689–1705.

Huiskamp, G. (2002). Negotiating communities of meaning in theory and practice: Rereading *Pedagogy of the Oppressed* as direct dialogic encounter. In J. J. Slater, S. M. Fain, & C. A. Rossatto, (Eds.), *The Freirean legacy: Educating for social justice* (pp. 73–94). New York: Peter Lang.

Hunt, M. O. (2007). African American, Hispanic and White beliefs about Black/White inequality, 1977–2004. *American Sociological Review 72*, 390–415.

Hunter-Boykin, H. (1992). Responses to the African American teacher shortage: "We grow our own" through the Teacher Preparation Program at Coolidge High School. *Journal of Negro Education, 61*(4), 483–495.

Hursh, D. (2005). The growth of high-stakes testing in the USA: Accountability, markets, and the decline in educational quality. *British Educational Research Journal, 31*(5), 605–622.

Hursh, D. (2007). Assessing No Child Left Behind and the rise of neoliberal education policies. *American Educational Research Journal, 44*, 493–518.

Hurtado, S., Engberg, M. E., Ponjuan, L., & Landreman, L. (2002). Students' precollege preparation for participation in a diverse democracy. *Research in Higher Education 43* (2), 163–186.

Iglesias, E.M., & Valdes, F. (1998) Religion, gender, sexuality, race, and class in coalitional theory: A critical & self critical analysis of LatCrit. *Chicano-Latino Law Review*, 19, 503–588.

Irizarry, J.G. (2007). "Home-growing" teachers of color: Lessons learned from a town-gown partnership. *Teacher Education Quarterly, 34*(4), 87–102.

Irvine, J. J. (1988). An analysis of the problem of the disappearing Black educator. *Elementary School Journal, 88*(5), 503–514.

Irvine, J. J. (2003). *Educating teachers for diversity: Seeing with a cultural eye.* New York: Teachers College Press.

Jacobson, M. F. (2006). *Roots too: White ethnic revival in post-civil rights America.* Cambridge:, MA Harvard University Press.

James, C. (1995). Multicultural and anti-racism education in Canada. *Race, Gender and Class* 2(3): 31–48.

James, C. (2001). Multiculturalism in the Canadian context. In C. A. Grant & J. L. Lei (Eds.). *Global constructions of multicultural education* (pp. 175–204). Mahwah, NJ: Lawrence Erlbaum.

James, C. E., & Haig-Brown. (2002). "Returning the dues." Community and the personal in a university-school partnership. *Urban Education, 36*(2), 226–255.

Jennings, L. B., & Smith, C. P. (2002). Examining the role of critical inquiry for transformative practices. *Teachers College Record, 104,* 456–481.

Johnson, D. D., & Johnson, B. (2002). High-stakes. Lanham, MD: Rowman & Littlefield.

Johnson, K. A. (2000). *The effects of advanced teacher training on student achievement.* Washington, D.C.: The Heritage Foundation.

Johnson, K.R. (1996–97). The social and legal construction of nonpersons. *Inter-American Law Review*, 28(2), 263–292.

Jones, M. G., Jones, B. D., & Hargrove, T. Y. (2003). *The unintended consequences of high-stakes testing.* Lanham, MD: Rowman & Littlefield.

Kailin, J. (1998/99). Preparing urban teachers for schools and communities: An anti-racist perspective. *High School Journal* 82 (2): 80–87.

Kanpol, B., & McLaren, P., Eds. (1995). *Critical multiculturalism: Uncommon voices in a common struggle.* Westport, CT.: Bergin & Garvey.

Kincheloe, J. L., & Steinberg, S. R. (1997). *Changing multiculturalism.* Buckingham: Open University Press.

Kincheloe, J. L., & Steinberg, S. R. (2006). *What you don't know about schools.* New York: Palgrave Macmillan.

King, J. E. 1992. Diaspora literacy and consciousness in the struggle against miseducation in the Black community. *Journal of Negro Education* 61 (3): 317–340.

King, J. E., Ed. (2005). *Black education: A transformative research and action agenda for the new century.* Washington, DC: AERA and Mahwah, NJ: Lawrence Erlbaum Associates.

Klein, N. (2008). *The shock doctrine: The rise of disaster capitalism.* New York: Henry Holt and Co.

Kliebard, H. M. (1982). Education at the turn of the century: A crucible for curriculum change. *Educational Researcher, (*11), 16–24.

Kliebard, H. M. 1995. *The struggle for the American curriculum,* 2nd ed. New York: Routledge.

Kluegel, J. R., & Smith, E. R. 1986. *Beliefs about inequality: Americans' views of what is and what ought to be.* New York: Aldine de Gruyter.

Knight, M. G. (2004). Sensing the urgency: Envisioning a Black humanist vision of care of teacher education. *Race Ethnicity and Education, 7*(3), 211–228.

Knoester, M., Ed. (2012). *International struggles for critical democratic education.* New York: Peter Lang.

Kohn, A. (1999). Forward . . . into the past. *Rethinking Schools,* 14(1). Retrieved from www.rethinkingschools.org/

Kossan, P. (2009, June 12). Arizona schools superintendent pushes ban on ethnic studies. *AZCentral.com*. Retrieved from www.azcentral.com/news/articles/ 2009/06/12/20090612 ethnicbanON0612.html

Krater, J., Zeni, J., & Cason, N. D. (1994). *Mirror images: Teaching writing in Black and White*. Portsmouth, NH: Heinemann.

Krater, J., & Zeni, J. (1995). Seeing students, seeing culture, seeing ourselves. *Voices from the Middle, 3*(3), 32–38.

Krull, E., Oras, K., & Sisack, S. (2007). Differences in teachers' comments on classroom events as indicators of their professional development. *Teaching and Teacher Education, 23*(7), 1038–1050.

Kumashiro, K. K. (2004a). *Against common sense: Teaching and learning toward social justice*. New York: RoutledgeFalmer.

Kumashiro, K. K. (2004b). Uncertain beginnings: Learning to teach paradoxically. *Theory into Practice, 93*(2), 111–115.

Ladson-Billings, G. (1994). *The dreamkeepers*. San Francisco: Jossey-Bass.

Ladson-Billings, G. (1995). Toward a theory of culturally relevant pedagogy. *American Educational Research Journal, 47*, 465–491.

Ladson-Billings, G. (1998). Just what is critical race theory and what's it doing in a nice field like education? *International Journal of Qualitative Studies in Education*, 11(1), 7–24.

Ladson-Billings, G. (1999). Preparing teachers for diverse student populations: A critical race theory perspective. *Review of Research in Education*, 24, 211–247.

Ladson-Billings, G. (2000). Racialized discourses and ethnic epistemologies. In N.K. Denzin & Y.S. Lincoln (Eds.) *Handbook of qualitative research* (2nd Edition) (pp. 257–277). Thousands Oaks, CA: Sage Publications, Inc.

Ladson-Billings, G., & Tate, W. (1995). Toward a critical race theory of education. *Teachers College Record*, 97, 47–68.

LaDuke, W. (1999). *All our relations: Native struggle for land and life*. Minneapolis, MN: Honor the Earth.

Lather, P. (1991). *Getting smart*. New York: Routledge.

Lau, K. F., Dandy, E. B., & Hoffman, L. (2007). The Pathways Program: A model for increasing the number of teachers of color. *Teacher Education Quarterly, 34*(4), 27–40.

Lave, J., & Wenger, E. (1991). *Situated learning: Legitimate peripheral participation*. Cambridge, UK: Cambridge University Press.

Lazar, A. (1998). Helping preservice teachers inquire about caregivers: A critical experience for field-based courses. *Action in Teacher Education 19*(4), 14–28.

Lea, V. (1994). The reflective cultural portfolio: Identifying public cultural scripts in the private voices of white student teachers. *Journal of Teacher Education, 55*(2), 116–127.

Lee, C. D. (1995). A culturally based cognitive apprenticeship: Teaching African American high school students skills in literary interpretation. *Reading Research Quarterly 30*, 608–630.

Lee, C. D. (2001) Is October Brown Chinese? A cultural modeling activity system for underachieving students. *American Educational Research Journal, 38* (1), 97–142.

Lee, C. D. (2006). "Every good-bye ain't gone": Analyzing the cultural underpinnings of classroom talk. *International Journal of Qualitative Studies in Education, 19*, 305–327.

Lee, C. D. (2007). *Culture, literacy and learning: Taking bloom in the midst of the whirlwind*. New York: Teachers College Press.

Lee, E. (1985). *Letters to Marcia: A teacher's guide to anti-racist education.* Toronto: Cross Cultural Communication Centre.

Lee, E. (1995). Taking multicultural, antiracist education seriously. In Levine, D. P., et al. (Eds.). *Rethinking schools: An agenda for change* (pp. 10–16). New York: New Press: Distributed by W.W. Norton.

Lee, E., Menkart, D., & Okazawa-Rey, M., Eds. (1998). *Beyond heroes and holidays: A practical guide to K-12 anti-racist, multicultural education and staff development.* Washington, D.C.: Network of Educators on the Americas.

Lee, O., & Luykx, A. (2005). Dilemmas of scaling up innovations in science instruction with non-mainstream students. *American Educational Research Journal, 42*(3), 411–438.

Lensmire, T. J. (2010). Ambivalent white racial identities: Fear and an elusive innocence. *Race Ethnicity and Education 13* (2), 159–172.

Leonard, J., Napp, C., & Adeleke, S. (2009). The complexities of culturally relevant pedagogy: A case study of two secondary mathematics teachers and their ESOL students. *High School Journal, 93*(1), 3–22.

Levine, D. P., Lowe, R., Peterson, B., & Tenorio, R., Eds. (1995). *Rethinking schools: An agenda for change.* New York: New Press: Distributed by W.W. Norton.

Lewis, A. E. (2001). There is no "race" in the schoolyard: Colorblind ideology in an (almost) all-White school. *American Educational Research Journal 38* (4), 781–811.

Lewis, C. W., James, M., Hancock, S., & Hill-Jackson, V. (2008). Framing African American students' success and failure in urban settings. *Urban Education, 43,* 127–153.

Lewis, K. M., Sullivan, C. M., & Bybee, D. (2006). An experimental evaluation of a school-based emancipatory intervention to promote African American well-being and youth leadership. *Journal of Black Psychology 32* (1), 3–28.

Linn, R. L. (2005, June 28). Conflicting demands of No Child Left Behind and state systems: Mixed messages about school performance. *Education Policy Analysis Archives, 13*(33). Retrieved from http://epaa.asu.edu/epaa/v13n33/

Linton, S. (1998). *Claiming disability.* New York: New York University Press.

Lipka, J. (1991). Toward a culturally based pedagogy: A case study of one Yup'ik Eskimo teacher. *Anthropology & Education Quarterly 22* (3), 203–223.

Lipka, J., & Adams, B. (2004). Culturally based mathematics education as a way to improve Alaska Native students' math performance. Appalachian Collaborative Center for Learning, Assessment, and Instruction in Mathematics. Retrieved from www.uaf.edu/mcc/award-recognition-and-oth/

Lipka, J., Hogan, M. P., Webster, J. P., Yanez, E., Adams, B., Clark, S., & Lacy, D. (2005a). Math in a cultural context: Two case studies of a successful culturally based math project. *Anthropology & Education Quarterly 36* (4), 367–385.

Lipka, J., Sharp, N., Brenner, B., Yanez, E. & Sharp, F. (2005b). The relevance of culturally based curriculum and instruction: The case of Nancy Sharp. *Journal of American Indian Education 44* (3), 31–54.

Lipman, P. (2004). *High stakes education.* New York: RoutledgeFalmer.

Littleton, D. M. (1998). Preparing professionals as teachers for the urban classroom. *Action in Teacher Education, 19*(4), 149–158.

Livingstone, D. W., Ed. (1987). *Critical pedagogy and cultural power.* South Hadley, MA: Bergin & Garvey.

Loewen, J. W. (1995). *Lies my teacher told me.* New York: New Press.

Logan, D. (2011, Oct. 24). *Summary of latest federal individual income tax data*. Tax Foundation. Retrieved from taxfoundation.org/article/summary-latest-federal-individual-income-tax-data-0.

Lomawaima, K. T., & McCarty, T. L. (2006). *"To remain an Indian:" Lessons in democracy from a century of Native American education*. New York: Teachers College Press.

Lopez, G. E. (2004). Interethnic contact, curriculum, and attitudes in the first year of college. *Journal of Social Issues 40* (1), 75–94.

Lortie, D. C. (1975). *Schoolteacher*. Chicago: University of Chicago Press.

Love, F. E., & Greer, R. G. (1995). Recruiting minorities in to teaching. *Contemporary Education, 67*(1), 30–32.

Lyall, K., & Sell, K. R. (2006). *The true genius of America at risk*. Westport, CT: Greenwood Publishing Group.

Lynn, M. (1999). Toward a critical race pedagogy: A research note. *Urban Education*, 33(5), 606–626.

Macedo, D. (1994). *Literacies of power: What Americans are not allowed to know*. Boulder, CO: Westview.

Macedo, D., & Bartolome, L. I. (1999). *Dancing with bigotry: Beyond the politics of tolerance*. New York: St. Martin's Press.

Mahan, J. M., & Stachowski, L. (1993–1994). Diverse, previously uncited sources of professional learning reported by student teachers serving in culturally different communities. *National Forum of Teacher Education Journal, 3*(1), 21–28.

Mansfield, E., & Kehoe, J. W. (1994). A critical examination of anti-racist education. *Canadian Journal of Education* 19(4): 419–430.

Marable, M. (2000). *How capitalism underdeveloped Black America: Problems in race, political economy, and society*. Cambridge, MA: South End Press.

Martin, A. M., & Hand, B. (2009). Factors affecting the implementation of argument in the elementary science classroom: A longitudinal case study. *Research in Science Education, 39*, 17–38.

Martin, B. (1999). Suppression of dissent in science. *Research in Social Problems and Public Policy, 7*, 105–135.

Marx, S. (2000). An exploration of preservice teacher perceptions of second language learners in the mainstream classroom. *Texas Papers in Foreign Language Education, 5*(1), 207–221.

Math in a Cultural Context (2010). University of Alaska Fairbanks. Retrieved from www.uaf.edu/mcc.

Matthews, C. E., & Smith, W. S. (1994). Native American related materials in elementary science instruction. *Journal of Research in Science Teaching 31* (4), 363–380.

Matsuda, M., Lawrence, C., Delgado, R., & Crenshaw, K., Eds. (1993). *Words that wound: Critical race theory, assaultive speech, and the first amendment*. Boulder, CO: Westview Press.

May, S. (1994). *Making multicultural education work*. Philadelphia: Multilingual Matters.

May, S. (1999). Critical multiculturalism and cultural difference: Avoiding essentialism. In S. May (Ed.), *Critical multiculturalism: Rethinking multicultural and antiracist education* (pp. 11–41). London: The Falmer Press.

May, S., & Sleeter, C. E. (2010). Introduction. In S. May & C. E. Sleeter (Eds.), *Critical multiculturalism: Theory & praxis* (pp. 1–18). New York: Routledge.

Mayhew, M. J., Grunwald, H. E., & Dey, E. L. (2005). Curriculum matters: Creating a positive climate for diversity from the student perspective. *Research in Higher Education 46* (4), 389–412.

Mayo, P. (1999). *Gramsci, Freire and adult education: Possibilities for transformative action*. London: Zed Books.

McAllister, G., & Irvine, J. J. (2002). The role of empathy in teaching culturally diverse students: A qualitative study of teachers' beliefs. *Journal of Teacher Education, 53*(5), 433–443.

McCarthy, C. (1995). Multicultural policy discourses on racial inequality in American education. In R. Ng, P. Staton, & J. Scane (Eds.), *Anti-racism, feminism, and critical approaches to education* (pp. 21–44). Westport, CT: Bergin & Garvey.

McCarthy, C. (1998). *The uses of culture*. New York: Routledge.

McCarty, T. L. (1993). Language, literacy, and the image of the child in American Indian classrooms. *Language Arts 70* (3), 182–192.

McCombs, B. L. (2003). A framework for the redesign of K-12 education in the context of current educational reform. *Theory into Practice, 42*(2), 93–101.

McLaren, P. (1991). Critical pedagogy: Constructing an arch of social dreaming and a doorway to hope. *Journal of Education 173* (1) 9–34.

McLaren, P. (1998). Revolutionary pedagogy in post-revolutionary times: Rethinking the political economy of critical education. *Educational Theory 48* (4), 431–462.

McLaren, P. (2000). *Che Guevara, Paulo Freire, and the pedagogy of revolution*. Lanham, MD: Rowman & Littlefield.

McLaren, P., & Mayo, P. (1999). Value commitment, social change, and personal narrative. *International Journal of Educational Reform 8* (4): 397–408.

McNeil, L., & Valenzuela, A. (2001). The harmful impact of the TAAS system of testing in Texas: Beneath the accountability rhetoric. In G. Orfield & M. L. Kornhaber (Eds.), *Raising standards or raising barriers: Inequality and high-stakes testing in public education* (pp. 127–150). New York: Century Foundation Press.

Mehan, H., Hubbard, L., & Datnow, A. (2010). A co-construction perspective on organizational change and educational reform. *Yearbook of the National Society for the Study of Education, 109*(1), 98–112.

Meier, D. (2004). NCLB and democracy. In D. Meier, & G. Wood (Eds.), *Many children left behind* (pp. 66–78). Boston: Beacon Press.

Meier, K.J., Stewart, J., & England, R.E. (1989). *Race, class and education: The politics of second generation discrimination*. Madison: University of Wisconsin Press.

Melnick, S., & Zeichner, K. (1996). The role of community-based field experiences in preparing teachers for cultural diversity. In K. Zeichner, S. Melnick, & M. L. Gomez (Eds.), *Currents of reform in preservice teacher education* (pp. 176–196). New York: Teachers College Press.

Memory, D. J., Coleman, C. L., & Watkins, S. D. (2003). Possible tradeoffs in raising basic skills cutoff scores for teacher licensure: A study with implications for participation of African Americans in teaching. *Journal of Teacher Education, 54*(3), 217–227.

Meyer, L. H., Penetito, W., Hynds, A., Savage, C., Hindle, R., & Sleeter, C. E. (2010). *Evaluation of the Te Kotahitanga programme, Final Report*. Wellington, NZ: Ministry of Education.

Meyer, R. J. (2002). *Phonics exposed*. Mahwah, NJ: Lawrence Erlbaum.

Miles, M. A. (2006). Introduction. In M. A. Miles, M. A. O'Grady, & K. R. Holmes (Eds.), *2006 index of economic freedom* (pp. 1–26). Washington, DC: Heritage Foundation.

Miller, D., & Macintosh, R. (1999). Promoting resilience in urban African American adolescents: Racial socialization and identity as protective factors. *Social Work Research, 3*, 159–169.

Milner, H.R. (2006). The promise of Black teachers' success with Black students. *Educational Foundations, 20* (3–4), 89–104.

Milner, H. R., IV. (2010). *Start where you are, but don't stay there: Understanding diversity, opportunity gaps, and teaching in today's classrooms*. Cambridge, MA: Harvard Education Press.

Milner, H. R., IV. (2011). Culturally relevant pedagogy in a diverse urban classroom. *Urban Review, 43*, 66–89.

Milner, H.R., & Howard, T.C. (2004). Black teachers, Black students, Black communities and *Brown*: Perspectives and insights from experts. *Journal of Negro Education, 33*(3), 285–297.

Ministry of Education. (2006). *Nga haeata matauranga: Annual report on Māori education.* Wellington, NZ: Ministry of Education.

Mitchell, R. (2010). Cultural aesthetics and teacher improvisation: An epistemology of providing culturally responsive service by African American professors. *Urban Education, 45*, 604–629.

Modood, T. (2007). *Multiculturalism: A civic idea.* Cambridge, UK: Polity Press.

Moll, L. C., & González, N. (1994). Lessons from research with language-minority children. *Journal of Reading Behavior, 26*, 439–456.

Modgil, S., Verma, G., Mallick, D., & Modgil, C., Eds. (1986). *Multicultural education: The interminable debate.* London: The Falmer Press.

Monk, D. H. (1994). Subject area preparation of secondary mathematics and science teachers and student achievement. *Economics of Education Review, 13*, 125–145

Montoya, M. (1994). Mascaras, trenzas, y grenas: Un/masking the self while un/braiding Latina stories and legal discourse. *Chicano-Latino Law Review*, 15, 1–37.

Montaño, T., Ulanoff, S., Quintanar-Sarellana, R., & Aoki, L. (2006). California Senate Bill 2042: The debilingualization and deculturalization of prospective bilingual teachers. *Social Justice, 32*(2), 103–121.

Montoya, M. E. (1997). Academic *mestizaje*: Re/Producing clinical teaching and re/framing wills as Latina praxis. *Harvard Latino Law Review*, 2, 349–373.

Moon, T. R., Brighton, C. M., & Callahan, C. M. (2003). State standardized testing programs: Friend or foe of gifted education? *Roeper Review, 25*(2), 49–60.

Morrison, K. A., Robbins, H. H., & Rose, D. G. (2008). Operationalizing culturally relevant pedagogy: A synthesis of classroom-based research. *Equity & Excellence in Education, 41*, 433–435.

Moule, J. (2004). Safe and growing out of the box: Immersion for social change. In J. Romo, P. Bradfield & R. Serrano (Eds.), *Working in the margins: Becoming a transformative educator* (pp. 147–171). Upper Saddle River, NJ: Merrill Prentice-Hall.

Nagda, B. A., Kim, C. W., & Truelove, Y. (2004). Learning about difference, learning with others, learning to transgress. *Journal of Social Issues 60* (1), 195–214.

Nasir, N. S., & Hand, V. H. (2006). Exploring sociocultural perspectives on race, culture, and learning. *Review of Educational Research, 76*, 449–475.

National Academy of Education. (2009). *Education Policy White Paper on Teacher Quality.* S. Wilson (Ed.). Washington, DC: Author. Retrieved from www.naeducation.org/Teacher_Quality_White_Paper.pdf

National Center for Education Statistics (2009). *The nation's report card: Long-term trends 2008.* Washington, D.C.: Institute of Education Sciences, U.S. Department of Education Retrieved from http://nationsreportcard.gov/ltt_2008/ltt0009.asp.

National Center for Education Statistics (2010). *The condition of education.* Washington, D.C.: Institute of Education Sciences, U.S. Department of Education. Retrieved from http://nces.ed.gov/programs/ coe/2010/section4/indicator27.asp

National Center for Education Statistics (2011). *The nation's report card: Reading 2011* (NCES 2012–457). Washington, D.C.: Institute of Education Sciences, U.S. Department of Education.

National Center for Education Statistics (2012). *The condition of education.* Washington, D.C.:

Institute of Education Sciences, U.S. Department of Education Retrieved from http://nces.ed.gov/programs/coe/index.asp

National Commission on Excellence in Education. (1983). *A Nation at Risk*. Washington, D.C.: U.S. Government Printing Office.

National Research Council. (1998). *Preventing reading difficulties in young children*. Washington, D.C.: National Academy Press.

Nelson, J. A., Bustamante, R. M., & Onwuegbuzie, A. J. (2008). The school-wise cultural competence observation checklist for school counselors. *ASCA, 11*, 207–217.

Nelson, L. (2012, April 5). U.S. Panel negotiates over rules for teacher preparation programs. *Inside Higher Ed*. Retrieved from www.insidehighered.com/news/2012/04/05/us-panel-negotiates-over-rules-teacher-preparation-programs

Ng, R., Staton, P., & Scane, J., Eds. (1995). *Anti-racism, feminism, and critical approaches to education*. Westport, CT: Bergin & Garvey.

Nieto, S. (1999). *The light in their eyes: Creating multicultural learning communities*. New York: Teachers College Press.

Nieto, S. (2000). Placing equity front and center: Some thoughts on transforming teacher education for a new century. *Journal of Teacher Education, 51*(3), 180–187.

Nieto, S., & Bode, P. (2007). *Affirming diversity: The sociopolitical context of multicultural education* (5th ed). Boston: Allyn & Bacon.

Noguera, P. A., & Akom, A. (2000). Disparities demystified. *Nation, 270*(22).

Noordhoff, K., & Kleinfeld, J. (1993). Preparing teachers for multicultural classrooms. *Teaching and Teacher Education, 9*(1), 27–39.

Norfolk Public Schools. (n.d.) *Glossary of terms from the No Child Left Behind Act of 2001*. Retrieved from http://www.nps.k12.va.us/NCLB/NCLB_glossary.htm.

North, C. (2008). What's all this talk about "social justice?" Mapping the terrain of education's latest catchphrase. *Teachers College Record 110* (6), 1182–1206.

Nykiel-Herbert, B. (2010). Iraqi refugee students: From a collection of aliens to a community of learners. *Multicultural Education, 17*(30), 2–14.

Oakes, J., Blasi, G., & Rogers, J. (2004). Accountability for adequate and equitable opportunities to learn. In K. Sirtonik (Ed.), *Holding accountability accountable: What ought to matter in public education*. New York: Teachers College Press.

Obidah, J. E. (2000). Mediating boundaries of race, class, and professional authority as a critical multiculturalist. *Teachers College Record 102* (6), 1035–1060.

O'Connor, C. (1997). Dispositions toward (collective) struggle and educational resilience in the inner city: A case analysis of six African-American high school students. *American Educational Research Journal 34* (4), 593–629.

Okihiro, G. Y. (1995). *Common ground: Reimagining American history*. Princeton: Princeton University Press.

Oliff, P., Mai, C., & Leachman, M. (2012). *New school year brings more cuts in state funding for schools*. Center on Budget and Policy Priorities. Retrieved from http://www.cbpp.org/cms/index.cfm?fa=view&id=3825

Oliva, M., & Staudt, K. (2003). Pathways to teaching: Latino student choice and professional identity development in a teacher training magnet program. *Equity & Excellence in Education, 36*, 270–279.

Oliva, M., & Staudt, K. (2004). Latino professional identity development. *Kappa Delta Pi Record, 41*(1), 38–241.

Omi, M., & H. Winant. (1986). *Racial formation in the United States.* New York: Routledge and Kegan Paul.

Padak, N. D., Stadulis, J. D., Barton, L.E., Meadows, F.B., & Padak, G.M. (1994). Mentoring with future urban teachers. *Urban Education, 29*(3), 341–353.

Pang, V.O., & Gibson, R. (2001). Concepts of democracy and citizenship: Views of African American teachers. *Social Studies, 92*(6), 260–266.

Pang, V. O., & Sablan, V. A. (1998) Teacher efficacy. In M. E. Dilworth (Ed.), *Being responsive to cultural differences* (pp. 39–58). Washington, DC: Corwin Press.

Parker, L. (1998). Race is . . . race ain't": An exploration of the utility of critical race theory in qualitative research in education. *International Journal of Qualitative Studies in Education,* 11(1), 7–24.

Parker, L., Deyhle, D., and Villenas, S. (Eds.) (1999). *Race is . . . race isn't: critical race theory and qualitative studies in education.* Boulder, CO: Westview Press.

Parker, W. C. (2003). *Teaching democracy.* New York: Teachers College Press.

Patchen, T., & Cox-Petersen, A. (2008). Constructing cultural relevance in science: A case study of two elementary teachers. *Science Education, 92,* 994–1014.

Penetito, W. (2010). *What's Māori about Māori education?* Wellington, NZ: Victoria University Press.

Perkins, J. (2004). *Confessions of an economic hit man.* San Francisco: Berrett Koehler Publishers.

Perry, T., & Fraser, J. W. (1993). *Freedom's plow: Teaching in the multicultural classroom.* New York: Routledge.

Peterson, B. (2000/2001). Planting the seeds of solidarity. *Rethinking Schools, 15*(2). Retrieved from http://rethinltingschools.org/archive/ l 5__02/ Seed152.shtml

Peterson, R. E., (1991). Teaching how to read the world and change it: Critical pedagogy in the intermediate grades. In C. E. Walsh (Ed.), *Literacy as praxis: Culture, language and pedagogy* (pp. 156–182). Norwood, NJ: Ablex.

Pew Research Center (2012). *The lost decade of the middle class.* Washington, DC: Pew Social and Demographic Trends.

Phillips, G., McNaughton, S., & MacDonald, S. (2004). Managing the mismatch: Enhancing early literacy progress for children with diverse language and cultural identities in mainstream urban schools in New Zealand. *Journal of Educational Psychology, 96,* 309–323.

Picower, B. (2009). The unexamined Whiteness of teaching: How White teachers maintain and enact dominant racial ideologies. *Race Ethnicity & Education 12* (2), 197–216.

Pipes, T. (2002). *Beneath the surface: Middle school students and diversity.* Unpublished master's thesis, California State University, Monterey Bay.

Poplin, M., & Weeres, J. (1992). *Voices from the inside: A report on schooling from inside the classroom.* Claremont, CA: Claremont Graduate School, Institute for Education in Transformation.

Posner, R.A. (1997). Narrative and narratology in classroom and courtroom. *Philosophy and Literature,* 21(2), 292–305.

Powell, R. R. (1996). Epistemological antecedents to culturally relevant and constructivist classroom curricula: A longitudinal study of teachers' contrasting worldviews. *Teaching and Teacher Education, 12*(4). 365–384.

Pruyn, M. (1994). Becoming subjects through critical practice: How students in one elementary classroom critically read and wrote their world. *International Journal of Educational Reform* 3 (1):

37–50.

Pruyn, M. (1999). *Discourse wars in Gotham West.* Boulder, CO: Westview.

Quellmalz, E. S., & Hoskyn, J. (1988). Making a difference in Arkansas: The multicultural reading and thinking project. *Educational Leadership 45* (7), 52–55.

Ramos, L. C. (2012). Devalued solidarity: A problem of education and identity. In C. E. Sleeter & E. Soriano Ayala (Eds.), *Building solidarity across communities of difference in education: International perspectives* (pp. 45–61). New York: Teachers College Press.

Rangel, J. (2007). The educational legacy of *El Plan de Santa Barbara*: An interview with Reynaldo Macías. *Journal of Latinos and Education 6* (2), 191–199.

Rastier, F. (1997). *Meaning and textuality.* (F. Collins & P. Perron, Trans.) Toronto: University of Toronto Press.

Rattansi, A. (1999). Racism, "postmodernism," and reflexive multiculturalism. In S. May (Ed.), *Critical multiculturalism: Rethinking multicultural and antiracist education* (pp. 77–112). London: The Falmer Press.

Ravitch, D., (1990). Diversity and democracy: Multicultural education in America. *American Educator* 14 (1): 16–20, 46–68.

Ravitch, D. (2001). Ex uno plures. *Education Next, 1*(3), 27–29.

Ravitch, D. (2002). September 11: Seven lessons for the schools. *Educational Leadership 60*(2), 6–9.

Richardson, R. C., Jr., & Skinner, E. F. (1992). Helping first-generation minority students achieve degrees. In L. S. Zwerling & H. B. London (Eds.), *First-generation students: Confronting the cultural issues, Vol. 80* (pp. 29–43). San Francisco: Jossey-Bass.

Rickford, A. (2001). The effect of cultural congruence and higher order questioning on the reading enjoyment and comprehension of ethnic minority students. *Journal of Education for Students Placed at Risk, 6*, 357–387.

Ricoeur, P. (1988). *Time and narrative, Vol. 3.* (K. Blamey & D. Pellauer, Trans). Chicago: University of Chicago Press.

Riding In, J., Cook-Lynne, E., Holm, T., & Red Horse, J. (2005). Reclaiming American Indian Studies. *Wicazo Sa Review 20* (1), 169–177.

Rios, F., & Montecinos, C. (1999). Advocating social justice and cultural affirmation. *Equity & Excellence in Education, 32*(3), 66–77.

Roderick, M., Jacob, B. A., & Bryk, A. S. (2002). The impact of high-stakes testing in Chicago on student achievement in promotional gate grades. *Educational Evaluation and Policy Analysis, 24*(4), 333–357.

Rodriguez, J. L., Jones, E. B, Pang, V. O., & Park, C. D. (2004). Promoting academic achievement and identity development among diverse high school students. *High School Journal, 87*, 44–53.

Roediger, D. R. (1991). *The wages of whiteness.* New York: Verso.

Rogoff, B. (2003). *The cultural nature of human development.* Oxford, UK: Oxford University Press.

Roithmayr, D. (1999). Introduction to critical race thoery in educational research and praxis. In l. Parker, D. Deyhle, and S. Villenas (Eds.), *Race is . . . race isn't: Critical race theory and qualitative studies in education.* Boulder, CO: Westview Press.

Romany, C. (1996). Gender, race/ethnicity and language. *La Raza Law Journal*, 9(1), 49–53.

Romero, A. (2008). Towards a critical compassionate intellectualism model of transformative urban education. Unpublished doctoral dissertation. Tucson: The University of Arizona.

Romero, A., Arce, S., & Cammarota, J. (2007). A barrio pedagogy: Identity, intellectualism, activism, and academic achievement through the evolution of critically compassionate intellectualism. *Race*

Ethnicity and Education 12 (2), 217–233.

Ross, F. (2001). Helping immigrants become teachers. *Educational Leadership, 58*(8), 68–71.

Ruiz, N.T. (1995). The social construction of ability and disability: Optimal and at-risk lessons in a bilingual special education classroom. *Journal of Learning Disabilities* 28: 491–502.

Saez, E. (2010). *Striking it richer: The evolution of top incomes in the United States.* Berkeley: University of California Berkeley. Retrieved from elsa.berkeley.edu/~saez/saez-UStopincomes-2010.pdf

Sakash, K., & Chou, V. (2007). Increasing the supply of Latino bilingual teachers for Chicago Public Schools. *Teacher Education Quarterly, 34*(4), 41–52.

Saltman, K. J. (2007). *Capitalizing on disaster: Taking and breaking public schools.* Boulder, CO: Paradigm Publishers.

Sanchez, T. R. (2007). The depiction of Native Americans in recent (1991–2004) secondary American history textbooks: How far have we come? *Equity & Excellence in Education* 40, 311–320.

Sanchez, V. (1998). Looking upward and inward: Religion and critical theory. *Chicano-Latino Law Review,* 19, 531–435.

Sanders, M. G. (1997). Overcoming obstacles: Academic achievement as a response to racism and discrimination. *Journal of Negro Education 66* (1), 83–93.

Savage, C., Hindle, R., Meyer, L. H., Hynds, A., Penetito, W., & Sleeter, C. E. (2011). Culturally responsive pedagogies in the classroom: Indigenous student experiences across the curriculum. *Asia-Pacific Journal of Teacher Education, 39*, 183–198.

Schlesinger, A. M., Jr. (1992). *The disuniting of America.* New York: Norton.

Schoenfeld, A H. (2004). The math wars. *Educational Policy, 18*(1), 253–286.

Schommer, M. (1990). Effects of beliefs about the nature of knowledge on comprehension. *Journal of Educational Psychology, 82*, 498–504.

Schommer, M. (1998). The role of adults' beliefs about knowledge in school, work, and everyday life. In M. C. Smith & T. Pourchot (Eds.), *Adult learning and development: Perspectives from educational psychology* (pp. 127–143). Mahwah, NJ: Erlbaum.

Seidl, B., & Friend, G. (2002). Leaving authority at the door. *Teaching and Teacher Education, 18*(4), 421–433.

Sellers, R. M., Chavous, T. M., & Cooke, D. Y. (1998). Racial ideology and racial centrality as predictors of African American college students' academic performance. *Journal of Black Psychology* 24 (1), 8–27.

Selwyn, D. (2005–2006). Teacher quality: Teacher education left behind. *Rethinking Schools, 20*(2). Retrieved from http://www.rethinkingschools.org/archive/20_02/left202.shtml

Sen, R. (2011, Nov. 1). Forget diversity, it's about "occupying" racial inequity. *Colorlines.* Retrieved from colorlines.com/archives/2011/11/forget_the_diversity_debate_its_about_occupying_racial_inequity.html

Shade, B. J., Boe, B. L., Garner, O., & New, C. A. (1998). The road to certification: A different way. *Teaching and Change, 5*(3–4), 261–275.

Shannon, P. (2001). "What's my name? A politics of literacy in the latter half of the 20th century in America," In P. Shannon (Ed.), *Becoming political, too: New readings and writings on the politics of literacy education* (pp. 112–141). Portsmouth, NH: Heinemann.

Sheets, R. H. (1995). From remedial to gifted: Effects of culturally centered pedagogy. *Theory into Practice, 34*, 186–193.

Shen, J. (1998). Alternative certification, minority teachers, and urban. *Education and Urban Society,*

31(1), 30–41.

Shields, C., Bishop, R., & Mazawi, A. (2005). *Pathologizing practices. The impact of deficit thinking on education.* New York: Peter Lang.

Shirts, G. (1969). *Star Power.* La Jolla, CA: Western Behavioral Sciences Institute.

Shirts, G. (1977). *BaFa BaFa.* La Jolla, CA: Western Behavioral Sciences Institute.

Shor, I. (1980). *Critical teaching and everyday life.* Boston: South End Press.

Shor, I. (1992). *Empowering education: Critical teaching for social change.* Chicago: University of Chicago Press.

Short, G., & Carrington, B. (1996). Anti-racist education, multiculturalism and the new racism. *Educational Review 48*(1), 65–77.

Siddle-Walker, V. (2000). Valued segregated schools for African American children in the South, 1935–1969: A review of common themes and characteristics. *Review of Educational Research, 70*(3), 253–285.

Simon, R. I. (1992). *Teaching against the grain: Texts for a pedagogy of possibility.* New York: Bergin & Garvey.

Simon, T.W. (1999). Racists versus anti-semites?: Critical race theorists criticized. *Newsletter on Philosophy, Law, and the Black Experience.* 98(2), 1–11.

Singer, A. (2012, Feb. 28). Cuomo, common core, and Pearson-for-profit. *Huffington Post.* Retrieved from http://www.huffingtonpost.com/alan-singer/cuomo-common-core-and-pearson_b_1293465.html.

Skrla, L., Scheurich, J. J., Johnson, J. F., Jr., & Koschoreck, J. W. (2001). Accountability for equity: Can state policy leverage social justice? *International Leadership in Education, 4*(3), 237–260.

Sleeter, C. E. (1992). *Keepers of the American dream.* London: The Falmer Press.

Sleeter, C.E. (1995a). An analysis of the critiques of multicultural education. In J. A. Banks & C. M. Banks (Eds.), *Handbook of Research on Multicultural Education* (pp. 81–94). New York: Macmillan.

Sleeter, C. E. (1995b). Reflections on my use of multicultural and critical pedagogy when students are white. In C. E. Sleeter & P. L. McLaren (Eds.) *Multicultural education, critical pedagogy and the politics of difference* (pp. 415–438). Albany: SUNY Press.

Sleeter, C. E. (2001a). *Culture, difference and power.* New York: Teachers College Press.

Sleeter, C. E. (2001b). Preparing teachers for culturally diverse schools: Research and the overwhelming presence of whiteness. *Journal of Teacher Education, 52*(2), 94–106.

Sleeter, C. E. (2002). State curriculum standards and the shaping of student consciousness. *Social Justice, 29*(4), 8–25.

Sleeter, C. E. (2003). Reform and control: An analysis of SB 2042. *Teacher Education Quarterly* 30(1), 19–30.

Sleeter, C. E. (2005). *Un-standardizing curriculum: Multicultural teaching in the standards-based classroom.* New York: Teachers College Press.

Sleeter, C. E. (2008). Preparing white teachers for diverse students. In Cochran-Smith, M., Feiman-Nemser, S., & McIntyre, J. (Eds.). *Handbook of Research in Teacher Education: Enduring issues in changing contexts,* 3rd ed. (pp. 559–582), New York: Routledge.

Sleeter, C. E., Ed. (2011). *Professional development for culturally responsive and relationship-based pedagogy.* New York: Peter Lang.

Sleeter, C. E., & Cornbleth, C., Eds. (2011). *Teaching with vision: Culturally responsive teaching in standards-based classrooms.* New York: Teachers College Press.

Sleeter, C. E., & Grant, C. A. (1991). Textbooks and race, class, gender and disability. In M.W. Apple & L. Christian-Smith, (Eds.) *Politics of the textbook* (pp. 78–110). New York: Routledge, Chapman and Hall.

Sleeter, C.E., & Grant, C.A. (2009). *Making choices for multicultural education: Five approaches to race, class and gender*, 6th ed. New York: Wiley.

Sleeter, C. E., & Montecinos, C. (1999). Forging partnerships for multicultural education. In S. May (Ed.), *Critical multiculturalism: Rethinking multicultural and anti-racist education* (pp. 113–137). London: The Falmer Press.

Sleeter, C. E., & Stillman, J. (2007). Navigating accountability pressures. In C. E. Sleeter (Ed.), *Facing accountability in education: Democracy and equity at risk.* New York: Teachers College Press.

Smith, L. T. (1999). *Decolonizing methodologies: Research and indigenous peoples.* London: Zed Books.

Solomon, R. P. (1997). Race, role modeling, and representation in teacher education and teaching. *Canadian Journal of Education, 22*(4), 395–410.

Solorzano, D. G. (1989). Teaching and social change: Reflections on a Freirean approach in a college classroom. *Teaching Sociology* 17: 218–225.

Solorzano, D.G. (1997). Images and words that wound: Critical race theory, racial stereotyping and teacher education. *Teacher Education Quarterly*, 24, pp. 5–19.

Solorzano, D.G. (1998). Critical race theory, race and gender microaggressions, and the experience of Chicana and Chicano scholars. *International Journal of Qualitative Studies in Education*, 11(1), 121–136.

Solorzano, D. G., & Delgado Bernal, D. (2001). Examining transformational resistance through a critical race and LatCrit theory framework: Chicana and Chicano students in an urban context. *Urban Education*, 36(3), 308–342.

Solorzano, D.G., & Villalpando, O. (1998). Critical race theory, marginality, and the experiences of students of color in higher education. In Torres, C. A. & Mitchell, T. R. (Eds.). *Sociology of education: Emerging perspectives* (pp. 211–224). New York: SUNY Press.

Solorzano, D., & Yosso, T. (2002). Critical race methodology: Counter-storytelling as an analytical framework for education research. *Qualitative Inquiry*, 8(1), 23–44.

SooHoo, S. (2004). We change the world by doing nothing. *Teacher Education Quarterly, 31*(1), 199–211.

Span, C. M. (2002). Black Milwaukee's challenge to the cycle of urban miseducation: Milwaukee's African American immersion schools. *Urban Education 37* (5), 610–630.

Stake, R. E. (2000). *The art of case study research.* Thousand Oaks, CA: Sage.

Stalvey, L. M. (1988). *The education of a WASP.* Madison: University of Wisconsin Press.

Stanley, T. (1998). The struggle for history: Historical narratives and anti-racist pedagogy. *Discourse: Studies in the Cultural Politics of Education* 19(1), 41–52.

Steele, C. M., & Aronson, J. (1995). Stereotype threat and the intellectual test performance of African Americans. *Journal of Personality and Social Psychology, 69*(5), 797–811.

Steiner-Khamsi, G. (1990). Community languages and anti-racist education: The open battlefield. *Educational Studies* 16 (1): 33–47.

Stevens, T., Agnello, M. F., Ramirez, J., Marbley, A., & Hammer, D. (2007). Project FUTURE: Opening the door to West Texas teachers. *Teacher Education Quarterly, 34*(4), 103–120.

Stillman, J. (2011). Teacher learning in an era of high-stakes accountability: Productive tension and critical professional practice. *Teachers College Record, 113*, 133–180.

Storz, M. G. (2008). Educational inequity from the perspectives of those who live it: Urban middle school students' perspectives on the quality of their education. *Urban Review, 40*, 247–267.

Students for Cultural and Linguistic Democracy (1996). Reclaiming our voices. In C. E. Walsh (Ed.). *Education reform and social change* (pp. 129–145). Mahwah, NJ: Lawrence Erlbaum.

Su, Z. (1997). Teaching as a profession and as a career: Minority candidates' perspectives. *Teaching and Teacher Education, 13*(3), 325–340.

Swanson, H. L, O'Connor, E., & Cooney, J. B. (1990). An information processing analysis of expert and novice teachers' problem solving. *American Educational Research Journal, 27*(3), 533–556.

Tate, W. (1994). From inner city to ivory tower: Does my voice matter in the academy? *Urban Education* 29: 245–269.

Tate, W. F. (1997). Critical race theory and education: History, theory, and implications. *Review of Research in Education, 22*, 195–247.

Taylor, B. M., Pearson, P. D., Peterson, D. S., & Rodriguez, M. C. (2003). Reading growth in high-poverty classrooms: The influence of teacher practices that encourage cognitive engagement in literacy learning. *Elementary School Journal, 104*(1), 3–28.

Taylor, D. (1998). *Beginning to read and the spin doctors of science: The political campaign to change America's mind about how children learn to read.* Urbana, IL: National Council of Teachers of English.

Tetreault, M. K. T. (1989). Integrating content about women and gender into the curriculum. In J. A. Banks & C. A. M. Banks (Eds.), *Multicultural education: Issues and perspectives* (pp. 124–144). Boston: Allyn & Bacon.

Tharpe, R., Estrada, P., Dalton, S.S., & Yamauchi, L.A. (2000). *Teaching transformed: Achieving excellence, fairness, inclusion and harmony.* Boulder, Co: Westview Press.

Thomas, C. D., & Williams, D. L. (2008). An analysis of teacher defined mathematical tasks: Engaging urban learners in performance-based instruction. *Journal of Urban Teaching and Research, 4*, 109–121.

Thomas, W., & Collier, V. (1999) *School Effectiveness for Language Minority Students.* George Washington University, Washington, D.C.: National Clearinghouse for Bilingual Education.

Thompson, A. (1997). For: Anti-racist education. *Curriculum Inquiry, 29*(1), 7–44.

Thompson, A. (2002). Entertaining doubts: Enjoyment and ambiguity in White, antiracist classrooms. In E. Mirochnik, & D.C. Sherman (Eds.). *Passion and pedagogy: relation, creation, and transformation in teaching* (pp. 431–452). New York: Peter Lang.

Tiedt, P. L., & Teidt, I. M. (1999). *Multicultural teaching*, 5th ed. Boston: Allyn & Bacon.

Tiezzi, L. J., & Cross, B. E. (1997). Utilizing research on prospective teachers' beliefs to inform urban field experiences. *The Urban Review, 29*(2),113–125.

Timperley, H., Wilson, A., Barrar, H., & Fung, I. (2007). *Teacher professional learning and development: Best evidence synthesis iteration.* New Zealand: Ministry of Education.

Tooley, J., & Dixon, P. (2006). The failures of state schooling in developing countries and the peoples' response. In M. A. Miles, M. A. O'Grady, & K. R. Holmes (Eds.), *2006 index of economic freedom* (pp. 27–37). Washington, DC: Heritage Foundation.

Torres-Karna, H., & Krustchinsky, R. (1998). The early entry program. *Teacher Education and Practice, 14*(1), 10–19.

Trainor, J. S. (2005). "My ancestors didn't own slaves": Understanding white talk about race. *Research in the Teaching of English 40* (2), 140–167.

Trelease, J. (2006). The Bushes and the McGraws. *Trelease on Reading*. Retrieved from www.trelease-on-reading.com/whatsnu_bush-mcgraw.html

Troyna, B. (1987). Beyond multiculturalism: Towards the enactment of anti-racist education in policy, provision and pedagogy. *Oxford Review of Education* 13 (3), 307–320.

Tyson, C. A. (2002). "Get up off that thing:" African American middle school students respond to literature to develop a framework for understanding social action. *Theory and Research in Social Education 30* (1), 42–65.

Underwood, P. S. (2009). *Effects of culturally responsive teaching practices on first- grade students' reading comprehension and vocabulary gains* (Unpublished doctoral dissertation). Florida State University, Tallahassee, FL.

U.S. Department of Education, National Center for Education Statistics. (2002). *Digest of Education statistics*. Washington, DC: U.S. Government Printing Office.

U.S. Department of Education, National Center for Education Statistics. (2007). *Schools and staffing survey*. Retrieved from nces.ed.gov/surveys/sass/tables/state_2004_18.asp

Valenzuela, A. (2005). Accountability and the privatization agenda. In A. Valenzuela (Ed.), *Leaving children behind* (pp. 263–294). Albany, NY: SUNY Press.

Valli, L., Croninger, R. G., Chambliss, M. H., Graeber, A. O., & Buese, D. (2008). *Test driven: High-stakes accountability in elementary schools*. New York: Teachers College Press.

Vasilaki, M. (2002). *A developmentally appropriate visual art program for K-1 students*. Unpublished master's thesis, California State University Monterey Bay.

Vasquez, J. M. (2005). Ethnic identity and Chicano literature: How ethnicity affects reading and reading affects ethnic consciousness. *Ethnic and Racial Studies 28* (5), 903–924.

Vecchio, D. (2004). Immigrant and ethnic history in the United States survey. *The History Teacher 37*(4), 494–500.

Veltri, B. T. (2008). Teaching or service? The site-based realities of Teach for America teachers in poor, urban schools. *Education and Urban Society, 40*(5), 511–542.

Vernez, G., Krop, R. A., & Rydell, C. P. (1999). *Closing the education gap: Benefits and costs*. Santa Monica, CA: RAND.

Villalpando, O. (2003). Self-segregation or self-preservation? A critical race theory and Latina/o critical theory analysis of a study of Chicana/o college students *International Journal of Qualitative Studies in Education* 16(5), 619–646.

Villegas, A. M., & Clewell, B. (1998). Increasing the number of teachers of color for urban schools: Lessons from the Pathway national evaluation. *Education and Urban Society, 31*(1), 42–61.

Villegas, A. M., & Lucas, T. (2002). *Educating culturally responsive teachers*. Albany, NY: SUNY Press.

Visweswaren, K. A. (1994). *Fictions of feminist ethnography*. Minneapolis: University of Minnesota Press.

Walker, H. (1989). Towards anti-racist, multicultural practice with under fives. *Early Child Development and Care* 41, 103–112.

Wang, J. (2001). The training of ethnic minority teachers: The NNU model. *Asia-Pacific Journal of Teacher Education and Development, 4*(2), 73–88.

Warburton, E. C., Bugarin, R., & Nuñez, A. (2003). *Bridging the gap: Academic preparation and post-secondary success of first-generation students*. Washington, DC: U.S. Department of Education, National Center for Educational Statistics.

Ware, F. (2006). Warm demander pedagogy. *Urban Education, 41*, 427–456.

Watahomigie, L. J., & McCarty, T. (1994). Bilingual/bicultural education at Peach Springs: A Hualapai way of schooling. *Peabody Journal of Education, 69*, 26–42.

Watkins, W. H. 1993. Black curriculum orientations: A preliminary inquiry. *Harvard Educational Review* 65 (3): 321–338.

Wei, R. C., Darling-Hammond, L., & Adamson, F. (2010). *Teacher professional development in the United States*. National Staff Development Council.

Weinberg, M. 1977. *A chance to learn: The history of race and education in the United States*. Cambridge; New York: Cambridge University Press.

Wellman, D. T. (1977). *Portraits of white racism*. Cambridge; New York: Cambridge University Press.

What Works Clearinghouse. (2006). Evidence standards for reviewing studies. Retrieved from http://whatworks.ed.gov/reviewprocess/standards.html

White, B. C. (2000). Pre-service teachers' epistemology viewed through perspectives on problematic classroom situations. *Journal of Education for Teaching, 26*(3), 279–306.

White, C. J., Bedonie, C., de Groat, J., Lockard, L., & Honani, S. (2007). A bridge for our children: Tribal/university partnerships to prepare indigenous teachers. *Teacher Education Quarterly, 34*(4), 71–86.

Wiggan, G. (2007). From opposition to engagement: Lessons from high achieving African American students. *The Urban Review 40* (4), 317–349.

Wiggins, R. A., & Follo, E. J. (1999). Development of knowledge, attitudes, and commitment to teach diverse student populations. *Journal of Teacher Education, 50*(2), 94–105.

Williams, R. (1997). Vampires anonymous and critical race practice. *Michigan Law Review*, 95. 741–765.

Wilson, B. L., & Corbett, H. D. (2001). *Listening to urban kids: School reform and the teachers they want*. Albany: State University of New York Press.

Wineberg, S. (2001). *Historical thinking and other unnatural Acts*. Philadelphia: Temple University Press.

Wing, A. K. (Ed.) (1997). *Critical race feminism: A reader*. New York: New York University Press.

Wink, J. (1997). *Critical pedagogy: Notes from the real world*. White Plains, NY: Longman.

Wink, J., & Putney, L. 2002. *A Vision of Vygotsky*. Boston: Allyn and Bacon.

Wixson, K.K., & Dutro, E. (1998). *Standards for primary-grade reading: An analysis of state frameworks*. Center for the Improvement of Early Reading Achievement. Ann Arbor: University of Michigan. Retrieved from www.ciera.org/library/reports/inquiry-3/3–001/3–001.pdf.

Wong, P. L., Murai, H., Berta-Ávila, M., William White, L., Baker, S., & Arellano, A. (2007). The M/M center: Meeting the demand for multicultural, multilingual teacher preparation. *Teacher Education Quarterly, 34*(4), 9–26.

Wood, G. (2004). A view from the field: NCLB's effects on classrooms and schools. In D. Meier, & G. Wood (Eds.), *Many children left behind* (pp. 33–52). Boston: Beacon Press.

Woodruff, P. (2005). *First democracy: The challenge of an ancient idea*. New York: Oxford University Press.

Woodson, C. G. (1933). *The mis-education of the Negro*. Washington, D.C.: Associated Publishers.

Yeakey, C. C., & Bennett, C. I. (1990). Race, schooling and class in American society. *Journal of Negro Education, 59*(1), 3–18.

Yopp, R. H., Yopp, H. K., & Taylor, H. P. (1992). Profiles and viewpoints of minority candidates in a teacher diversity project. *Teacher Education Quarterly, 19*(3), 29–48.

Young, E. (2010). Challenges to conceptualizing and actualizing culturally relevant pedagogy: How viable is the theory in classroom practice? *Journal of Teacher Education, 61*, 248–260.

Young, J. (1995). Multicultural and anti-racist teacher education. In R. Ng, P. Staton, & J. Scane (Eds.). *Anti-racism, feminism, and critical approaches to education* (pp. 43–63). Westport, CT: Bergin & Garvey.

Yosso, T. (2002). Toward a critical race curriculum. *Equity and Excellence in Education, 35*(1), 93–107.

Zapata, J. T. (1988). Early identification and recruitment of Hispanic teacher candidates. *Journal of Teacher Education, 39*(1), 19–23.

Zeichner, K. (2003). The adequacies and inadequacies of three current strategies to recruit, prepare, and retain the best teachers for all students. *Teachers College Record, 105*(5), 490–519.

Zeichner, K. M., & Conklin, H. G. (2005). Teacher education programs. In Cochran-Smith, M., & Zeichner, K. M. (Eds.). *Studying teacher education* (pp. 645–736). Mahwah, NJ: Lawrence Erlbaum Associates.

Zozakiewicz, C., & Rodriguez, A. J. (2007). Using sociotransformative constructivism to create multicultural and gender-inclusive classrooms: An intervention project for teacher professional development. *Educational Policy, 21*, 397–425.

Zumwalt, K., & Craig, E. (2005). Teachers' characteristics: Research on the demographic profile in studying teacher education. In Cochran-Smith, M., & Zeichner, K. M. (Eds.) *Studying teacher education* (pp. 111–156). Mahwah, NJ: Lawrence Erlbaum Associates.

Index

Questions about the
Purpose(s) of Colleges
and Universities

Norm Denzin,
Shirley R. Steinberg
General Editors

What are the purposes of higher education? When undergraduates "declare their majors," they agree to enter into a world defined by the parameters of a particular academic discourse—a discipline. But who decides those parameters? How do they come about? What are the discussions and proposed outcomes of disciplined inquiry? What should an undergraduate know to be considered educated in a discipline? How does the disciplinary knowledge base inform its pedagogy? Why are there different disciplines? When has a discipline "run its course"? Where do new disciplines come from? Where do old ones go? How does a discipline produce its knowledge? What are the meanings and purposes of disciplinary research and teaching? What are the key questions of disciplined inquiry? What questions are taboo within a discipline? What can the disciplines learn from one another? What might they not want to learn and why?

Once we begin asking these kinds of questions, positionality becomes a key issue. One reason why there aren't many books on the meaning and purpose of higher education is that once such questions are opened for discussion, one's subjectivity becomes an issue with respect to the presumed objective stances of Western higher education. Academics don't have positions because positions are "biased," "subjective," "slanted," and therefore somehow invalid. So the first thing to do is to provide a sense—however broad and general—of what kinds of positionalities will inform the books and chapters on the above questions. Certainly the questions themselves, and any others we might ask, are already suggesting a particular "bent," but as the series takes shape, the authors we engage will no doubt have positions on these questions.

From the stance of interdisciplinary, multidisciplinary, or transdisciplinary practitioners, will the chapters and books we solicit solidify disciplinary discourses, or liquefy them? Depending on who is asked, interdisciplinary inquiry is either a polite collaboration among scholars firmly situated in their own particular discourses, or it is a blurring of the restrictive parameters that define the very notion of disciplinary discourse. So will the series have a stance on the meaning and purpose of interdisciplinary inquiry and teaching? This can possibly be finessed by attracting thinkers from disciplines that are already multidisciplinary, for example, the various kinds of "studies" programs (women's, Islamic, American, cultural, etc.), or the hybrid disciplines like ethnomusicology (musicology, folklore, anthropology). But by including people from these fields (areas? disciplines?) in our series, we are already taking a stand on disciplined inquiry. A question on the comprehensive exam for the Columbia University Ethnomusicology Program was to defend ethnomusicology as a "field" or a "discipline." One's answer determined one's future, at least to the extent that the gatekeepers had a say in such matters. So, in the end, what we are proposing will no doubt involve political struggles.

For additional information about this series or for the submission of manuscripts, please contact Shirley R. Steinberg, msgramsci@gmail.com. To order other books in this series, please contact our Customer Service Department at: (800) 770-LANG (within the U.S.), (212) 647-7706 (outside the U.S.), (212) 647-7707 FAX, or browse online by series at: www.peterlang.com.